Colonial Crossings

For my parents, Alan and Lidie Howes

Contents

Acknowledgements

The essays collected here were written over a period of a dozen years or more, and during that time I have incurred many pleasurable debts. For their help, expertise, intellectual stimulation and friendship I would like to thank Derek Attridge, Claire Connolly, Elizabeth Butler Cullingford, Luke Gibbons, Margaret Kelleher, Kevin Kenny, Siobhán Kilfeather, Vera Kreilkamp, Robin Lydenberg, Marc Manganaro, Lisa Salem Manganaro, John McClure, Paul Muldoon, Kevin O'Neill, Bruce Robbins, Ray Ryan, Rob Savage, James Smith, Clair Wills and Chris Wilson.

Earlier versions of the essays collected here appeared in the following publications:

'Tears and Blood: Lady Wilde and the Emergence of Irish Cultural Nationalism', Journal X, 1, 2 (1997), 203–23; reprinted in Tadhg Foley and Seán Ryder, eds., Ideology and Ireland in the Nineteenth Century (Dublin: Four Courts Press, 1998), 151–72;

'Discipline, Sentiment, and the Irish-American Public: Mary Anne Sadlier's Popular Fiction', Éire-Ireland, 40, 1–2 (2005), 140–69;

'William Carleton's Literary Religion', in James H. Murphy, ed., Evangelicals and Catholics in Nineteenth-Century Ireland (Dublin: Four Courts Press, 2005), 107–22;

'Misalliance and Anglo-Irish Tradition in Le Fanu's Uncle Silas', Nineteenth-Century Literature, 47, 2(1992), 164–86;

'Tradition, Gender, and Migration in 'The Dead': or, How Many People Has Gretta Conroy Killed?', Yale Journal of Criticism, 15, 1 (2002), 149–71;

'Goodbye Ireland I'm Going to Gort: Geography, Scale, and Narrating the Nation', in Marjorie Howes and Derek Attridge, eds., Semicolonial Joyce (Cambridge: Cambridge University Press, 2000), 58–77;

'Postcolonial Yeats: Culture, Enlightenment, and the Public Sphere', Field Day Review, 2 (2006), 55–74.

I would like to thank the various publishers for permission to reprint them in amended form.

I am especially indebted to Seamus Deane and Breandán Mac Suibhne for wanting to publish this book, and for their persistent patience, and patient persistence, during the whole process.

As always, my greatest thanks are owed to my family. I am grateful to my husband Paul and our daughter Alex for their loving support and frequent reminders that there is far more to life than work.

This book is dedicated, with love and gratitude, to my parents, Alan and Lidie Howes.

Introduction

In their Preface to *The Cambridge Companion to Modern Irish Culture*, Joe Cleary and Claire Connolly invoke the figure of the crossroads to describe the intersection of tradition and modernity in Ireland:

> Today, the old rural national image is on the wane and the country currently likes to represent itself as a thriving, energetic, cosmopolitan place ... The revels of the comely maidens dancing at the crossroads of the local townland now are ended or linger only as national kitsch; the country prefers instead a corporate quick-step on a global crossroads between Boston, Bermuda and Berlin.[1]

The crossroads functions as a clichéd figure for an idealized conception of traditional Ireland, as a modern emblem of Ireland's place in a globalizing world, and as a sign for the meeting of the two. It also embodies much about the content and variety of some of this book's other preoccupations: forms of belonging and collectivity, migration and geographical movement, individual authors' negotiations with literary genres and intellectual traditions, the intersection of categories like gender and nationality, and the relationship between Irish studies and postcolonial studies.

All the writers discussed here were born in Ireland, all of them wrote about Ireland, and each one imagines national belonging differently. The essay on Lady Wilde examines her engagement with the nationalism of Young Ireland and offers some observations about where that nationalism intersected with, and diverged from, the nationalism of Daniel O'Connell. The chapter on William Carleton looks at his efforts to render the characteristic qualities and narratives of the Irish Catholic peasantry, proposing a re-evaluation of the role of religion and genre in those efforts. The discussion of Mary Anne Sadlier describes the forms of belonging and estrangement that characterized the Irish-American identity her works imagined for immigrants. The piece on J. S. Le Fanu sketches the contours of a troubled Anglo-Irish community and tradition. The Joyce essays argue that he critiques Revivalist nationalism and insistently imagines alternative, ambiguous forms of national belonging. And the Yeats chapter takes up that writer's engagement with the Irish people as a national public.

---

1   Joe Cleary and Claire Connolly, eds., *The Cambridge Companion to Modern Irish Culture* (Cambridge, 2005), xi

Theorists of the nation have often remarked that national belonging is characterized by incoherence, contradiction, or paradox, and the essays here treat nationality less as an idea to be represented than as a set of problems to grapple with. Such grappling involves recognizing that the national intersects with other categories: gender, sexuality, class, and religion. Wilde confronts the difficulties of a specifically middle-class nationalism that both needed and feared the Irish masses, and Joyce examines how representations of women inform conceptions of national community. Wrestling with the problem of the national also involves thinking about the bases for different kinds of collectivity — physical bodies, forms of feeling, or the dictates of reason. The essays on Carleton and Joyce's Gretta Conroy take up the reading of bodies in relation to national narratives, the discussion of Wilde distinguishes a nationalist erotics from other kinds of national affect, and the chapter on Yeats tracks the oscillation between reason and feeling as the basis for a national community in his work and thought.

Much of the most influential work on nationalism since Benedict Anderson's *Imagined Communities* has come out of postcolonial studies, a field whose usefulness for scholars of Irish literature, culture, or history has been hotly contested in the last few decades.[2] Most of the essays in this volume are informed by those debates, but do not engage them directly. The exception is the Yeats essay, which tries to shift the terms of contemporary debates about Yeats and the postcolonial and offers an extended argument about how we might conceive of the relationship between postcolonial studies and the literature of the Irish Literary Revival differently. One impetus behind that essay lay in my sense that debates over whether or not Ireland, or Yeats, should be considered postcolonial had begun to reach the limits of their usefulness. This is illustrated, for example, in the final chapter of Stephen Howe's *Ireland and Empire*, which conducts a thorough critique of postcolonial work in Irish studies, yet concludes with an acceptance of the utility of some postcolonial models.[3] Most of the essays here, however, assume (rather than argue) that postcolonial work offers useful ideas and paradigms for the study of Irish culture.[4]

Belonging and collectivity only exist in relation to distance and separation; migration and other forms of geographical movement are major preoccupations of many of the essays here as well. Anderson's original account of nationalism observed the importance of communications and transportation systems, and the key role played by the 'creole pilgrimages' of colonial functionaries, in the creation of national forms of consciousness.[5] His later arguments extend that importance further, offering the claims that 'exile is the nursery of nationality' and that nationalism is 'a project for coming home from exile'.[6] The (now familiar) idea that nationality arises from geographical movement, and other kinds of 'displacement', rather than from rootedness, is most explicitly and extensively taken up in 'Goodbye Ireland I'm Going to Gort', which argues that in Joyce's works the nation emerges most vividly where it crosses paths with other spatial scales, such as the local, the regional, and the global. On the other hand, the overall dialectic this idea suggests between going 'away' (in some way or another) and producing ideas of 'home' (of one kind or another) informs much of the work in this volume. In retrospect,

---

2   Benedict Anderson, *Imagined Communities: Reflections on the Origin and Spread of Nationalism*, rev. edn. (London and New York, 1991)
3   See Stephen Howe, *Ireland and Empire* (Oxford, 2000), esp. 229–43.
4   I have pursued a more direct engagement with recent debates over postcolonial and Irish studies elsewhere; see Marjorie Howes, 'Yeats and the Postcolonial', in Marjorie Howes and John Kelly, eds., *The Cambridge Companion to W. B. Yeats* (Cambridge, 2006); 'Joyce, Colonialism, and Nationalism', in Derek Attridge, ed., *The Cambridge Companion to James Joyce*, 2nd edn. (Cambridge, 2004); and (with Derek Attridge) Introduction, in Derek Attridge and Marjorie Howes, eds., *Semicolonial Joyce* (Cambridge, 2000).
5   Anderson, *Imagined Communities*, 114
6   Benedict Anderson, *The Spectre of Comparisons: Nationalism, Southeast Asia and the World* (London and New York, 1998), 59, 65

it is this dialectic, rather than Anderson's literary interests and his well-known claims about the novel form, that has been most enabling for the discussions collected here.[7]

Migration and geographical movement are important to many of these essays for other reasons as well. Both Joyce chapters emphasize the complex transactions between real and imagined journeys that go into the production of literary representations of migration. And both engage with the profoundly gendered nature of geographical movement, in its real and imagined dimensions. What emerges is a set of competing national narratives; some are historically more conventional or canonical than others, and each of them structures the relationships among migration, gender, and nationality differently. These essays identify a continuum of migration that is freighted with cultural meanings about home, ranging from the movements involved in the labour of domestic servants and the travels of schoolchildren to transatlantic emigration. The discussion of Sadlier takes up the most explicit or 'classic' emigration narratives, and examines how a middle-class Catholic intellectual responded to the political and literary challenges posed by the Famine emigrants to the United States. Here again, different conceptions of geographical movement intersect. And an interest in thinking about geographical space, not just as an emptiness to be traversed, but as having its own depths and complexities, is pursued in 'Goodbye Ireland I'm Going to Gort'.

The writers studied here range from the ultra-canonical Yeats and Joyce through the somewhat canonical Le Fanu and Carleton to the largely neglected Wilde and Sadlier. The Yeats and Joyce essays seek to enter critical dialogues (or, to use a less flattering term, industries) that are full of stimulating and sophisticated scholarship. These chapters respond to particular contemporary developments in critical fields, such as the rise of interest in Joyce as a writer who engaged intensely, if ambivalently, with Irish nationalism and debates over how best to characterize Yeats's relationship to the colonial and postcolonial. Both developments sprang at least partly from the increasingly busy intersection between Irish studies and postcolonial studies. The discussions of Carleton and Le Fanu attempt to remedy perceived gaps in the existing scholarly literature. The former reads Carleton's representations of religion through some generic and formal features of his writing, rather than through the much-discussed question of his personal relation to Catholicism. The latter proposes to move beyond the opposition between Irish/political and psychoanalytic/sexual readings of the Anglo-Irish gothic by arguing that, for particular historical and colonial reasons, Le Fanu structured his anxieties about Anglo-Irish identity through representations of femininity and female sexuality. In the essays on Wilde and Sadlier I hope to generate scholarly interest in a pair of women writers who were tremendously popular in their day but have yet to be rediscovered by literary and cultural historians. Until recently, Irish studies has been fairly slow to engage in such acts of retrieval; the publication of volumes 4 and 5 of *The Field Day Anthology of Irish Writing* indicates the growth of interest in such material and demonstrates just how much there is to be uncovered and explored.[8] In addition, much research remains to be done on popular literature produced by and for the Irish. The questions and complexities offered by such writing differ from the questions and complexities offered by Yeats and Joyce, who were undeniably superior writers according to a whole range of criteria, but they can be equally compelling.

The lesser-known works often raise questions about the crossroads where individual writers confront the requirements of generic conventions. The essays on Wilde, Sadlier, and Carleton all

---

7   Jonathan Culler has pointed out that many literary and cultural critics invoke Anderson's claims about the novel's form in order to lend authority to their own very different arguments about national content and themes in literature. See Jonathan Culler, 'Anderson and the Novel', in Jonathan Culler and Pheng Cheah, eds., *Grounds of Comparison: Around the Work of Benedict Anderson* (New York and London, 2003).

8   Angela Bourke et al., eds., *The Field Day Anthology of Irish Writing*, vols. 4–5, *Women's Writing and Traditions* (Cork and New York, 2002)

trace those writers' negotiations with the dominant traditions of sentimental literature. Gothic literature, millenarian thought, and oral traditions are discussed more briefly. Still, in reading these essays together, one can see that generic conventions, while often rigid in themselves, can be put to surprisingly flexible and multiple uses. Popular genres are certainly produced and consumed differently in various locations, but they are also profoundly international in their formal regularities and their circulation. Investigating the issues surrounding these genres helps place Irish writers in a global rather than a purely national frame. It is far more useful, for example, to examine Sadlier in relation to the American didactic fiction of the 'feminine fifties', and sentimental traditions more generally, than to try to confine her to a specifically Irish literary tradition. If one impulse behind these essays is the wish to examine how different writers engage with ideas about Ireland and Irishness, another, equally important, impulse emerges in the later essays: the desire to show that such engagements are best studied in comparative and transnational frames that take account of the way the local, the national, and the global all cross paths.

Blood and Tears: Lady Wilde

Young Ireland marked the emergence of an Irish nationalism that was more ethnic and cultural than civic and constitutional. Although it fizzled out as an organization after the abortive rising of 1848, it had enduring cultural and political legacies. The poetry of Young Ireland was arguably the most popular body of literature in Ireland in the latter half of the nineteenth century. Later developments in Irish nationalism owed a great deal to the version of Ireland embodied in the verse of *The Nation*, in which the ballad and the song were the favoured modes of transmission.[1] David Lloyd and Seán Ryder have sketched out its major features: it was overwhelmingly bourgeois, organized around the production of identity, and heavily gendered, equating true nationalist subjectivity with masculinity.[2] These features, far from rendering Young Ireland ideologically simple or monologic, determined the shape of its complexities and contradictions.[3] The aim of this essay is to illuminate previously neglected aspects of Young Ireland's cultural nationalism.

Lady Wilde was born Jane Elgee in 1821, to a conservative, middle-class, Protestant family in Wexford. She married William Wilde in 1851, and became Lady Wilde when he was knighted in 1864. She was one of a number of nationalist poets that came to prominence after Thomas Davis's death in 1845. Under the pen-name 'Speranza', she published poetry and prose in *The Nation*; the poems were collected in 1864 as *Poems by Speranza*. By then she had secured her reputation as one of the most inflammatory writers of the Young Ireland movement.[4] Much of her other work has been

---

1   Chris Morash, Introduction in *The Hungry Voice: The Poetry of the Irish Famine* (Dublin, 1989), 30

2   For extended discussions of these features, see David Lloyd, *Anomalous States: Irish Writing and the Post-Colonial Moment* (Durham, NC, 1993) and *Nationalism and Minor Literature: James Clarence Mangan and the Emergence of Irish Cultural Nationalism* (Berkeley, CA, 1987), and Seán Ryder, 'Gender and the Discourse of "Young Ireland" Cultural Nationalism', in T. P. Foley et al., eds., *Gender and Colonialism* (Galway, 1995), 210–24.

3   On Young Ireland's origins, development, and intellectual structures, see Richard Davis, *The Young Ireland Movement* (Dublin and Totowa, NJ, 1987); George Boyce, *Nationalism in Ireland* (London, 1991), 154–91; David Cairns and Shaun Richards, *Writing Ireland: Colonialism, Nationalism and Culture* (Manchester, 1988), 22–41; Seamus Deane, 'Poetry and Song 1800–1890' and 'The Famine and Young Ireland', in Seamus Deane, ed., *The Field Day Anthology of Irish Writing*, 3 vols. (Derry, 1991), vol. 2, 1–114, 115–208.

4   The authorities considered her anonymous 1848 essay 'Jacta Alea Est' [The Die is Cast] seditious enough to warrant prosecution, and tried Charles Gavan Duffy as its author. When Elgee (as she then was) disrupted his trial by standing up in the gallery and claiming authorship, the government declined to prosecute her, and four different juries refused to convict Duffy. For an account of the incident, see Richard Ellmann, *Oscar Wilde* (New York, 1988), 9.

forgotten.[5] After the failure of the 1848 Rising, both she and William became disillusioned with Irish nationalism; later she concentrated increasingly on other literary projects and on her aspirations to run a literary salon. In the late nineteenth century, she was generally acknowledged as an important, if eccentric, figure in the Dublin literary and social scene. When her son, Oscar Wilde, toured the United States in 1882, headlines in New York's Irish Nation lamented, 'Speranza's Son ... Phrasing about Beauty while a Hideous Tyranny Overshadows His Native Land'.[6] Ten years later, when W. B. Yeats wanted to praise the fiery eloquence of Maud Gonne's political speeches, he dubbed her 'the new Speranza'.[7]

Like many nineteenth-century women writers of sentimental fiction or parlour poetry, Wilde was considerably more visible to her contemporaries than she was to later cultural critics. Although her contributions to The Nation were nearly as popular as those of Davis, its most charismatic writer, she has been largely neglected by studies of Irish cultural nationalism as well.[8] To the extent that she has entered literary history, Wilde has done so primarily as a figure defined by her gendered 'excesses' — emotional, political, and stylistic.[9] These excesses are usually characterized as a surfeit of sentimentalizing emotion and an extravagant interest in violence, bloodshed and death: a constant sense that the history of Ireland was, as she wrote in a pamphlet on 'The American Irish', 'an endless martyrology written in tears and blood'.[10] Wilde's preoccupation with the dramatic shedding of tears and blood reveals her particular engagements with the major structures and contradictions that distinguished Young Ireland from the Old Ireland of Daniel O'Connell. In a letter to his constituents, O'Connell wrote:

> My plan is peaceable, legal, constitutional; it is part of that general scheme by which I incessantly contemplate the regeneration of Ireland, and her restoration to national dignity from her present provincial degradation, without a crime, without an offence, without a tear, and, above all, without the possibility of shedding one drop of human blood.[11]

In Wilde's works, in contrast, Young Ireland's tenuous relation to the Irish masses, which it both idealized and distrusted, its interest in and anxieties about subject constitution, and the masculinism of its ostensibly transcendent nationalist subject, are negotiated and structured through representations of tears and blood.

5   She translated Sidonia the Sorceress (1847–48), a novel by Wilhelm Meinhold, in 1849 and Lamartine's Pictures of the First French Revolution (1848) and The Wanderer and His Home (1850) in 1850; she published The Glacier Land in 1852 and The First Temptation in 1853. Poems: Second Series; Translations appeared in 1866. In 1880 she completed and published a book her husband had begun before his death, Memoir of Gabriel Béranger. Driftwood from Scandinavia appeared in 1884, Ancient Legends, Mystic Charms and Superstitions of Ireland in 1887, and Ancient Cures, Charms, and Usages of Ireland in 1890. Notes on Men, Women, and Books (1891) and Social Studies (1893) were collections of essays, all, or nearly all of which, had appeared earlier in journals.

6   Ellmann, Oscar Wilde, 195

7   'The New Speranza', in George Bornstein and Hugh Witemeyer, eds., Letters to the New Island (New York, 1989), 61

8   See Davis, Young Ireland Movement, 85.

9   Thomas Flanagan, in his The Irish Novelists, 1800–1850 (New York, 1959), 325, quoted in Ellmann, Oscar Wilde, 18, describes her as 'the silliest woman who ever lived' and Terry Eagleton's play St. Oscar (Derry, 1989) pokes fun at her vehement and sentimentalizing nationalism. Her work is included in a number of turn of the century anthologies; for a list see Morash, Writing the Irish Famine, 112. Later in the twentieth century, however, her work was seldom anthologized. Kathleen Hoagland's 1000 Years of Irish Poetry (Old Greenwich, CT, 1981) includes only her most famous poem, 'The Famine Year', and A. A. Kelly omits her from Pillars of the House: An Anthology of Verse by Irish Women from 1690 to the Present (Dublin, 1987) on the grounds that her poetry 'appears turgid to the modern ear' (19). She does not appear in the first three volumes of The Field Day Anthology but she is included in the fourth volume and in A. Leighton and M. Reynolds, eds., Victorian Women Poets: An Anthology (Oxford, 1995).

10 Reprinted in Horace Wyndham, Speranza: A Biography of Lady Wilde (London and New York, 1951), 205–39

11 M. F. Cusack, ed., The Speeches and Public Letters of the Liberator, 2 vols. (Dublin, 1875), vol. 2, 414–15

Tears

Wilde's nationalist poems are awash with tears — the tears of men, women and children; the tears of poets, patriots and peasants; the tears of sufferers, spectators and gods. These tears structure an important aspect of Young Ireland's construction of its project as subject constitution. David Lloyd's *Nationalism and Minor Literature* offers a ground-breaking and insightful examination of this project. While Lloyd's work focuses mainly on issues of identity and unity in the work of James Clarence Mangan — unity as homogeneity between the individual and the nation; identity as the consistency of the subject over time — another way to think about subject constitution is as the production and organization of affect. Of course, most nationalisms are primarily 'about' feeling; the question is how particular nationalisms conceptualize and organize it. In most accounts, their engagement with the question of feeling takes the form of an erotics.[12] This tends to produce two related narratives of the relationship between gender and nationalism, both focusing on the representation of the nation as a woman. In the first, the nation-as-woman is an eroticized lover, and her patriots worship her with an ecstatic heterosexual devotion. In the second, the nation is figured as an idealized mother whose purity secures her sons' faithfulness and mediates their potentially dangerous homosocial attachments to each other.[13] The distinction between these narratives is one of degree and emphasis, rather than kind; both involve suppressing homosexual desire between men and presenting heterosexual love as the appropriate model of national affect. Such narratives do form an important part of Young Ireland's cultural production, but they do not exhaust the functions of gender in nationalist writing, nor do they encompass all the ways in which cultural nationalism engaged with the question of national feeling. In addition, women writers often have an especially problematic relationship to such iconography.[14] While these representational patterns are not wholly absent from Wilde's work, they do not structure it in a significant way. Young Ireland also employed a different set of tropes for conceptualizing and organizing national feeling, one that was arguably more congenial to women writers. Through representations of tears, her poetry illustrates this alternative conception of cultural nationalism as subject constitution and that project's relation to gender and class boundaries.

While O'Connell wanted to achieve his political goals without shedding blood or tears, he was no less sentimental than Young Ireland; his nationalism simply imagined a different relation between nationality and feeling. O'Connell's movement relied upon a combination of feeling and reason.[15] His nationalism was largely a modernizing, Enlightenment project; several critics have argued that disciplined, mass, constitutional politics in Ireland and Britain originated with his movement.[16] He emphasized the calm rationality of his own political arguments — 'I am cool, and quiet, and deliberate;

---

12 The Introduction to *Nationalisms and Sexualities* observes, 'Whenever the power of the nation is invoked — whether it be in the media, in scholarly texts, or in everyday conversation — we are more likely than not to find it couched as a *love of country*: an eroticized nationalism'; see Andrew Parker et al., eds., *Nationalisms and Sexualities* (New York, 1992), 1. Influential books like George Mosse's *Nationalism and Sexuality: Middle-Class Morality and Sexual Norms in Modern Europe* (Madison, WI, 1985) and Klaus Theweleit's *Male Fantasies, Volume I: Women Floods Bodies History*, trans. Stephen Conway (Minneapolis, MN, 1987) take as their starting points the assumption that the feelings associated with nationalism are best conceptualized in erotic terms.

13 See, for example, C. L. Innes, *Woman and Nation in Irish Literature and Society, 1880–1935* (Athens, GA, 1993); Elizabeth Butler Cullingford, '"Thinking of Her … as … Ireland": Yeats, Pearse, and Heaney', *Textual Practice*, 4 (1990), 1–21; Joseph Valente, 'The Myth of Sovereignty: Gender in the Literature of Irish Nationalism', *English Literary History*, 61, 1 (1994), 189–210; and Ryder, 'Gender'.

14 For a discussion of the Irish case, see Eavan Boland, *A Kind of Scar: The Woman Poet in a National Tradition* (Dublin, 1989).

15 As a young man, the two books he was most influenced by were William Godwin's *Caleb Williams* (1794) and Henry Mackenzie's *The Man of Feeling* (1771), representing the cults of rational improvement and of sensibility, respectively; see Oliver MacDonagh, *The Hereditary Bondsman: Daniel O'Connell, 1775–1829* (London, 1988), 39.

16 See Davis, *Young Ireland Movement*, 2, and Terry Eagleton, *Heathcliff and the Great Hunger: Studies in Irish Culture* (London, 1995), 274.

no bursts of passion sway my Soul' — and exhorted his followers to legal, orderly agitation.[17] On the other hand, O'Connell also employed, and was shaped by, the nineteenth-century discourses of sentimentalism and melodrama. His speeches, especially at the 'monster meetings' of the 1840s, were often calculated to arouse the passions of his audiences, and did so quite effectively. Even his written effusions, in a letter to his followers, on the death of Thomas Davis aspired to the status of a spontaneous, unmediated outpouring of feeling: 'I can write no more — my tears blind me.'[18] The main difference between O'Connell and Young Ireland, then, was that for O'Connell, although nationalism involved feeling, feeling was not the quintessential mark of national subjectivity. This was because O'Connell had little investment in Irish culture or identity as bases for political action or arrangements; his Irish nationalism was not primarily a project of subject constitution. He viewed the decline of the Irish language with equanimity, and, as Oliver MacDonagh observes, he would have found such concepts as 'anglicization' or 'mental colonialism' incomprehensible.[19] For O'Connell, nationality was a matter of location rather than feeling. 'The Irish people' simply meant all the inhabitants of Ireland, and the power and legitimacy of his movement rested on its mass character, rather than on its 'Irish' character. He liked to intone, 'I speak the voice of seven millions.'[20]

For Young Ireland, speaking the voice of the Irish was more complicated. Many critics have remarked on the doubleness that characterizes discourses of the nation; these discourses assert that the nation already exists, and at the same time they seek to create it.[21] This doubleness assumed a particularly virulent form for Young Ireland. On one hand, an anti-colonial nationalism has to work harder to illustrate the pre-existence of the nation than a statist nationalism, and in the case of Ireland, sectarian division provided glaring evidence that a unified nation did not already exist. On the other hand, Young Ireland arose under circumstances that made the task of a didactic, transformative nationalist project particularly difficult, so, in addition, the possibilities for creating the nation appeared slim.[22] For Young Ireland, 'the Irish people' was a problematic, paradoxical entity, made up of subjects that were already, ineradicably constituted as national, and, at the same time, stood in dire need of such constitution.

Wilde's representations of tears encapsulate this ambiguity. In some instances, tears are the mark of a suffering and passive populace who lack national consciousness or feeling (these two being virtually equivalent for romantic nationalism). Such tears indicate the masses' inadequate response to their own conditions of oppression, conditions that cry out for political action. One poem asks,

> But can we only weep, when above us thus lour
> The death-bearing wings of the angels of power.[23]

Another criticizes the 'abject tears, and prayers submissive' of the people who refuse to rise.[24] In 'Who

---

17 Cusack, *Speeches and Public Letters*, vol. 2, 373
18 Quoted in Oliver MacDonagh, *The Emancipist: Daniel O'Connell, 1830–47* (New York, 1989), 272. MacDonagh, *Hereditary Bondsman*, 194, also notes that, for most of his life, O'Connell's favourite writer was Thomas Moore, famous for his tearful sentimentalities on the subject of Ireland and the Irish.
19 MacDonagh, *Emancipist*, 137
20 Cusack, *Speeches and Public Letters*, vol. 1, 517
21 See Lloyd, *Anomalous States*, esp. 'Adulteration and the Nation'; Eagleton, *Heathcliff and the Great Hunger*, esp. 'Culture and Politics from Davis to Joyce'; and Homi Bhabha's influential formulation in 'DissemiNation: Time, Narrative, and the Margins of the Modern Nation', in Homi Bhabha, ed., *Nation and Narration* (New York and London, 1990), 291–322.
22 R. Radhakrishnan, 'Nationalism, Gender, and Narrative', in Parker et al., *Nationalisms and Sexualities*, 89, succinctly sums up this dilemma in the context of Indian nationalism: 'The masses can neither be bypassed (for they are the real India) nor can they be legitimated qua people.'
23 'Foreshadowings' in *Poems by Speranza*, 2nd edn. (Glasgow, n.d.), 18; volume hereafter cited as PS
24 'Have Ye Counted the Cost' in PS, 34

Will Show Us Any Good?' tears literally blind the masses to their true identity and interests:

> Suffering Ireland! Martyr-Nation!
> Blind with tears thick as mountain mist;
> Can none amidst all the new generation
> Change them to glory, ...'[25]

Tears as the sign of colonial abjection are often gendered feminine; the same poem describes a passive Ireland as the 'Saddest of mothers'.[26] Such representations fit smoothly into the mainstream of literature produced by other Young Irelanders such as Davis or Mangan. Another *Nation* poet put it this way:

> Serf! with thy fetters o'erladen,
> Why crouch you in dastardly woe?
> Why weep o'er thy chains like a maiden,
> Nor strike for thy manhood a blow?[27]

Like Wilde, 'Mary' (Ellen Downing) and 'Eva' (Mary Eva Kelly) of *The Nation* also exhorted their men to nationalist fortitude by denigrating a weak and tearful femininity as the alternative; as Seán Ryder has observed, their poetry 'differs little from that of their male colleagues in its reproduction of bourgeois nationalist gender relations — the difference being that it often articulates such relations from a woman's point-of-view'.[28]

Not all Irish woe was dastardly; Young Ireland's writers frequently invoked the tears of the suffering to describe the brutalities of English rule and the horrors of the Great Famine of the 1840s. Mary Eva Kelly's 'A Scene for Ireland' describes a starving mother's inability to feed her baby:

> She has no food to give it now
> Save those hot tears outgushing.[29]

But such a literature of Irish misery still equated weeping with helplessness, and thus lent itself to appropriation by a version of imperial sentimentality, exemplified by writers such as Ernest Renan and Matthew Arnold, that constructed the Irish as sensitive, romantic, and politically inept. Thomas Moore's *Irish Melodies* illustrates the potential ease of such appropriations. Moore's work was sufficiently nationalist to make him a favourite of O'Connell and a target of the conservative English press. But Moore was a liberal unionist, and his poems were immensely popular in the drawing rooms of England several decades before they became well-known in Ireland. Although he sometimes took up a nationalist call to armed resistance, at other times Moore's portrait of the Irish as the nation of the smile and the tear meant that Irish cultural production expressed the suffering of the Irish with such lyrical poignancy that

> Thy masters themselves, as they rivet thy chains,

---

25 PS, 59
26 PS, 60
27 'The Gathering of Leinster' in *The Spirit of the Nation*, pt. 2 (Dublin, 1843), 17
28 Ryder, 'Gender', 219
29 Quoted in Morash, *The Hungry Voice*, 61

Shall pause at the song of their captive, and weep.[30]

This image perfectly captures the classic mode and dynamics of imperial sentimentality, in which the empire nostalgically cathects that which it is in the process of destroying.

Wilde's works attempt to navigate between the nationalist Scylla of tears that indicate contemptible helplessness and the imperial Charybdis of tears that indicate moving helplessness that nevertheless remains helpless by transferring the imperative to nationalist subject constitution and action to the spectator or reader. Such a transfer is implicit in Young Ireland's laments for Irish suffering and their privileging of popular forms like the ballad. It also accords with Young Ireland's project, discernible in a number of its intellectual structures, to transform the history of Irish suffering, national and individual, into a source of, and blueprint for, a gloriously victorious future. But Wilde theorized, more thoroughly than many of her contemporaries, the processes and mechanisms through which tears undergo this transformation. In her works, tears constitute a spectacle of suffering capable of generating national feeling and spurring nationalist action; they also signify that a viewer is reacting properly to that spectacle. As this description suggests, such representations of weeping are generically related to the late eighteenth-century discourses of sensibility and their sentimental Victorian descendants, though they do not coincide completely with either. Terms like 'sensibility' and 'sentimentality' are notoriously hard to define; their political implications are even more slippery. Sensibility could be organized around individualistic, democratic, and liberal principles, or it could be mobilized in the service of 'natural' social and political hierarchies.[31] The politics of sentimentality are similarly uncertain and in contention.[32] The various formulations of these discourses shared a conviction of the immediately political significance of feeling, and a concomitant conception of feeling as the basis of the social bond. Thus when Edmund Burke attacked the French Revolution, whose excesses are widely supposed to have irrevocably tainted the vocabulary of sensibility after the 1790s, he did it by claiming sensibility's terms as his own without acknowledging them, lamenting the elimination of natural sentiments and affections as the basis for a hierarchical and harmonious social order.[33]

Burke, Wilde, and various Victorian sentimentalists shared a double interest in feeling as a spectacle to be observed, and as the response that a particular kind of spectacle should produce in the ethically and politically enlightened observer. The tears of the suffering object and the tears of the observing subject go together; the former produces the latter. Wilde's often millenarian vocabulary tended to interchange an earthly observer with a heavenly one. One poem urges,

Let us lift our streaming eyes
To God's throne above the skies,
He will hear our anguish cries.[34]

In 'The Voice of the Poor', the speaker claims:

30 'Oh! Blame Not the Bard' in *The Poetical Works of Thomas Moore* (New York, 1852), 237
31 See Chris Jones, *Radical Sensibility: Literature and Ideas in the 1790s* (London and New York, 1993); Claudia Johnson, *Equivocal Beings: Politics, Gender and Sentimentality in the 1790s: Wollstonecraft, Radcliffe, Burney, Austen* (Chicago, IL, 1995); and Anne Vincent-Buffault, *The History of Tears: Sensibility and Sentimentality in France* (New York, 1991).
32 For example, Ann Douglas, *The Feminization of American Culture* (New York, 1988) argues for the reactionary nature of sentimental fiction's tendency to reinforce nineteenth-century stereotypes of women, while Jane Tompkins, *Sensational Designs: The Cultural Work of American Fiction 1790–1860* (Oxford, 1985) argues for its revolutionary potential because it relocates the crucial scene of social and political transformation in the sphere traditionally associated with women: the heart and hearth. For another discussion of Victorian sentimentality, see Fred Kaplan, *Sacred Tears: Sentimentality in Victorian Literature* (Princeton, NJ, 1987).
33 See Johnson, *Equivocal Beings*, esp. Introduction.
34 'A Supplication' in PS, 17

If the angels ever hearken, downward bending,
They are weeping, we are sure,
At the litanies of human groans ascending
From the crushed hearts of the poor.[35]

Similarly, 'Ruins' predicts that the weeping of the poor will 'Start the angels on their thrones'.[36] If God and the angels could be trusted to respond with the appropriate sympathetic tears to the weeping of the oppressed, members of the Protestant Ascendancy could not. 'The Faithless Shepherds' castigates the landed aristocracy for its cruel indifference to the plight of the poor during the Famine by asserting that the Ascendancy (like many contemporary descriptions of Famine victims) are the walking dead:

Dead! — Dead! Ye are dead while ye live
Ye've a name that ye live — but are dead.

This ethico-political (or national) death-in-life manifests itself as an absence of feeling — 'For the heart in each bosom is cold / As the ice on a frozen sea' — and a lack of sympathetic tears: 'With your cold eyes unwet by a tear, / For your Country laid low on your bier'.[37] The absence of national feeling indicates the corruption of the current régime and presages its violent demise, just as the presence of such feeling in heaven suggests that the nationalist revolution is divinely directed or sanctioned.

'The Brothers', subtitled 'A scene from '98', presents a spectacle, an execution, and revolves around its potential ability to generate national feeling, measured in tears, and the nationalist action such tears should also produce. In so far as it is cast as an exemplary or paradigmatic spectacle, the kind of scene supremely suited to produce the desired sentiments, we might also think of the poem as Wilde's equivalent to Burke's famous description of Marie Antoinette in *Reflections on the Revolution in France*. The prisoners, 'two noble youths,' are 'in pride of life and manhood's beauty' and bear their fate with exemplary heroism. Christ-like, they are 'Pale martyrs' who die for the sake of their fellow Irish. The poem emphasizes its narrative of events as a national spectacle whose significance lies primarily in its effect on its audience. The first stanza describes the 'pale and anxious crowd' which will witness the execution, before introducing the brothers, and positions the reader among the spectators: 'You can see them through the gloom.' The second stanza also insists on the importance of the crowd for whom the emotional effect of the spectacle is measured in tears:

All eyes an earnest watch on them are keeping,
Some, sobbing, turn away,
And the strongest men can hardly see for weeping,
So noble and so loved were they.

The syntax equates watching and weeping, spectatorship and sympathy:

There is silence in the midnight — eyes are keeping
Troubled watch till forth the jury come;
There is silence in the midnight — eyes are weeping —
'Guilty!' is the fatal uttered doom.

---

35 PS, 14
36 PS, 40
37 PS, 45–46

The crowd's lamentations are an index to their level of feeling, but tears alone are not enough; true national feeling must express itself in action. As in Wilde's other representations of weeping as the mark of colonial abjection, tears that do not generate politically conscious resistance are feminizing:

Oh! the rudest heart might tremble at such sorrow,
The rudest cheek might blanch at such a scene:
Twice the judge essayed to speak the word — to-morrow —
Twice faltered, as a woman he had been.

The judge is moved, but the inadequacy of his feelings, which manifests itself as feminine weakness, is structural as well as personal, springing from his position as the imperial official presiding over the brothers' conviction and execution.

Wilde's poem thus explicitly rejects, in conventionally gendered terms, the imperial sentimentality of a writer like Moore, which figures the captors weeping over the chains of their victims as a positive conception of national feeling or identity. The penultimate stanza juxtaposes the crowd's passive weeping with the active intervention imagined by the narrator, a more advanced nationalist who sounds oddly like Burke:

Yet none spring forth their bonds to sever
Ah! methinks, had I been there,
I'd have dared a thousand deaths ere ever
The sword should touch their hair.
It falls! — there is a shriek of lamentation
From the weeping crowd around;
They're stilled — the noblest hearts within the nation —
The noblest heads lie bleeding on the ground.

The crowd's tears cannot prevent the spilling of the heroes' blood. For the first time in the poem, the spectacle is in the distant past. At the same time, the execution scene is presented as a kind of perpetual present, embodied in the heads that refuse to decay and in the continued appeal of the spectacle to nationalist sensibilities:

Years have passed since that fatal scene of dying,
Yet, lifelike to this day,
In their coffins still those severed heads are lying,
Kept by angels from decay.
Oh! they preach to us, those still and pallid features —
Those pale lips yet implore us, from their graves,
To strive for our birthright as God's creatures,
Or die, if we can but live as slaves.

Having transferred the burden of reacting properly to the scene from the weeping but passive crowd to the narrator, the poem then transfers this burden to its readers. The poem itself, as well as the events it features, exists as a permanent national spectacle, waiting for the reader in whom it will inspire sentiments and actions like the narrator's. Wilde locates the power to constitute the subject of Irish nationalism simultaneously in the timeless spectacle, which should produce it automatically in anyone, and in the contingencies of the poem's particular readership.[38]

Weeping is thus a figure for the doubleness of the nation; it can signify either the plenitude and force of the spirit of the nation, or its devastating absence. As a way of structuring Young Ireland's anxieties about cultural nationalism as subject constitution — defined as the production and organization of feeling — this ambiguity generates a problematic that differs substantially from the problematics produced by an erotics of nationalism. The erotics of nationalism raise the threat of homosexual (as opposed to homosocial) bonds between men, the possibility that the patriot will choose his wife over her sexual rival, the nation, and the spectre of the woman-as-nation whose sexual betrayal or rape is equivalent to colonial conquest. The tearful strand of nationalism exemplified in Wilde's work, however, grapples with the danger that the signs of national feeling are ambiguous, their meanings contingent on who displays them. Wilde's work manages this ambiguity by constructing taxonomies of feeling based on gender and class distinctions. Thus Young Ireland's representations of tears also occupy the intersection between its drive towards a transcendent national unity and its need to maintain the divisions that unity supposedly transcended.

Men and Women; Leaders and Peoples

Wilde's work is structured by two hierarchies of tears — the tears of men over the tears of women, and the tears of patriot leaders over the tears of the masses. While O'Connell's movement was largely for and populated by men, he was well aware of the potential intersections between feminine sentimentality and political reform. He was passionately opposed to slavery, and once claimed that Thomas Moore's *Captain Rock* was to the struggle for Catholic Emancipation what Harriet Beecher Stowe's *Uncle Tom's Cabin* was to the abolition of slavery.[39] Maurice R. O'Connell has argued that the logic of Young Ireland's romantic cultural nationalism, which emphasized the uniqueness of peoples, militated against its sharing O'Connell's Enlightenment, universalist concern with American slavery and other instances of oppression outside Ireland.[40] I would add that this emphasis on identity, whose supposedly ungendered national subject was actually a male subject, also militated against Young Ireland embracing Stowe's 'feminine' brand of reform. Like Stowe, Wilde insists that political change begins with and depends on conversion, a change of heart. Unlike Stowe, however, Wilde does not locate this change in the feminine, domestic sphere of the hearth, or give women any special power to effect it. In Wilde's taxonomy of tearfulness, the most ethically and politically laudable tears are mainly the privilege of middle- and upper-class men.[41]

Wilde's acceptance of Young Ireland's equation of true nationalist subjectivity with masculinity meant that while weeping as a sign of powerlessness or a lack of political consciousness is often feminized in her work, tears as evidence of positive national feeling are associated with masculinity:

Meekly bear, but nobly try,
Like a man with soft tears flowing.[42]

38 PS, 7–9
39 MacDonagh, *Emancipist*, 17
40 Maurice R. O'Connell, 'O'Connell, Young Ireland, and Negro Slavery: An Exercise in Romantic Nationalism', *Thought*, 64, 253 (1989), 130–36
41 Similarly, Johnson, *Equivocal Beings*, 14, argues that, rather than feminizing culture, politics, or men, the late eighteenth-century discourses of sensibility entailed the masculinization of formerly feminine traits; those traits were legitimized only because and only in so far as they were recoded masculine.
42 'Man's Mission' in PS, 26

Similarly, while the tears of the populace often reveal their despair and pre-political stupor, the tears of patriot leaders embody the riches they can offer the nation:

> And woe to you, ye poor —
> Want and scorn ye must endure;
> Yet before ye many noble jewels shine
> In the sand.
> Ah! they are patriots' tears — even mine —
> For Fatherland![43]

This impulse towards hierarchy and differentiation within the boundaries of the nation was the inevitable companion to Young Ireland's drive towards various kinds of unity — political, aesthetic, and ethical. Since the nation was always in the process of being forged, the nationalization of the masses was always incomplete. This was particularly true for Young Ireland, given its relative lack of organic connections to the Irish masses. O'Connell's movement, in contrast, had been more genuinely popular, with the emergent Catholic middle classes, particularly in cities and rural towns, as its backbone of support.[44] Young Ireland never achieved the popular following that O'Connell enjoyed; the enormous early success of *The Nation* depended in part upon O'Connell's Repeal Association, which distributed it. In addition, although O'Connell continued to have a popular following, the Famine destroyed his political machine.[45]

Accordingly, a number of scholars have read Young Ireland's project as an attempt to create in culture a unity that did not exist in the political sphere.[46] Thus Young Ireland's founding premise of a unified spirit of the nation located in the Irish masses arose as the chances of it achieving such unity and politicizing the masses were actually receding. But this compensatory response created its own contradictions; it is less often observed that nationalization had to be incomplete, or it risked undoing some of cultural nationalism's other founding premises.[47] Its healthy respect for property and general economic conservatism (with a few exceptions) set limits on Young Ireland's unifying, assimilative ideals, and led it to privilege the leading role of the bourgeois intellectual. As Wilde wrote in an essay on an anthology of Irish songs, 'The utterances of a people, though always vehement, are often incoherent; and it is then that men of education and culture are needed to interpret and formulate the vague longings and ambitions of the passionate hearts around them.'[48] For Young Ireland, the relationship between leaders and peoples demanded both that the masses assimilate themselves to the model of the leaders, and that this assimilation remain perpetually deferred.

As a result, the figure of the nationalist leader carries enormous weight for Young Ireland, embodying both an ideal of unity and the continued significance and the superiority of the bourgeois intellectual. Wilde's work is obsessed with leaders — the current dearth of effective national leaders, the qualities and techniques associated with leadership, the nature of the relationship between leaders and peoples.

---

43 'Our Fatherland' in PS, 99

44 R. F. Foster, *Modern Ireland 1600–1972* (London, 1988), 300, observes that O'Connell's origins, which 'blended Gaelic clansmen and local Catholic gentry', allowed him to assert his organic connection to them successfully.

45 Boyce, *Nationalism in Ireland*, 171

46 See, for example, Deane, 'Poetry and Song 1800–1890', 1, in which he argues that 'The political rhetoric could not be translated into action because it bespoke a unity of purpose that did not exist.'

47 The fact that this formulation echoes the ambivalence Bhabha has identified in imperialist discourses of native assimilation reminds us once again of cultural nationalism's formal similarities to imperialism. See Homi Bhabha, *The Location of Culture* (London and New York, 1994), esp. 'Of Mimicry and Man: The Ambivalence of Colonial Discourse'.

48 Quoted in Wyndham, *Speranza*, 160

Her poems refer to leaders with epithets such as 'poet-prophet', 'poet-priest', 'prophet-leader', and 'patriot leader'; her leaders are heroic, Christ-like, or God-like.[49] At the same time, her works constantly return to the faults of the masses who have failed to assimilate themselves to the model offered by such leaders. 'Have Ye Counted the Cost?' sneers,

> Let the masses pass on scorning,
> Seek not courage in their mind;
> Self-devotion, patriot fervour,
> Spring not from the craven kind.[50]

When she became frustrated with the national movement, she blamed the populace, writing to Duffy, 'I do not blame the leaders in the least. In Sicily or Belgium they would have been successful.'[51]

Along with other Young Irelanders, Wilde subscribed to Thomas Carlyle's dictum that the history of the world is a series of biographies — the biographies of great men. She wrote biographical essays about a number of figures, including Thomas Moore and Daniel O'Connell. David Lloyd has explored Young Ireland's preoccupation with biography and autobiography, arguing that for Irish cultural nationalism the hero's biography represents a repetition of the nation's history, prefigures its destiny, and asserts the seamless continuity of the individual with the nation.[52] Wilde's essay on O'Connell exemplifies this pattern. His life, she wrote, was

> one long gladiatorial wrestle against oppression and bigotry in which every step was a combat, but every combat a victory. ... The life of O'Connell is, indeed, the history of Ireland for nearly a century ... He lived through all, incarnated all, and was the avenger, the apostle, and the prophet of her people.[53]

This view of Irish history as a series of gladiatorial triumphs was, to say the least, counter-intuitive, and may seem particularly perverse in the wake of the Famine. In contrast, for O'Connell, the history of Ireland was a history of Irish patience and reason in the face of British cruelty and provocation. O'Connell's life, for Wilde, was part of the incomplete process of resistance, as well as an image of its successful completion; it embodied a history of suffering and defeat and provided a diagram of victorious revolution. The contradictions that inhabit such a formulation are compounded by the leader's relationship to the people, whom the leader must both represent and exceed.

Wilde's works foreground the question of the leader's success or failure in transforming the masses, invariably imagining this transformation occurring when the leader breathes the spirit of the nation into the populace through his passionate oratory. Thomas Davis's essays emphasized the skill of past Irish orators and encouraged present would-be leaders to study the character of their audiences and the techniques of oratory. Wilde described O'Connell's powers as an orator using a language of the mythical and the magical:

> Never, perhaps, since sirens gave up sitting and singing upon rocks, did such witch-music fall on the ear of listener. The effect was magical — it acted like some potent spell; ... Men were charmed,

---

49 PS, 25, 28, 39, 53
50 PS, 34
51 Quoted in Wyndham, *Speranza*, 31
52 Lloyd, *Nationalism and Minor Literature*, 59–60
53 Wilde, 'Daniel O'Connell', in *Notes on Men, Women and Books*, 180–97

subdued, enchanted — forgot everything but him, and could not choose but listen, love him, and swear to do or die for him.[54]

O'Connell was famous, in Ireland and abroad, for his oratorical skills, but he was not inclined to think of himself as a siren. He theorized his effect on his audiences and his role as a leader in very different terms. O'Connell was well aware that print capitalism, particularly the daily plebiscite of the newspaper, made the rise of his modern popular nationalism possible; this was later famously theorized by Benedict Anderson.[55] In 1839 he threatened his colleagues in Parliament by asking whether they realized 'that the Irish people almost universally were now readers? — that where newspapers formerly hardly went out of the great towns, they were now to be found in every village, and almost in every cabin?'[56] For O'Connell, the Irish people were no less a people, and no less a political force, for being apparently isolated, each in his or her own cabin. Luke Gibbons has pointed out that Anderson's argument requires some modification in relation to Ireland and other colonized nations which had important traditions of resistance in oral culture.[57] In addition, newspapers like The Nation were often passed around and read aloud to groups. So, while Irish newspapers were central to O'Connell's movement, and their effective circulation and cultural authority was far greater than sales figures suggest, they were closely connected to oral culture. But O'Connell did not privilege speech over writing, and he explicitly theorized the importance of print culture, rather than his own siren-like powers, to his nationalist project.[58]

Although Young Ireland consciously promoted and exploited print media, set up Repeal reading rooms, and lauded its literary projects as part of the national struggle, its rhetoric, in contrast to O'Connell's, went to some lengths to conceal its dependence on print. Cultural nationalism's representations of the nation erased the mediated national community created by print and visualized by O'Connell as each Irish citizen reading a newspaper at home, and replaced it with the physical immediacy of an orator addressing a crowd. Young Ireland's definition of the leader as orator cast him less as the people's representative than as their hypnotist, or, as Wilde put it, their siren. Although the people formed a natural and inevitable national community, they needed the leader's magical eloquence to make them aware of their nationhood and give it political force. To imagine the orator relying on logic, persuasion or choice in mobilizing the people was tantamount to recognizing the nation as constructed and contingent, so Young Ireland described its orators using a language of mystical transformation, in which the masses simply 'woke up' from the nightmare of their own ignorance and passivity. Wilde asks in one poem,

> Then, trumpet-tongued, to a people sleeping,
> Who will speak with magic command [?][59]

Another poem calls for a leader to 'Pass the word that bands together — / Word of mystic conjuration' and predicts the result:

> And, as fire consumes the heather,
> So the young hearts of the nation

54 Wilde, 'Daniel O'Connell', 188–89
55 Boyce, Nationalism and Ireland, 160; Anderson, Imagined Communities, 32–46
56 Cusack, Speeches and Public Letters, vol. 1, 536
57 Luke Gibbons, 'Identity Without a Centre: Allegory, History and Irish Nationalism', in Transformations in Irish Culture (Cork, 1996), 134–48
58 MacDonagh, Hereditary Bondsman, 208
59 'Who Will Show Us Any Good' in PS, 61

Fierce will blaze up, quick and scathing, 'gainst the stranger and the foe.[60]

The hearts of the masses respond automatically, irrationally and uncontrollably, like a field set ablaze, their reaction unmediated by distance, time, or thought.

As the repositories of the spirit of the nation and the instruments of that spirit's emergence in the people, poets and leaders were interchangeable in Wilde's work. 'The Young Patriot Leader' describes the hero's eloquence as an overpowering natural (and ultimately supernatural) force, capable of achieving the transformation of the heart that sentimentalists like Stowe imagined in less violently martial terms:

As a tempest in its force, as a torrent in its course,
So his words fiercely sweep all before them,
And they smite like two-edged swords, those undaunted thunder-words,
On all hearts, as tho' angels did implore them.[61]

Similarly, 'A Remonstrance' asserts:

Flashes from Poet's words
Electric light, strong, swift, and sudden, like
The clash of thunder-clouds, by which men read
God's writing legibly on human hearts.[62]

In Wilde's works, the words of patriot leaders and poets burn, smite, act as 'thunder crashes' or 'God's thunder'; they are both physical objects with concrete effects and fetishes, magical objects with absolute power to transform listeners.[63] The greater and more God-like the orator's transformative powers, however, the greater his distance from the masses with whom he was eventually supposed to be merged. Young Ireland's emphasis on the unmediated character of the orator's effect on the people formed the very vehicle through which it inscribed his absolute separation from them. Conversely, it was O'Connell's faith in the mediation of print that made it possible for him to imagine himself a member of the Irish nation, similar to other members.

Most of Wilde's works emphasize that the masses have yet to be transformed by the spirit of the nation. Her exhortatory language attempts to generate that spirit among her readers. The didactic impulses of Young Ireland's project are well known. But in Wilde's case, representations of gender play a particularly important role in organizing those impulses. The recalcitrance of the masses, and the necessary, continued separation of the leader from them, is expressed in the discrepancy between the women poet and the male patriot leader. 'Who Will Show Us Any Good?' laments:

Alas! can I help? but a nameless singer —
Weak the words of a woman to save;
We wait the advent of some light-bringer.[64]

---

60 'Forward!' in PS, 31
61 PS, 28–29
62 PS, 52
63 PS, 24, 30
64 PS, 61

The female poet is the pale, inadequate shadow of the true inspirer of the nation, the patriot leader. The doubleness of the nation, which exists eternally yet remains to be created, is mapped onto a gender gap between them.

The first poem in *Poems by Speranza*, 'Dedication. To Ireland', introduces the volume by emphasizing this discrepancy. The opening stanza, written entirely in the conditional tense, details how the speaker would like to inspire the nation, but also implies that she cannot:

> My Country, wounded to the heart,
> Could I but flash along thy soul
> Electric power to rive apart
> The thunder-clouds that round thee roll,
> And, by my burning words uplift
> Thy life from out Death's icy drift,
> Till the full splendours of our age
> Shone round thee for thy heritage —
> As Miriam's, by the Red Sea strand
> Clashing proud cymbals, so my hand
> Would strike thy harp,
> Loved Ireland!

The second stanza confesses:

> I can but look in God's great face,
> And pray Him for our fated race,
> To come in Sinai thunders down,
> And, with His mystic radiance, crown
> Some Prophet-Leader ...

The poem turns on the speaker's gender, which renders her an inferior substitute for a true poet-leader:

> The woman's voice dies in the strife
> Of Liberty's awakening life;
> We wait the hero heart to lead,
> The hero, who can guide at need.

The poem's last stanza affirms the efforts made by the 'woman's hand' of the speaker, while insisting on their limited efficacy.[65] Even the reference to Miriam indicates that she will never achieve the status of a true poet-prophet. Miriam was Moses' sister, and her only prophecy was a song of praise for Moses after he parted the Red Sea. Later, she was punished by God for complaining that Moses had too much power; Wilde's speaker is unlikely to incur punishment for a similar offence.

Like the other women writers of *The Nation*, Wilde did not explicitly critique or resist the major structures of Young Ireland's cultural nationalism. Instead, she inhabited their contradictions in a particular way. Wilde emphasized a sentimental rather than an erotic model of national feeling, but

---

65   PS, iii–iv

did not make the claims to specifically feminine power found in other sentimental literatures. She used Young Ireland's gender conventions to mediate a bourgeois nationalism's necessary but problematic separation from the people, embodied in the weak feminine tears of the masses and the worthy, masculine tears of the true patriot. Similarly, rather than explicitly assert the worth of the woman writer, Wilde employed the figures of the woman poet and the male patriot to inscribe the doubleness of the nation and the ambiguous status and potential the masses had for Young Ireland. But if Wilde found a despairing, pre-national people problematic, she hardly found a mobilized, nationalist people less so, as is illustrated in her representations of blood.

Blood

O'Connell alternatively condemned violence and appeared to condone it. Although the British political classes viewed him as a figure who deliberately aroused the passions of the mob, O'Connell feared and distrusted the masses who supported him, hated social unrest, and condemned revolutions and agrarian secret societies.[66] His speeches and essays counselled legal agitation, orderly mass demonstrations, and non-violence: 'Let there be no riot, no outrage, no violation of the law, and above all, no despair. We are eight millions.'[67] He repeatedly insisted that 'the best possible political revolution is not worth one single drop of human blood'.[68] Much of O'Connell's pacifist politics was based, however, on the implicit threat of a mass uprising. His speeches sometimes employed martial language, especially when he wanted to whip up popular feeling at the monster meetings of the early 1840s. The meetings themselves, which scholars have compared to people's festivals, religious revivals, and theatrical spectacles, bristled with potential mass violence, and encapsulated the tensions between violence and non-violence in the movement. They were elaborately staged, with much pomp and pageantry, and audiences responded passionately to O'Connell's famed oratorical skills. Crowds were often organized into ranks and marched in step, in a display of quasi-military discipline that suggested their potential to become a real army.[69] It was this combination of O'Connell's ability to mobilize the passions of the masses and his skill in controlling them, in the manner of an inspired military leader, that many contemporary observers found particularly threatening.

In some respects, Young Ireland's war-like rhetoric stated plainly what O'Connell had been careful to suggest obliquely. The devastation of the Famine, England's largely uncaring and inept handing of the crisis, and the revolutions across Europe in 1848 had radicalized many previously moderate Irish nationalists. Wilde began contributing to The Nation just after the Famine began and, as the crisis worsened, nationalist writers confronted the issue of how to represent death and suffering on an unprecedented, and nearly unrepresentable, scale. Blood, like tears, can illustrate the violent abjection of a colonized people, and the 'excessive' carnage in Wilde's work is, in part, a response to the ethical imperative to render the excessive carnage of the Famine adequately.[70] Like tears, blood has other functions in Wilde's work as well.

Wilde's representations of tears were inflected by the dominant discourses of feeling, but her representations of blood were informed by the major impulses of contemporary religious discourses,

---

66 MacDonagh, Emancipist, 229–31, and Hereditary Bondsman, passim.

67 Cusack, Speeches and Letters, vol. 2, 394

68 Cusack, Speeches and Letters, vol. 2, 441

69 See MacDonagh, Emancipist, 229–31, and Davis, Young Ireland Movement, 41. Some people in the south of Ireland interpreted an 1828 meeting and the agitation surrounding it as preparation for a rising; see Boyce, Nationalism in Ireland, 141.

70 For insightful discussions of these issues, see Chris Morash's Writing the Irish Famine (Oxford, 1995) and his Introduction to Hungry Voice.

the importance of which, as Maria Luddy has shown, can hardly be overestimated as a shaping force in the lives of publicly active nineteenth-century Irish women.[71] Her preoccupation with blood, violence and death was structured by a Protestant millenarianism in which the Apocalypse signals the end of this world, judgment, and the beginning of the new millennium. Chris Morash has pointed out that Irish Protestantism was heavily indebted to millenarian thought in the nineteenth century, and that interest in millennial prophecy was especially high in the late 1840s. Morash argues that although millenarian thought among most Protestants was reactionary and anti-Irish, it also offered Young Ireland a way of narrating the Famine that exposed the massive suffering it caused while also casting it as an apocalyptic harbinger of a utopian world.[72] In addition, Young Ireland's conception of the nationalization of the masses as a magical transformation, its fetishistic emphasis on the power of words, and its vagueness about how revolutionary change was actually to come about are all characteristics Eric Hobsbawm associates with millenarian movements.[73]

Wilde's millenarianism and her interest in biography functioned in similar ways: they enabled her to write the history of the nation and the individual as both a record of oppression and a blueprint for victory. The cataclysmic nature of the suffering involved in the Famine becomes an index to the radical nature of the transformation it heralds. Poems such as 'Foreshadowings' graft the vocabularies and structures of millenarian thinking onto a discourse of nationalist resistance.[74] The poem begins, 'Oremus! Oremus! [Let us pray!] Look down on us, Father!' and conflates the Horsemen of the Apocalypse with imperial coercion and famine:

> On rushes the war-steed, his lurid eyes flashing;
> There is blood on the track where his long mane is streaming, ...
> There's a tramp like a knell — a cold shadow gloometh —
> Woe! 'tis the black steed of Famine that cometh.

'Signs of the Times' claims, 'By our prophets God is speaking, in Sinai's awful thunders, / By pestilence and famine, in fearful signs and wonders', and describes the rough beast that slouches towards Ireland as a successor to the French Revolution:

> On its brow a name is written — France read it once before,
> And like a demon's compact, it was written in her gore —
> A fearful name — thrones trembled as the murmur passed along —
> RETRIBUTION, proud oppressors, for your centuries of wrong.[75]

The signs of a better world are literally 'written' — both determined and predicted — in violence, blood and gore. The Irish might be suffering horribly, but God — and the nationalists whose divine sanction was indicated by the interchangeability of the earthly and heavenly avengers that her poems constantly invoke — would judge the oppressors and avenge their crimes.

Analyses of cultural nationalism often associate its more violent-minded formulations with its nostalgic, mythologizing, backward-looking impulses.[76] But Young Ireland's nostalgia for lost origins

71 Maria Luddy, *Women and Philanthropy in Nineteenth-Century Ireland* (Cambridge, 1995), 2
72 Morash, *Writing the Irish Famine*, chs. 4–5
73 Eric Hobsbawm, *Primitive Rebels: Studies in Archaic Forms of Social Movement in the 19th and 20th Centuries* (New York, 1965), chs. 4–6
74 PS, 17–19
75 PS, 21–23
76 See, for example, Richard Kearney, *Myth and Motherland* (Derry, 1984).

and pristine precolonial culture did not prevent it from needing, and embracing, however ambivalently, a modernizing, nineteenth-century narrative of progress. Hobsbawm points out that millenarianism is the most 'modern' of 'primitive' social movements, and can be fairly easily harnessed in the service of modern political revolutions. Wilde's bloody millenarianism coexists with her commitment to progress, most often imagined as the 'onward march of nations' through history.[77] 'Who Will Show Us Any Good?' asserts, 'Ireland rests mid the rush of progression, / As a frozen ship in a frozen sea', and laments, 'we alone of the Christian nations / Fall to the rear in the march of Man'.[78] In fact, her bloody rhetoric offers an alternative, apocalyptic narrative of progress rather than a backward-looking resistance to it. 'The Year of Revolutions' asks,

> Shall we, oh! my Brothers, but weep, pray, and groan,
> When France reads her rights by the flames of a Throne?
> Shall we fear and falter to join the grand chorus,
> When Europe has trod the dark pathway before us?[79]

The apocalypse of the Famine and the nationalist apocalypse it prefigures propel Ireland forward along the path of civilization.

Wilde imagined violence and bloodshed as both the mark of oppression and a sign that the nationalist cause was advancing. But while the tears that indicate the weakness of the masses become the enlightened tears of the patriot or reader/spectator, her representations of blood usually revolved entirely around the masses, organizing her conception of the masses' role, once mobilized, in nationalist politics. This conception was the logical complement to Young Ireland's impulses to limit (as well as to achieve) the merging of leaders and peoples. Her version of O'Connell's disciplined army, that is, of the Irish people mobilized as an effective political force, was a raging mob. She assumed that mass politics was by nature violent and irrational, so when she imagined the successful transformation of the masses, she emphasized the unthinking and bloodthirsty propensities of the masses so transformed. Often, the mobilized populace becomes part of the landscape itself, taking the form of some blindly powerful and destructive force. 'Signs of the Times' lists the 'signs apocalyptic' of a coming upheaval, comparing disturbances among the people to surging oceans and tempest-tossed forests:

> When mighty passions, surging, heave the depth of life's great ocean —
> When the people, sway like forest trees, to and fro in wild commotion.[80]

'Forward!' threatens, 'And the heaving myriad surges, / To and fro in tumult swaying, / Threaten death to all who vainly would oppose them in their might', while 'The Year of Revolutions' exhorts, 'On, on in your masses dense, resolute, strong'.[81] Wilde's descriptions of violent nationalist mobs as blazing fields, human oceans, windswept forests, thunder clouds and other powerful natural phenomena fit them into millenarian narratives of upheaval. They also embody Young Ireland's anxious conceptualization of mass politics as irrational and bloody.

Wilde's conception of mass politics as crowd violence made a transition from tears to blood an inviting figure for the nationalization of the masses. 'France in '93' compares the French bread riots

77 PS, 69
78 PS, 61
79 PS, 35
80 PS, 21
81 PS, 31, 36

of the 1790s to the cry of the starving Irish during the Famine, and describes the transformation of the abject people into a savage agent of crowd violence. The first stanza presents the lower classes as crude and lacking national consciousness:

> Hark! the onward heavy tread —
> Hark! the voices rude —
> 'Tis the famished cry for Bread
> From a wildered multitude.

The 'wildered multitude' signifies its helplessness and despair by weeping: 'Thousands wail and weep with hunger.' The second stanza traces their transformation into 'an armed multitude', which has exactly the same 'heavy tread' and 'voices rude' as the despairing crowd. The only visible mark of their transformation is that they have stopped shedding tears and begun shedding blood:

> Bloody trophy they have won,
> Ghastly glares it in the sun —
> Gory head on lifted pike.
> Ha! they weep not now, but strike.

Young Ireland's didactic impulses notwithstanding, they have not been enlightened; they have simply become enraged.

The poem gleefully addresses the guilty, aristocratic victims of the crowd's revenge, threatening and taunting them, as in

> Calculating statesmen, quail;
> Proud aristocrat, grow pale;
> Savage sounds that deathly song

or

> What! coronetted Prince or Peer,
> Will not the base-born slavelings fear?

Throughout, the poem emphasizes the violent savagery of the revolution it depicts. The crowd's power lies not in the threat of disciplined action but in their blind, uncontrollable hunger for violence:

> Blindly now they wreak revenge —
> How rudely do a mob avenge!

The poem emphasizes hunger as the source of the riot, repeating words like 'famished' and 'bread'. In Wilde's apocalyptic reading of the Famine, the masses' hunger for food — which represents their colonial subjugation — and their hunger for violence — which represents their mobilization as an effective political force — become indistinguishable. The dismembered bodies of aristocrats become strange fruit, to borrow a phrase from a later description of mob violence:

Ghastly fruit their lances bear —
Noble heads with streaming hair.

The speaker imagines the carnage of the riot in terms of a savage 'harvest' of aristocratic blood:

Royal blood of King and Queen
Streameth from the guillotine;
Wildly on the people goeth,
Reaping what the noble soweth.

Thus the lines 'Hunger now, at last, is sated / In halls where once it wailed and waited' have multiple referents: food, blood, blood as food.[82] While national feeling among the male patriot leaders manifests itself as tears, national feeling among the masses manifests itself as a blind bloodlust as deep and instinctive as the hunger for which it is a metonym.

Current criticism often theorizes cultural nationalism's project of subject constitution as the formation of a centred subject whose autonomy prefigures national autonomy, and whose national feelings are embodied in unmistakable signs, such as love of country. Wilde's work illustrates that, at the same time, Young Ireland's bourgeois nationalism also produced different, more unsettling versions of national subject constitution, particularly in relation to the Irish masses, although their representation is typical of the crowd or the mob in much nineteenth-century political and racial discourse. In this version, the signs of national feeling are ambiguous, their meanings contingent and shifting. This subject's bodily integrity is tenuous — defined through shedding tears, spilling blood, even ingesting blood — and its autonomy dissolves into the unreasoning mind of the crowd. These divergent conceptions of subject constitution marked Young Ireland's ambivalence about the Irish masses; subject constitution as the achievement of individual integrity, autonomy and stable signification was the province of the élite. The necessary complement to Young Ireland's drive towards unity, its dreams of assimilation, and its faith in the people as the embodiments of the spirit of the nation was its reliance on class and gender hierarchies, its will to separate bourgeois leaders and intellectuals from the populace, and its fear that the masses could not be constituted as national subjects, or that they could only be constituted as threatening, ambiguous kinds of national subjects. As a woman writer engaging with a deeply masculinist tradition, Wilde had cause to be particularly sensitive to the latter set of impulses — those that emphasized disjunction, distrust and hierarchy. The major tropes and patterns of Wilde's work embody, rather than resist, many of Young Ireland's gender conventions. Through those conventions, however, Wilde illustrated with particular clarity the disintegrative and divisive aspects of the contradictory formulations that distinguished Young Ireland from Old.

82 PS, 53–55

Literary Religion: William Carleton

William Carleton is regularly cast as a central figure in the development of Irish literature. Terry Eagleton, for example, calls him 'the finest nineteenth-century novelist of all' and says that his *Traits and Stories of the Irish Peasantry* 'can surely lay claim to the status of premier work of the century's literature'.[1] Carleton is often described as an important precursor of Joyce and Roy Foster has recently written an essay arguing his importance for the early Yeats.[2] His centrality for later writers and the problems his work raises are most often formulated through references to ethnography, religion, and literary form. Most critics agree that the importance of *Traits and Stories* is primarily ethnographic, and that the two major problems that hindered Carleton's project, and the capacity of later readers to appreciate it, are his vexed relation to Catholicism and his formal unevenness. Seamus Deane claims that the tales in *Traits and Stories* were 'truly memorable for the power with which they evoked the life of the Irish peasantry' but that 'most of Carleton's writings are miscellanies of prose styles, with stylistic breaks even in the midst of a single sentence'.[3] Declan Kiberd remarks that 'part of Carleton's achievement as a writer would be his rendition of a social panorama, a cross-section of peasant types,' but also comments: 'it is sometimes said that a single Carleton sentence seems to have been written in two very different styles by two very different men'.[4] And Barbara Hayley characterizes the tales as 'a mixture of folklore and melodrama'.[5] Scholars may be fairly united on the subject of Carleton's formal fragmentation, but they are more divided on the subject of his religion and its impact on his role in the creation of an Irish national literature.

Traits *and Stories* first appeared as an anonymous collection of eight stories in 1830. The critical reception was overwhelmingly favourable, and the book was admired by many readers, from Karl Marx

1   William Carleton, *Traits and Stories of the Irish Peasantry*, 2 vols. (Gerrards Cross, 1990 [1830–33]); hereafter cited as TS; Terry Eagleton, *Heathcliff and the Great Hunger: Studies in Irish Culture* (London, 1995), 207

2   Seamus Deane, *A Short History of Irish Literature* (London, 1986), 112, comments that 'the beginnings of the Joycean complex are discernible' in Carleton's representations of the Irish peasantry, and Paul Muldoon, *To Ireland, I* (Oxford, 2000), 25, asserts that 'Carleton contains a powerful combination of intimacy with, and enmity towards, his subject matter that would not be seen again until Joyce'. Roy Foster, 'Square-built Power and Fiery Shorthand: Yeats, Carleton and the Irish Nineteenth Century', in *The Irish Story: Telling Tales and Making it up in Ireland* (Oxford, 2002), 113–26.

3   Deane, *Short History*, 108–09

4   Declan Kiberd, *Irish Classics* (Cambridge, MA, 2000), 266, 274

5   Barbara Hayley, *Carleton's* Traits and Stories *and the 19th Century Anglo-Irish Tradition* (Gerrards Cross, 1983), 1

to Crofton Croker.[6] It proved very popular, going through a number of editions, often expanded, re-arranged, and/or revised, over the next fourteen years.[7] By the time he wrote the Preface to the 1842 edition, Carleton was explicitly casting his work as part of a burgeoning effort to create a truly national literature for Ireland. He lamented, in particular, the 'political' effects of the stage Irishman found in English letters, which, he said, 'passed from the stage into the recesses of private life, wrought itself into the feelings until it became a prejudice'.[8] He connected the literary situation with much-discussed political problems, claiming that previously Ireland had been labouring 'under all the dark privations of a literary famine' and that Ireland's literary men had, by writing for the English market, become literary and intellectual 'absentees'. He claimed that greater mutual knowledge between the Irish and the English was already leading to mutual respect, and praised the *Dublin University Magazine* as a 'neutral spot in a country where party feeling runs so high, on which the Roman Catholic Priest and the Protestant parson, the Whig, the Tory, and the Radical, divested of their respective prejudices, can meet in an amicable spirit'. He predicted that 'Ireland in a few years will be able to sustain a native literature as lofty and generous, and beneficial to herself, as any other country in the world can boast of'.[9]

Several features of Carleton's argument in the Preface to *Traits and Stories* — his integrationist bent, his project to rescue the Irish from detractors and misunderstandings and to exhibit their positive characteristics, his belief that literature could heal the rifts of the political world, his determination to help establish a national literature, and the fact that he addressed himself, at least partly, to a non-Irish audience — give him something in common with the national tales written by authors such as Sydney Owenson or Maria Edgeworth. But if, as Ina Ferris and Joep Leerssen suggest, such tales in the early nineteenth century treated Ireland as an exotic, unknown place, in which the protagonist is nearly always an outsider who learns to put aside previous prejudices and forges a sympathetic connection to Ireland, Carleton's stories do not. They oscillate between the perspectives of insider and outsider.[10] Indeed, Carleton's Preface goes to some lengths to establish his status as an insider or native informant, claiming, as many later commentators would, that he can accurately describe the Irish peasantry because he knows them and is one of them.

Carleton bolsters this claim to authenticity by recounting his biography and using his parents as exemplary figures for the peasantry as a whole. Each parent embodies a different conception of the peasantry and Irish folk culture, however. In a famous passage, which Carleton reproduced in his autobiography, his father represents the Irish country people as an inexhaustible mine of cultural vitality, perpetually available, coexisting comfortably with English language and culture. He knows the Old and New Testaments by heart, and

his memory was a perfect storehouse, and a rich one, of all that the social antiquary, the man of letters, the poet, or the musician, would consider valuable. As a teller of old tales, legends, and historical anecdotes he was unrivalled, and his stock of them was inexhaustible. He spoke the Irish and English languages with nearly equal fluency. With all kinds of charms, old ranns, or poems, old prophecies, religious superstitions, tales of pilgrims, miracles, and pilgrimages, anecdotes of blessed priests and friars, revelations from ghosts and fairies, was he thoroughly acquainted.

---

6   Eileen A. Sullivan, *William Carleton* (Boston, MA, 1983), 59
7   Hayley offers a definitive account of this process.
8   TS, vol. I, iii
9   TS, vol. I, iv–v, vii
10 See Ina Ferris, *The Romantic National Tale and the Question of Ireland* (Cambridge, 2002) and Joep Leerssen, *Remembrance and Imagination: Patterns in the Historical and Literary Representations of Ireland in the Nineteenth Century* (Cork, 1996).

As a result, Carleton says, he never came across a bit of Irish popular culture that was completely new to him. Carleton's mother, on the other hand, represents a conception of Irish peasant culture as fading, inaccessible, and incompatible with English. She was especially good at keening, 'had a prejudice against singing the Irish airs to English words' and some of her untranslated songs 'have perished with her'. Those that were not lost with her are only partly known and interpretable: 'At this day I am in possession of Irish airs, which none of our best antiquaries in Irish music have heard, except through me, and of which neither they nor I myself know the names.'[11]

Carleton's father represents retention and accessibility; through him, Carleton possesses the secrets of Irish culture. On the contrary, his version of his mother is organized around loss and obscurity; even the cultural artefacts — the songs — he possesses directly through her cannot be fully known or accessed. Both conditions are the condition of an insider, but the latter is that of an insider who has been dispossessed of something that properly belongs to him. In one, the insider's culture is vigorous and living; in the other, it is fractured and dying. This division bears a family resemblance to a dilemma that Joep Leerssen has argued was central to the language revival later in the century: 'the choice between the return to the pristine example of antiquity, or the vigour of the living demotic tradition'.[12] When his extremely accomplished and wide-ranging account of how various thinkers represented Ireland in the nineteenth century mentions Carleton, which is not very often, Leerssen sees him as part of the Romantic tendency to take the peasantry out of the present and the political realm and locate them in various timeless realms, such as the past or folklore.[13] I would add that Carleton carefully constructed his own claims to authenticity and attached those claims to two competing (and equally Romantic) conceptions of the national, folkloric past: one that saw it as continually available for salvage and another that saw it as constantly slipping away.

Debates over the extent to which the authenticity Carleton claimed was genuine have often centred around his relation to religion. Born Catholic, Carleton converted to Protestantism, married a Protestant, produced some extremely anti-Catholic works early in his career, and later moderated his views, adopting a more liberal Protestantism and expressing considerable sympathy and admiration for Catholics. In 1826, before he began publishing his short stories, he wrote a letter to his friend William Sisson, deputy librarian of Marsh's Library in Dublin, and included a memorandum to be forwarded to Robert Peel, who was then Home Secretary. The memorandum is an argument against Catholic Emancipation, which was of course then being hotly debated. Carleton drew connections between terrorist violence and the movement for Catholic Emancipation, said he could prove a link between O'Connell's Catholic Association and illegal secret societies, and accused the Catholic clergy of condoning, or at least tolerating those societies.[14] In the cover letter to Sisson, Carleton once again offers to provide proof, and says: 'according to the present operation of Roman Catholic politics, the question of Emancipation is singularly mixed up with the immediate and personal interests of its most violent and outrageous supporters'. And later he comments:

> But the *Priests* are those whom I principally fear, not more from the habitual dissimulation of their character, than from *my knowledge* of the unforgiving fire which burns within them. Black, malignant, and designing, systemically treacherous and false, [they] are inherently inimical to Protestants, they brood over their purposes with a hope of revenge sharpened by the restraint which compels them to conceal it, and concentrated within their souls from want of expansion.

11 TS, vol. 1, vii–ix, x, xi
12 Leerssen, *Remembrance and Imagination*, 196
13 Leerssen, *Remembrance and Imagination*, 164
14 See Robert Lee Wolff, *William Carleton, Irish Peasant Novelist: A Preface to His Fiction* (New York and London, 1980), 20.

Carleton goes on to say that he would rather see his children dead than 'under the dreadful yoke of Romish influence'.[15] This was two years before he began writing for Caesar Otway's anti-Catholic *Christian Examiner*.

Later in life, and after the debate over Catholics had died down in the wake of Emancipation, Carleton seems to have moderated these views, though Barbara Hayley cautions us against exaggerating this change. Carleton did expunge some particularly virulent passages from early anti-Catholic stories when he reprinted them, wrote sympathetically of the plight of the Irish Catholic country people, and harshly criticized Protestant landlords.[16] In his autobiography, begun when he was seventy-four and never completed, he recalled that in the County Tyrone of his youth 'there was then no law *against* an Orangeman, and no law *for* a Papist', and he claimed 'although I conscientiously left the church, neither my heart nor my affections were ever estranged from the Catholic people, or even from their priesthood'.[17]

Not surprisingly, given these contradictory views, arguments about Carleton's role as a founder of modern Irish literature have always been troubled by the question of his relation to Catholicism. When Yeats edited *Stories from Carleton* for the Walter Scott publishing house in 1889, his Introduction took up the problem of Carleton and religion.[18] Yeats acknowledged that Carleton had 'drifted' into Protestantism (though the Peel memorandum hardly suggests a 'drift'), but claimed that 'his heart, anyway, soon returned to the religion of his fathers; and in him the Established Church proselytizers found their most fierce satirist'. This did not stop *The Nation* from reviewing the book negatively on account of Carleton's apostasy. A small controversy ensued, in which Yeats tried to intervene by reviewing his own book in the *Scots Observer*; this ploy, not surprisingly, did not really work. Yeats had the sense to print the review anonymously, but scholars agree that we have sufficient evidence that Yeats wrote it. As Foster points out, Yeats 'steadfastly argued that Carleton remained essentially Catholic; and that this was somehow part of his essential authenticity', a view of the relationship between Irishness and Catholicism he would later abandon. For Yeats, Carleton was above all an ethnographer and a social historian — as part of this controversy, he wrote a letter to the editor of *The Nation* titled 'Carleton as an Irish Historian'. Foster argues that Yeats's work in the 1890s contained a surprising number of echoes from Carleton, and that Yeats found in Carleton's work the 'clarity and lack of sentimentality' that he was trying to establish in his own poetry. Yeats claimed, 'There is no wistfulness in the works of Carleton. I find there, especially in his longer novels, a kind of clay-cold melancholy.' In this way, Carleton was for Yeats the imperfect precursor of Synge: 'On one level, he might seem to come within Yeats's imposed ban on stereotypical and unsubtle national image-making. In another way, however, Carleton was capable of his own version of the uncompromisingness, originality, rigour, "salt and savour" which Yeats missed in the Davis school and found in Synge.'[19] In a later review of Carleton's autobiography Yeats explicitly cast Carleton as a founding figure of Irish national literature, calling him the 'creator of a new imaginative world, the demiurge of a new tradition'.[20]

Current scholarship on Carleton, somewhat surprisingly, often feels compelled to take up the question of Carleton, authenticity, the national tradition, and religion in similar terms. This means that often critics treat Carleton as an ethnographer and pose the question of religion in his works in terms of his criticisms of, or loyalty to, Catholicism. Robert Lee Wolff, for example, asserts that Carleton's

15 See David Krause, *William Carleton the Novelist: His Carnival and Pastoral World of Tragicomedy* (New York and Oxford, 2000), 69.
16 Hayley, *Carleton's Traits and Stories*, xi, points out, however, that he did not expunge them all, and that he even added some anti-Catholic passages to early stories for republication.
17 William Carleton, *The Autobiography* (Belfast, 1996 [1896]), 37, 92
18 The volume included 'The Poor Scholar', 'Tubber Derg', 'Wildgoose Lodge', 'Shane Fadh's Wedding', and 'The Hedge School'.
19 Foster, 'Square-built Power', 117–19, 124
20 *Uncollected Prose by W. B. Yeats*, vol. 1, ed. John P. Frayne (London and New York, 1970), 394

'attacks on the faith and its clergy were by no means "very little" or even all "early"' and emphasizes the Protestantism of the early works in particular.[21] David Krause's recent book goes out of its way to refute such claims, arguing that Carleton 'paradoxically and emotionally remained loyal to his Catholic heritage'. And Krause criticizes scholars like Wolff who, he says, assess Carleton's work in religious rather than fictional terms.[22] Critics have continued to debate the issue in these terms, I think, because what is at stake is Carleton the ethnographer — his authenticity in terms of representing the peasantry, folk culture, and a foundation of the national tradition. If scholars conclude that Carleton is in some fundamental way an anti-Catholic writer, then his portraits of the Catholic country people begin to look increasingly like condescending stereotypes. If, on the other hand, scholars argue that he remained loyal to Catholicism on some essential level, a level usually characterized as emotional, unconscious, or paradoxical, it becomes possible to recuperate a kind of anthropological accuracy in his works.

But Carleton's imagination is at once literary and religious. It is possible to offer a different set of terms for thinking about Carleton's representations of Catholicism and folk culture. His stories share with much sentimental fiction and melodrama a relative lack of interiority or psychological complexity. It is more useful to see their treatment of popular religion as 'lived religion' rather than ideology and to focus on externals like practice rather than interior states — on what people do, rather than what they 'believe'. Thus faith and materiality, the sacred and the profane, appear as intertwining, not opposed, realities. In Carleton's stories this manifests itself most clearly in his representations of bodies and rituals.

Reading Bodies

Carleton's most famously anti-Catholic text, 'The Lough Derg Pilgrim', was his first publication; as is well known, it appeared in 1828 in Otway's *Christian Examiner*. Later, when Carleton reprinted it, he expunged some of the more offensive passages, but plenty remain. The story is a Protestant parable, full of the vocabularies and images that were standard in anti-Catholic discourses, narrated with irony and condescension by an older and wiser speaker looking back upon a period of youthful folly. One of Carleton's arguments is that the pilgrimage, and Catholicism as a whole, are hypocritical and fraudulent, that they are composed of a series of empty forms and bodily gestures that are devoid of meaningful content or true religious consciousness, that conceal human weakness and immorality — thus, they perform the same function as the dissimulating priests in the letter to Sisson. In his autobiography, Carleton recounts an incident when, temporarily down and out in Dublin, he spent the night in a cellar inhabited by beggars:

> Crutches, wooden legs, artificial cancers, scrofulous necks, artificial wens, sore legs, and a vast variety of similar complaints, were hung up upon the walls of the cellars, and made me reflect upon the degree of perverted talent and ingenuity that must have been necessary to sustain such a mighty mass of imposture.[23]

21 Wolff, *William Carleton, Irish Peasant Novelist*, 5
22 Krause, *William Carleton the Novelist*, 37, 77. Similarly, James Murphy observes that 'Carleton was not strongly religious, was never part of the establishment and always retained a sense of Catholic grievance'; see his *Ireland: A Social, Cultural and Literary History 1791–1891* (Dublin, 2003), 83.
23 Carleton, *Autobiography*, 165

For Carleton, the Catholic body is like the bodies of these beggars. It is a kind of prosthesis, a deceptive shell that performs ritual falsehoods.

In the story, Catholic bodies have an independent existence that reveals the impostures of the pilgrimage. Before he goes to Lough Derg, the narrator, who is, he says, 'completely ignorant' of religion, acquires a reputation for piety by praying louder and fasting longer than his competitors. Once he begins the stations, bodily pain strips the ritual of genuine religious significance: 'I was absolutely stupid and dizzy with the pain, … I knew not what I was about, but went through the forms in the same mechanical spirit which pervaded all present'. He occupies 'an inverted existence, in which the soul sleeps, and the body remains awake', and his body produces involuntary groans and shrieks. We are also told that 'the language which a Roman Catholic of the lower class does not understand, is the one in which he is disposed to pray'. By the time he confesses, he says he could not remember 'a tithe of my sins' and that 'the priest, poor man, had really so much to do, and was in such a hurry, that he had me clean absolved before I had got half through the preface, or knew what I was about'.[24] The narrator has also been impersonating a priest; his two travelling companions take him for one (or, rather, they pretend to), and he does not undeceive them. Catholicism is a religion of false exteriors, mechanical rites performed in ignorance of their meaning. The interior states it does foster are morbid manifestations of a gothic imagination worthy of Charles Robert Maturin's *Melmoth the Wanderer*. (Carleton knew Maturin's works, and even met him once in Dublin.) During the vigil, the speaker has been told that pilgrims who fail to stay awake will be damned in the next world and go mad in this one, and his body prays while he sleeps: 'After all, I really slept the better half of the night; yet so indescribably powerful was the apprehension of derangement that my hypocritical tongue wagged aloud at the prayers, during these furtive naps.'[25]

In Carleton's story the body functions as the site where the cruelty and emptiness of Catholic doctrine and Catholic rituals reveal themselves. The narrator comments, 'I verily think that if mortification of the body, without conversion of the life or heart — if penance and not repentance could save the soul, no wretch who performed a pilgrimage here could with a good grace be damned.' But the body is also the site of unconscious resistance to those doctrines and rituals, and the foundation of a superior religion. The battle between the forces of Catholic superstition and Protestant rationality is fought out on the level of the body, between, for example, the body's natural and beneficial urge to sleep and the hypocritical tongue's mechanical delivery of prayers that mean nothing. As the narrator walks towards the lake, his body rebels against the unnaturally sombre and morbid frame of mind he is forcing himself into with Catholic prayers:

> Despite of all the solemnity about me, my unmanageable eye would turn from the very blackest of the seven deadly offences, and the stoutest of the four cardinal virtues, to the beetling, abrupt, and precipitous rocks which hung over the lake as if ready to tumble into its waters … I was taken twice, despite of the most virtuous efforts to the contrary, from a *Salve Regina*, to watch a little skiff, which shone with its snowy sail spread before the radiant evening sun, and glided over the waters, like an angel sent on some happy message. In fact, I found my heart on the point of corruption, by indulging in what I had set down in my vocabulary as the lust of the eye.[26]

This lust of the eye, and the obstinacy of the body generally, signify an alternative religion, one that is in accordance with nature rather than violating it. In a common literary formulation, it is connected

24 TS, vol. 1, 240, 256–57, 261–63
25 TS, vol. 1, 261
26 TS, vol. 1, 251, 257

with the beauties of the natural world. Earlier in the walk, the narrator describes the beauties of the natural setting:

> The rapid martins twittered with peculiar glee, or, in the light caprice of their mirth, placed themselves for a moment upon the edge of a scaur, or earthy precipice, in which their nests were built, and then shot off again to mingle with the careering and joyful flock that cut the air in every direction. Where is the heart which could not enjoy such a morning scene?

But the narrator's 'mistaken devotion' has rendered him immune to what he calls 'those sensations which the wisdom of God has given as a security in some degree against sin, by opening to the heart of man sources of pleasure, for which the soul is not compelled to barter away her innocence, as in those of a grosser nature'.[27] Ultimately, it is the narrator's body and not his mind (and in these passages, the pleasures of his body) that is naturally Protestant. While this aligns Protestantism with a natural world obedient to God's plan, it also threatens to open Protestantism to the treachery and falsehood of the Catholic body. Interestingly, Carleton's autobiography recalls that William Sisson, 'in consequence of some dreadful accident, lost the greater portion of one leg and thigh; but so admirably was this replaced, that to an ordinary eye he looked like a man afflicted only with slight lameness'.[28]

So bodies need to be read carefully; the ordinary eye might miss their true meaning. How does one distinguish between the beggar impostures in the cellar and the upstanding librarian? This issue is taken up in 'The Lough Derg Pilgrim' in several scenes illustrating what is perhaps best thought of as the question of Catholic versus Protestant readership or spectatorship. To the discerning eye, the narrator's body and clothing indicate the ludicrous nature of his quest, his pretensions, and his religious imagination. It is an index to the kind of knowledge that the older narrator has and the younger self lacks; his body tells us what he does not yet know — that his quest is ridiculous:

> I ... cut an original figure, being six feet high, with a short grey cloak pinned tightly about me, my black cassimere small-clothes peeping below it — my long, yellow, polar legs, unincumbered with calves, quite naked; a good hat over the cloak — but with no shoes on my feet, marching gravely upon my pilgrimage.

Some people he passes smile or laugh at his appearance, and he concludes that these were 'Protestant grins', while Catholics read his exterior differently, taking him for a priest and showing respect.[29] The story contains an implied Protestant spectator/reader, who coincides with the educated, older and wiser narrator. And the narrator explicitly contrasts the reader's 'free, manly, cultivated understanding' with the feelings of his younger self upon reaching the site. A related instance of Catholic credulity leading to misreading of the body occurs in Carleton's 'Phelim O'Toole's Courtship', in which Phelim's besotted parents are convinced that the ravages of small pox have made his face more, rather than less, attractive.

In Carleton's religio-literary imagination, then, bodies figure in several ways: as the deceptive exteriors of Catholicism, as the natural, God-given foundation of rational Protestantism, and as objects that demand interpretation and therefore provide indexes that separate the discerning from the credulous viewer or reader. Much of Carleton seeks to unmask their deceptive appearances, to point to the fake wens and artificial legs hanging on the wall. But he also suffers from the apprehension

---

27 TS, vol. 1, 243
28 Carleton, *Autobiography*, 189
29 TS, vol. 1, 244, 248

that appearances, bodies, and clothing, and perverse readings of them, contain a slippery truth and power of their own. 'In such a world as this, where outsides are so much looked to,' he muses in his autobiography, 'what good was my intellect to me when in shabby apparel? What person could discover it in a man with a seedy coat upon his back, when that man was a stranger? We ought not to expect impossibilities.'[30] In 'Phelim O'Toole's Courtship', Phelim is actually irresistible to the women he courts. He becomes engaged to three of them; his parents' fond reading of his exterior is correct in a sense.

Much previous criticism has treated Carleton's bodies (often more or less by implication) in the context of a combination of the carnivalesque and the tragic. They function as evidence of a living, vital, community and tradition, eating, drinking, fighting, courting, while, in other moments, they register the maiming of that community by poverty, famine, and ill-governance. John Wilson Foster, for example, comments, 'For all the deprivation suffered by Carleton's people, they are a rich and lively assortment, even in the throes of hunger and sickness they have a feverish energy.'[31] But if we attend more specifically to Carleton's representations of religion, on the one hand, and to their relation to the literary (as opposed to the ethnographic) features of his writing, on the other, a related but somewhat different picture emerges. Carleton's Catholic body is a sign of corruption, of a dying culture, but it is also the sign of a culture that survives by imposing its appearances on reality in a wily and sometimes unsettling fashion. It reasserts itself, not in the religious realm, but in questions of readership and audience, and in plot structures that illustrate the power of exteriors or the power of a Catholic reading of the body. Carleton embeds that distinction between folk culture as vital and folk culture as fading, as realized in his parents, in representations of the body; that body is a source not simply of vitality or impoverishment, but of ambiguity.

Re-writing Rituals

In general terms, Carleton's religio-literary imagination combines a focus on the externals of appearances and lived religion with questions of literary form and readership. He takes two important Catholic rituals — marriage and pilgrimage to a holy well — and reformulates their sacred meaning by using the tropes of melodrama and sentimental fiction. Thus the literary and the religious, the secular and the sacred, are crossed.

Unlike 'The Lough Derg Pilgrim', 'Shane Fadh's Wedding' (first published in 1830) is narrated by one of the country people — Shane himself — rather than by an educated Protestant observer. Much of the interest of the story revolves around Carleton's comic, ethnographic exploration of Irish country wedding customs. But the story also displays an interest in marriage as a sacrament. Shane and Mary want to get married, but Mary's father opposes the match. So they decide to run away together in order to force his consent, a practice that, Carleton tells us, is common in the Irish countryside. And he bears this out by delineating the customs surrounding it in much the same humorous, ethnographic mode that he uses to describe the wedding itself. When the couple are about to go to Shane's uncle's house to spend the night, however, the tone shifts abruptly into a different register, and the following scene takes place:

30 Carleton, *Autobiography*, 177–78
31 Quoted in Krause, *William Carleton the Novelist*, 36–37

'Well, Mary,' says I, 'a-cushla-machree, it's dark enough for us to go; and, in the name of God, let us be off.'

The crathur looked into my face, and got pale — for she was very young then: 'Shane,' says she, and she thrimbled like an aspen lafe, 'I'm going to trust myself with you for ever — for ever, Shane, avourneen,' — and her sweet voice broke into purty murmurs as she spoke; 'whether for happiness or sorrow God he only knows. I can bear poverty and distress, sickness and want with you, but I can't bear to think that you should ever forget to love me as you do now; or that your heart should ever cool to me: but I'm sure,' says she, 'you'll never forget this night, and the solemn promises you made me, before God and the blessed skies above us.'

We were sitting at the time under the shade of a rowan-tree, and I had only one answer to make — I pulled her to my breast, where she laid her head and cried like a child, with her cheek against mine. My own eyes weren't dry, although I felt no sorrow, but — but — I never forgot that night — and I never will.[32]

This exchange constitutes the sacred aspect of the marriage, set apart from the profane festivities that surround it in situation, tone, and vocabulary. It solemnizes their union in much the same way a church wedding would. It echoes the ceremony fairly directly — 'in poverty and distress, sickness and want', and it is here, not at the actual wedding ceremony, that we see Shane make a solemn promise to Mary before God. The scene connects their union to the sacred by using the language and imagery of sentimental fiction. Yeats may have found the later Carleton unsentimental, but this story combines Carleton's humorous, ethnographic mode with some of the classic tropes of sentimentality. Shane's and Mary's hearts are so full that words are inadequate, as evidenced by Mary's inarticulate murmurs and Shane's wordless response. In sentimental fiction, the language of the body — turning pale, trembling, weeping — signifies deep emotion and moral worth, and the tableau of Mary with her head on Shane's breast, her cheek to his cheek, employs the kind of suggestive but controlled eroticism that characterizes many of the discourses of feeling.

All these characteristics are also to be found in Sydney Owenson's *The Wild Irish Girl*, but there is an important difference between the two texts. In Owenson, Catholic ritual is picturesque and seductive but to be rejected, a beautiful set of exterior forms concealing interior corruption and danger. Horatio muses:

What a religion is this! How finely does it harmonize with the weakness of our nature; how seducingly it speaks to the senses; how forcibly it works on the passions; how strongly it seizes on the imagination; how interesting its forms; how graceful its ceremonies, how awful its rites … Who would not become its proselyte, were it not for the stern opposition of reason — the cold suggestions of philosophy.[33]

On the other hand, the romance between Horatio and Glorvina is frequently cast in religious terms, and his romantic devotion is explicitly described as religious devotion. On May Day, for example, Horatio and his 'lovely votarist' participate in a kind of natural marriage ceremony, in which she gives him a rose and he pledges to her. He later refers to the occasion as a 'sacred covenant'. A few pages after the ceremony, Horatio and Father John witness an old woman performing the pattern at a holy well, and Father John describes to Horatio Lough Derg and the 'votarists' who visit it.[34] The connection here

32 TS, vol. 1, 56
33 Sydney Owenson [Lady Morgan], *The Wild Irish Girl* (Oxford, 1999 [1806]), 50
34 Owenson, *Wild Irish Girl*, 140, 153–54

between two kinds of devotion is explicit — and purely metaphorical. Owenson uses the vocabulary of religion to describe Horatio's romantic commitment and the transformation Glorvina causes in him, rescuing him from his corruption and ennui.

In contrast, Carleton uses the language of sentimental fiction in order to re-create the sacred aura that he has expunged from the actual wedding ceremony. He does not make religion a metaphor for romantic love. In many of his stories, he represents Catholic practices in a manner that we might think of as revising Victor Turner's formulation of the 'liminal' — a rite or condition that is removed from everyday life and in which established social rules and hierarchies are temporarily suspended. Liminality produces what Turner calls 'communitas', an unmediated, egalitarian community among participants. Obviously there is a connection to a Bakhtinian carnivalesque here, too. Several scholars, including Diarmuid Ó Giolláin, have read patterns at Irish holy wells partly in these terms.[35] Carleton's popular festivals do display these features to some extent. But the actual religious rituals themselves are often stripped of their associations with the sacred. That is to say, they are stripped of their associations with whatever enables them to offer access to the liminal. Instead, they usually replicate the hierarchies and conflicts of the profane world. Another example here would be 'The Station', which, in its original form in particular, gave Carleton the opportunity to denounce the practice of confession and to illustrate the myriad class and social distinctions in the rural community.

To return to 'Shane Fadh's Wedding'; when the narrative arrives at Shane and Mary's actual wedding ceremony, Carleton takes pains to include it, but barely to narrate it at all, and to overshadow it completely with Shane's anxiety to prevent the other men present from beating him to the first kiss. Shane recounts,

> While the priest was going over the business, I kept my eye about me, and, sure enough, there were seven or eight fellows all waiting to snap at her. When the ceremony drew near a close, I got up on one leg, so that I could bounce to my feet like lightning, and when it was finished, I got her in my arm, before you could say Jack Robinson, and swinging her behind the priest, gave her the husband's first kiss.[36]

The next man to get a kiss is the priest, who shoves back the other participants bodily to claim his privilege. The sacred element of the marriage has been transferred to the sentimental language of the scene under the rowan tree, so here the ceremony appears as 'going over the business', and as part of the profane world. This transaction between the sacred and the profane, the ethnographic and the sentimental, is also evidenced by Carleton's revisions over time. Barbara Hayley shows that many of the sentimental passages were added or augmented as part of the revisions Carleton undertook as he sought to moderate some of the anti-Catholic tenor of his work.[37] So adding sentiment and looking upon Catholic ritual more tolerantly advanced in his writings together.

We find a similar transfer of the energies of the sacred to the realm of domestic affections and family life in 'Tubber Derg; or, The Red Well'. We also find a similar substitution of a partially secularized ritual for an explicitly Catholic one. This story, which first appeared as 'Landlord and Tenant' in 1831 in the *National Magazine*, is a story about bad landlords, tenant rights and the virtues of industriousness, faith, and charity. In the text, Tubber Derg is not, or not explicitly, a holy well where one would make a pattern. But it is clear that Carleton wanted to suggest holy wells in 'Tubber Derg', and he gave an

---

35 See Diarmuid Ó Giolláin, 'The Pattern', in J. S. Donnelly, Jr., and Kerby A. Miller, eds., *Irish Popular Culture, 1650–1850* (Dublin, 1999), 201–21.

36 TS, vol. I, 65

37 Hayley, *Carleton's Traits and Stories*, 43

extended description of a pattern at a holy well in 'Phelim O'Toole's Courtship'. Most holy wells in Ireland were named after saints, but not all of them were, and Carleton's name — Red Well — and the description of the water invokes the penitential aspects of the patterns as well as foreshadowing Owen McCarthy's trials and hardships: 'as the traveller ascended ... towards the house, he appeared to track his way in blood, for a chalybeate spa arose at its head, oozing out of the earth, and spread itself in a crimson stream over the path in every spot whereon a foot-mark could be made'.[38] This also provides an echo of Carleton's description in 'Phelim O'Toole's Courtship', a large part of which is disapproving and includes the sight of 'men and women ... washing the blood off their knees, and dipping such parts of their body as were afflicted with local complaints into the stream'.[39]

But the well in 'Tubber Derg' is a different kind of sacred site — one that represents the prelapsarian domestic bliss in which Owen McCarthy and his family live when the story opens, and which is ruined by the economic collapse that occurred after 1814 and the callousness of Owen's landlord and the landlord's agent. The story opens with an idealized description of the valley containing the well and Owen's house, and with the domestic tableau of a contented Owen surrounded by his family: 'a little chubby urchin at his knee, and another in his arms ... whilst Kathleen his wife, with her two maids, each crooning a low song, sat before the door, milking the cows'. Then it documents the decline of the family's circumstances, a function of the 'national depression', to the point where a desperate Owen decides to travel to Dublin to beg his absentee landlord for clemency in person. At the start of this secular pilgrimage, his favourite child runs after him and asks for another kiss. However, his quest is also described in terms of a popular religious pilgrimage — 'He had done his duty — he had gone to the fountain-head, with a hope that his simply story of affliction might be heard' — and it even suggests the penitential nature of such pilgrimages when he is pushed down the stairs by the landlord's servant and suffers a wound on his head. But it is not successful, and while he is away, his family is evicted and the child dies. He is haunted by her request for a last kiss, which he takes as a prophecy or foreshadowing of her death.[40]

Carleton spends a lot of time describing Owen's grief over the loss of his home and his child — and, because she is buried at Tubber Derg, they are metonyms for one another — and his continuing determination to establish a moral, respectable, and financially secure life for his remaining family. The main point is not simply that Carleton employs the languages and tropes of sentimentality, which he does, but that they have a particular relation to religion here, signified by the fact that the story rewrites the holy well into an emblem of a sacred domestic space, and sends Owen on two journeys that are profane, but are also imbued with the religion of domesticity. This conjunction of the religious and the domestic is also indicated, for example, when his wife, Kathleen, wonders whether their luck has turned for the better because Alley, the dead child, is interceding for them in heaven, and the narrator comments: 'there was something beautiful in the superstition of Kathleen's affections; something that touched the heart and its dearest associations'.[41] The superstition of the affections is an apt phrase for this kind of rewriting of the sacred as the domestic. We might also call it a species of syncretism that is both religious and literary.

Owen's second pilgrimage takes him back to Tubber Derg, and to the girl's grave, where his neighbours, grateful for his charity and help in earlier days, have put up the gravestone he could not afford when she was buried, turning a private burial site into a public sacred space. Owen prays at

38 Michael P. Carroll, *Irish Pilgrimage: Holy Wells and Popular Catholic Devotion* (Baltimore, MD, 1999), 25; Carleton, TS, vol. 2, 364. A chalybeate stream contains iron, which causes the water to turn a rusty-red.

39 TS, vol. 2, 194

40 TS, vol. 2, 365, 372, 379, 381, 399

41 TS, vol. 2, 399

the grave for the dead child to 'pray for us before God, an' get him an' his blessed Mother to look on us wid favour an' compassion'. This pilgrimage is successful. Immediately afterwards, Owen is given the chance to rent a farm near the well, and builds a new house on it that resembles 'that of Tubber Derg in its better days' as closely as possible and ends his days happily, surrounded by his family, in a repetition of the original tableau: 'Kathleen and two servant maids were milking, and the whole family were assembled about the door'. The moral of the story, according to Owen, is never to give up one's trust in God, and Carleton contrasts him to 'many of his thoughtless countrymen' who should learn from his example.[42]

To argue that the religious ambiguity of bodies and the rewriting of Catholic ritual and the sacred in sentimental and domestic terms is characteristic of Carleton's religio-literary imagination shifts the ground of critical discussions of Carleton and religion away from questions of authenticity and his loyalty (or lack thereof) to Catholicism. This shift can also help account for some of the formal divisions and transitions that characterize Carleton's writing in *Traits and Stories*, such as the combination of the carnivalesque and the sentimental, or Carleton's uncertainty about whether the culture he sought to document was fading away, or whether it was re-inventing itself in new forms and new practices. Further, it can show how his work anticipated the ethnographic modernism of Yeats and Synge, particularly their concern for popular modes of religious and sentimental sensibility. The difficult and obscure interior zones represented by Carleton's views on religion, or the question of his authenticity, are still worthwhile subjects of study and debate. But scholars should also now begin to examine the exteriors, bodies, and rituals that preoccupied his religio-literary imagination.

42 TS, vol. 2, 409, 414

Discipline and Sentiment: Mary Anne Sadlier

Mary Anne Sadlier was the most popular and influential Irish-American writer (or, perhaps more accurately, Irish-North American writer, as she is sometimes claimed as part of Canadian literature) of the Famine generation.[1] Sadlier wrote a number of novels that are set in Ireland; she also wrote a number of novels about Irish migration to the New World. Among the few scholars who discuss her, the consensus is that these novels are, to use Charles Fanning's phrase, 'practical fiction for immigrants'.[2] Such scholars assume or claim that her novels offer practical advice to Famine immigrants about how to negotiate between assimilation and ethnic and religious particularism in the New World, that they convey the 'functional ideology' of how such immigrants actually pursued this negotiation, and that, in spite of their unfortunate didactic moralizing, they have sociological value because they give us information about the everyday lives of Irish immigrants in mid and late nineteenth-century America. None of these propositions is exactly wrong, but all are flawed or misleading to some extent. There are some alternative frameworks that better illuminate what kind of didactic fiction Sadlier's novels represent (or what it means to describe them as didactic), what relation they bear to the popular literatures and the political ideologies of the period, and how they engage with the history of Irish migration to the New World.

Sadlier was born Mary Anne Madden in County Cavan in 1820 and raised by her father, who was a fairly comfortable merchant. She began publishing poetry in a London magazine at age eighteen. Her father died in 1844, and Mary Anne migrated to Montreal, where she met and married James Sadlier, who was managing the Canadian office of the Catholic publishing company that he and his brother had founded in New York in 1837. When the D. and J. Sadlier Company bought out the list of the pioneering Irish-American publisher John Doyle in 1853, the company became the largest Catholic publishing house in North America. Sadlier and her family lived in Montreal until 1860, when they

---

1   There are no reliable circulation figures for Sadlier's novels. Discussing the difficulty of dating first editions of her work, Willard Thorpe, 'Catholic Novelists in Defense of Their Faith, 1829–1885', *Proceedings of the American Antiquarian Society*, 78 (1968), 99, comments that 'her earlier novels were evidently read to pieces'. There is also some question about her intended and actual audiences. Most scholars have assumed that she wrote primarily for the Catholic Irish-American community, though Katherine Egan, '"White", If "Not Quite": Irish Whiteness in the Nineteenth-Century Irish-American Novel', *Éire-Ireland*, 36, 1–2 (2001), 66–81, has suggested that she also had Protestant America in mind.
2   See Charles Fanning, *The Irish Voice in America: 250 Years of Irish-American Fiction*, 2nd edn. (Lexington, KY, 2000), chs. 3–4.

moved to New York. Between the time of her marriage and that move, she produced six children and began her prolific career as a novelist, essayist, and translator. Most of her novels were serialized in Irish-American periodicals like Thomas D'Arcy McGee's *American Celt*, the Boston *Pilot*, or the New York *Tablet* (which succeeded the *American Celt* and was bought by the Sadlier Company in 1857) before being published in book form. By the time the Sadliers moved to New York, she was, according to Fanning, 'established as the best known Irish Catholic voice in American letters' and was a leading light of the Catholic social and intellectual circle that included McGee, the influential Catholic editor of the *Quarterly Review*, Orestes Brownson, and New York's outspoken and combative Archbishop John Hughes.[3] Her husband died in 1869, and she ran the New York branch of the Sadlier Company for a time, but was apparently forced out of the business by a nephew at some point, and during the 1880s she moved back to Canada. She died in 1903.

Sadlier's circum-atlantic life and publishing career, her fairly privileged connections with the Catholic publishing and Church establishments, and her commitment to the creation of new forms of popular literature indicate some important features of the particular historical moment to which her novels responded. Her works do not merely reflect transatlantic experience or culture; they seek to theorize it, to intervene in it, to constitute it. This project is best analysed in relation to two sets of historical developments. The first is the expansion and institutionalization of Irish America, and the establishment of the transatlantic equation between Irishness and Catholicism, a set of developments that began about 1830, and accelerated its pace during the 1840s and 1850s. The second set of developments involves instabilities and conflicts that threatened to impede the first set: the influx of potentially uncooperative Famine immigrants, on the one hand, and the political hostility embodied in nativism and Know-Nothingism, on the other. Sadlier's literary endeavours responded to this historical context. She also structured those literary endeavours in order to create a Catholic popular literature that could compete with other popular American cultural forms of the period: the most important of these was the fictional tradition represented by the massively popular sentimental, didactic fiction by women, such as Harriet Beecher Stowe's *Uncle Tom's Cabin*, Maria Susanna Cummins's *The Lamplighter*, and Susan Warner's *The Wide, Wide World*. Her engagement with this tradition, and her revisions of it, take up a number of important contemporary ideas about education, citizenship, community, privacy, and the public.

Catholic Irish America Goes Public

The expansion and institutionalization of Irish America had a number of components. Most of them involved the consolidation of a group identity, based upon a combination of religion and ethnicity, that asserted itself through new public institutions, new kinds of access to and claims upon the American public sphere, and new forms of publicity for Irish Catholic America. The number of American Catholic periodicals increased only from six to seven between 1836 and 1840, but had risen to fifteen by 1845. According to Robert Hueston, 'A new era in Catholic apologetics began as public lectures, sponsored by the increasing number of Catholic educational and social societies, became popular.'[4] Various organizations were created to help Irish immigrants in the United States: the Irish Emigrant Society of New York held its first meeting in 1841, and the society established the Emigrant Industrial

---

3   Fanning, *Irish Voice*, 115
4   Robert Francis Hueston, *The Catholic Press and Nativism, 1840–1860* (New York, 1976), 37

Savings Bank in 1850.[5] Another aspect was the growth of an institutionalized and transatlantic Irish-American nationalism. New York became the American headquarters for the Repealers, Young Ireland, and other organizations dedicated to aiding the cause of the Irish in Ireland. The alliance between the Irish and the Democratic Party was solidifying; by the 1840s, most Irish Americans were voting Democrat, and Irish nationalism became a factor in urban politics in places like New York and Boston. In the late 1830s and early 1840s, the schools question generated a major controversy, in New York in particular. Catholics complained about Protestant proselytizing and anti-Catholic prejudice in the public schools. Revisions to the school system in 1842, an apparent victory for Catholics, did not fully meet their demands, and the controversy had aroused enormous anti-Catholic hostility. By the mid-1840s the Church was emphasizing the need for the creation of separate Catholic educational and charitable institutions.

In tandem with the development of these new public institutions, new civic space, and new claims on the public sphere, the American Catholic Church became increasingly powerful and increasingly Irish. Kevin Kenny observes that the equation of Irishness with Catholicism on both sides of the Atlantic should not be taken for granted and did not always exist:

> it was part of a cultural process that reached fruition only in the mid and late nineteenth century, when the general social transformation wrought by the Great Famine was accompanied by a 'devotional revolution' in Irish and Irish-American Catholicism. Before that, the hold of the Catholic Church over the Irish people was often surprisingly tenuous. Moreover, the Catholic Church in America was anything but Irish in tone and leadership before the 1830s.

John Hughes became bishop of New York in 1842, and set about transforming Irish immigrants into avid churchgoers — with remarkable success. He also created and promoted a wide range of Catholic institutions, building more churches, helping to set up Catholic social services and parochial schools, and abolishing the lay trustee system (a system that was a kind of republican innovation), reasserting an emphasis on ecclesiastical authority and hierarchy.[6]

These were also years when anti-Catholic sentiment in the United States was particularly virulent. The nativist crusades of the 1830s and 1840s, and the Know-Nothings of the 1850s were explicitly anti-Irish and anti-Catholic. As Kenny observes, 'most nativists at this time were opposed not to immigration generally, but to Irish Catholic immigrants in particular'.[7] In 1834 rioters set fire to a convent in Massachusetts, and nativist mobs attacked Irish Catholics in Philadelphia, Richmond, and Charleston in 1844 and 1845. Much popular culture, especially sensationalist popular literature, offered forms of anti-Catholic pornography (there were also, of course, other forms and targets, like anti-Mormon narratives). Perhaps the most famous example is Maria Monk's nativist convent narrative *The Awful Disclosures of Maria Monk*, which claimed to be a non-fictional exposé of the horrifying secret life of a Montreal convent.[8] It includes many of the standard features of anti-Catholic literature on both sides of the Atlantic: sexual depravity, infanticide, abuse of the confessional, and victims who are forbidden to read the Bible and are forced to abandon their individual sense of right and wrong and to submit to the absolute and tyrannical authority of corrupt priests. It dwells at length on the excessive severity

5   See Hasia Diner, '"The Most Irish City in the Union": The Era of the Great Migration, 1844–1877', in Ronald H. Bayor and Timothy Meagher, eds., *The New York Irish* (Baltimore and London, 1996), 92. The best general history of the Irish in America is Kevin Kenny's *The American Irish: A History* (London and New York, 2000).
6   Kenny, *American Irish*, 71, 76
7   Kenny, *American Irish*, 115
8   Maria Monk, *The Awful Disclosures of Maria Monk* (London, 1997 [1836])

and macabre variety of the physical punishments and penances to which the nuns were subjected. First published in 1836, it sold 300,000 copies before the American Civil War, becoming the best-selling work of fiction in nineteenth-century America after *Uncle Tom's Cabin*.[9]

Hostile public attitudes were one potential problem for the emerging Catholic Irish-American establishment; Irish Americans themselves were another. Most of them did not, of course, move in the fairly privileged circles Sadlier belonged to. They embodied very different models of transatlantic culture. Even pre-Famine Irish immigrants were the poorest social group in the United States after African Americans and Native Americans.[10] They were also the most urbanized people in the country. As Lawrence McCaffrey observes, 'Irish Catholics had the painful and dubious distinction of pioneering America's urban ghettos.'[11] By 1834, the Five Points neighbourhood in New York had already become famous as a centre of crime, violence, drunkenness and prostitution, and, as Tyler Anbinder reports, the press had begun to publish 'lengthy exposés about the neighborhood'.[12] Charles Dickens visited Five Points in 1842, accompanied by 'two heads of the police' for protection. He encountered two Irish labourers 'in holiday clothes' on Broadway, looking for the shipping office at which they could pay their homesick mother's fare back to Ireland. He also remarked on the menial but crucial jobs that fell to Irish labourers: 'It would be hard to keep your model republics going, without the countrymen and countrywomen of those ... labourers. For who else would dig, and delve, and drudge, and do domestic work, and make canals and roads, and execute great lines of Internal Improvement!'[13] The massive waves of Famine immigrants were generally literate, and were not the very poorest people in Ireland. But they were poorer, less anglicized, and less skilled than previous immigrant generations. They were less able to cope, at least in respectable ways, with the challenges of the New World, and more likely to wind up in trouble. The Irish were overrepresented in slums, jails, charitable institutions, and mental hospitals. Their reputation for a host of social pathologies, many of them particularly urban pathologies, became more firmly established in the popular mind.[14]

The Famine immigrants were obviously a potential power base for the Irish Catholic establishment that was coming into being, but they were also a potential threat or recalcitrant force. As more and more of them poured into North America, and nativism developed itself into the fevered anti-Irish Catholic pitch of Know-Nothingism in the early 1850s, Catholic intellectuals like Sadlier and Brownson worried openly about elevating the tone of the Irish Catholic community in America and creating a new kind of didactic popular literature. In July of 1849 Brownson published an article in his *Quarterly Review*, calling for the creation of a popular Catholic literature. Such works, he said, 'would amuse, interest, instruct, cultivate in accordance with truth the mind and the affections, elevate the tone of the community, and, when they did not directly promote virtue, they would still be powerful to preserve and defend innocence, often a primary duty'. He went on to explain:

> Purely spiritual culture is amply provided for; but owing to the barbarism of past ages, and the incredulity and license of the last century and the present, secular culture in union with the Christian spirit is, and ever has been, only partially provided for, and but imperfectly attained. It seems to us that the best way for our Catholic writers to serve the cause of truth and virtue is to devote themselves, not to controversial or ascetic works, of which we have enough, but to the

9   Kenny, *American Irish*, 80
10 Kenny, *American Irish*, 61
11 Lawrence J. McCaffrey, *The Irish Catholic Diaspora in America* (Washington, DC, 1976), 66
12 Tyler Anbinder, *Five Points* (New York, 2001), 23
13 Charles Dickens, *American Notes for General Circulation* (London, 2000 [1842]), 91, 99
14 For an extended discussion of this issue, see Kerby A. Miller, *Emigrants and Exiles: Ireland and the Irish Exodus to North America* (Oxford and New York, 1985), ch. 7.

Christian secular culture of the age.[15]

In January 1850, Patrick Donahoe's Boston *Pilot* began serializing the first of Sadlier's historical novels set in Ireland, *The Red Hand of Ulster*. That same month, Brownson published another editorial in which he suggested that someone ought to 'write a tale entitled the Orphan of New York or the Orphan of Boston — the Irish Orphan or the Catholic Orphan — which should be adapted to the condition of the poor orphan *boys* among ourselves'. Donahoe responded by offering a prize of fifty US dollars and serialization in the *Pilot* for the best such novel; Brownson judged the contest, and Sadlier's first novel of Irish America, *Willy Burke; or, The Irish Orphan in America*, won. Brownson praised the work in the *Quarterly Review* as an indication that 'a new literature, equally popular, but far more Catholic and healthy, is beginning to make its appearance among us'.[16] The novels discussed in this essay were among her most popular. *The Blakes and the Flanagans* was serialized in the *American Celt* in 1850 and published in book form in 1855; it was the only one of her novels to be translated into German. *Bessy Conway; or, The Irish Girl in America* was published in book form in 1861, and went through more American editions than any of her other novels with American settings.

Sadlier's fiction promoted the institutionalization of a middle-class Irish Catholic American community and culture, in order to enable new kinds of civic space and public life for Catholics, and to ward off the threat that the Famine immigrants might pose to these endeavours. She did this by creating a new kind of popular, Christian, secular culture. One of her later novels, *Elinor Preston* (1861), explicitly states her commitment to helping Irish Catholic America 'go public' in respectable and empowering ways. The narrator gives a glowing description of Montreal as a city whose public space is visibly Catholic, a place where one can 'see the clergy, secular and regular, walking abroad in the habits of their different orders ... appearing here and there in the moving diorama of the crowded streets'. She continues, 'All this was, of course, new to me, and it had an indescribable charm for one who, though brought up a Catholic and among Catholics, had never seen such public manifestations of Catholicity.'[17] But what should such novels look like, and how would they influence their readers? Sadlier's works participate in and revise some of the didactic traditions of the massively popular sentimental fiction by women that dominated the literary marketplace in the United States during this time, culminating in what literary historians have called the 'feminine fifties'.[18] Each novel engages with different aspects of the historical context, and each takes up and revises different elements of sentimental fiction. *The Blakes and the Flanagans* addresses institutions, education, and citizenship; *Bessy Conway* addresses urban pathology, a model of influence through female purity and piety, and oral culture and community.

Sensational Design and Severe Punishment: *The Blakes and the Flanagans*

The Preface to *The Blakes and the Flanagans* announces the novel's didactic mission, while also outlining the possible tensions created by the effort to be both Catholic and popular. 'Reader,' it begins, 'there is a moral contained in this story, and you will not read far till you find it out.' 'The world,' Sadlier explains, is 'divided into two great classes, believers and unbelievers: the children of the one true Church, and the children of the world.' She goes on to distinguish her work from other popular literature of the

15 Quoted in Agnes Brady McGuire, 'Catholic Women Writers', *Catholic Builders of the Nation: A Symposium of the Catholic Contribution to the Civilization of the United States*, vol. 4, *Catholics in the Liberal Professions* (Boston, MA, 1923), 185–86
16 Quoted in Fanning, *Irish Voice*, 118
17 Mary Anne Sadlier, *Elinor Preston* (New York, 1861), 238; hereafter cited as EP
18 The phrase was first used by Fred L. Pattee in *The Feminine Fifties* (New York, 1940).

time, which contains 'hair-breadth scapes by flood and field', and says,

> I do not profess to write novels — I cannot afford to waste time pandering merely to the imagination, or fostering that maudlin sentimentality, which is the ruin of our youth both male and female … One who has Eternity ever in view, cannot write mere love-tales; but simple, practical stories embodying grave truths, will be read by many, who would not read *pious books*.[19]

Her discomfort with the novel form is something that much sentimental fiction of the period shared, and her wish to reach the masses who would not read pious books but would be instructed and amused by Christian popular culture accords with the requirements laid out by Brownson.

The first chapter of *The Blakes and the Flanagans* sets the beginning of the novel in about 1825, 'before Nativism had developed itself into Know Nothingism'. The novel traces the fortunes, over the next several decades, more or less up until the time of writing, of two immigrant families. Both are Catholic. The Flanagans send their children to Catholic school, while the Blakes send their children to the local ward school. Miles Blake considers himself a good Catholic, and thinks that 'churches ought to be built and repaired' and 'the priest decently supported', but he finds Catholic America's other institutional projects unnecessary: 'Schools, or convents, or the like, were, in his opinion, by no means necessary'.[20] This original distinction between the wise Flanagans and the foolish Blakes is embodied over and over again in the subsequent narrative; the fortunes of the respective families, and the contrasts between them, grow directly out of this fateful decision. As the Preface suggests, the moral of the narrative is immediately apparent, and the unfolding of the novel merely serves to illustrate it repeatedly.

Chapter titles like 'The Two Schools', 'The Tree Begins to Bear Fruit', and 'Effect Follows Cause' emphasize these narrative principles of repeated contrast and inevitable trajectory. In successive chapters, a fashionable party at the Blakes' house goes awry when the Blakes embarrass their children by being too Irish, and a party at the Flanagans illustrates their commitment to old-fashioned Irish culture, community, and family hierarchy. This contrast is enforced on another level; at the latter party, the Blakes are 'thinking of a painful contrast' when the Flanagans' son Edward suggests an Irish reel to please his parents, and moments later their own children are brought to their minds 'by force of contrast'.[21] In another important contrast, the Flanagans' young daughter Susie dies young, in a scene heavily reminiscent of the death of Stowe's little Eva. 'Her last moments were of the most exquisite happiness,' reports the narrator, who comments:

> It was a beautiful sight to see the tranquil and happy death of that fair young girl surrounded by loving hearts and tearful eyes, and fervent suppliants petitioning God on her behalf. She was passing away from the earth in the freshness and beauty of her youth, and there was no horror, nothing painful in the transition.

The Blakes' daughter Eliza, who has married a Protestant and neglected her religion, dies in childbirth, shrieking for a priest who arrives too late.[22] Chatty and familiar in tone, the novel is also peppered with sententious observations and exhortations to the reader, like 'Ah! Surely it is a pitiable thing to hear Catholic parents complain of so much time being lost in Catholic schools in teaching and learning of Christian doctrine!' Sadlier's closing remarks 'beg all Catholic parents to "look on this picture, and on

---

19 Mary Ann Sadlier, *The Blakes and the Flanagans* (New York and Boston, MA, 1858), ii; hereafter cited as BF
20 BF, 10–12
21 BF, 169, 173
22 BF, 324, 384

this"', and to send their children to Catholic schools.[23]

These narrative features do not make for suspenseful reading. But they highlight Sadlier's connections to other American didactic and sentimental literature of the feminine fifties. Other features Sadlier's fiction shared with that tradition include plot structures that are both utterly contrived and utterly predictable; a lack of interest in complex characterization and psychological depth; an absence of irony and ambiguity; a conviction that the emotions of the heart and the involuntary language of the body — blushing, fainting, and, above all, tears — indicate moral and spiritual worth; and a preoccupation with death, judgment, heaven, and hell. Perhaps the most obvious and helpful comparison is Stowe's *Uncle Tom's Cabin*, which was written and serialized soon after passage of the Fugitive Slave Act of 1850, and published in book form in 1852. In her well-known recuperative reading of that novel, Jane Tompkins characterizes *Uncle Tom's Cabin*, not as a traditional novel, but as a 'typological narrative' in which all the events and characters, because they are related to an unchanging divine order, endlessly mirror that order and one another. Tompkins observes,

> The truths Stowe's narrative conveys can only be re-embodied, never discovered, because they are already revealed from the beginning. Therefore, what seem from a modernist point of view to be gross stereotypes in characterization and a needless proliferation of incident, are essential properties of a narrative aimed at demonstrating that human history is a continual re-enactment of the sacred drama of redemption.[24]

Characters in such fiction are defined, not psychologically, but 'soteriologically, according to whether they are saved or damned', a definition Sadlier's Preface echoes in sectarian terms. Such didactic fiction accords the exemplary figures, events, and virtues it revolves around 'the power to work in, and change, the world'.[25]

The Blakes and the Flanagans does not merely have didactic ambitions; it is obsessed with theories of education, scenes of instruction, the process of learning, and the means of discipline, and it entered a literary marketplace in which other popular works were similarly obsessed. The major political issue it takes up is the schools question, and it argues strenuously for separate Catholic schooling for Catholic children. The second chapter, entitled 'The Two Schools', compares the Catholic and ward schools. At the ward school, Henry Blake is constantly getting into fights with other boys because they say insulting things about 'papists' and the 'dirty Irish'. The schoolmaster, Mr. Simpson, is a smooth and well-dressed hypocrite who is 'even smoother and more oily' to Catholic boys than to other children. His supposedly pluralistic approach to religious diversity in his classroom — 'Here you are all on the same footing' — is blatantly contradicted by his anti-Catholic prejudices. His secularism is anathema to Sadlier's ideal of religious training, as is his determination to cast religion as a matter of individual choice. He tells Henry that 'The Great Creator of all things left man to his own free will in order that he might choose a religion for himself, but he is not in a condition to choose until he reaches man's estate.' This advice echoes the claims made by one of Henry's classmates, Hugh Dillon, whose life will inevitably turn out badly, that 'I'm an American born, and, as for religion, I have as much right to choose for myself as anyone else.' The narrator describes the violence implicit in Simpson's prejudiced authority over his Catholic students by comparing him to a well-known stereotype of the dandified but violent and uncouth Irishman: he is 'a gentleman whose dexterity in "handling" the faith of young Papists was well-nigh equal to that of our friend Pat, of Donnybrook notoriety, in handling "his sprig

23 BF, 114, 391
24 Jane Tompkins, *Sensational Designs: The Cultural Work of American Fiction 1790–1860* (New York and Oxford, 1985), 134
25 Tompkins, *Sensational Designs*, 130, 135

of Shillelah"'.[26] Henry's sister Eliza, meanwhile, receives as a reward for good conduct an anti-Catholic history book, while at the Catholic school the prize is a copy of *Lives of the Saints*.

Mr. Lanigan, the Catholic schoolteacher, has a shabby appearance and the violence of his authority is overt rather than covert: 'The boys were all afraid of Mr. Lanigan, for he held them in strict subjugation.' His advice to parents is 'Apply the rod, sir, when your boys are young, and keep a tight rein on them when they begin to grow up, and my name isn't Jeremiah Lanigan if you don't have them as Catholic as your heart could wish', a pedagogical theory the novel endorses. Applying the rod is a subject that comes up repeatedly in the novel, and is one of the hallmarks of the kind of Catholic education embodied in the admirable Mr. Lanigan, though no actual scenes of manual correction are represented.[27] Later we are told that Lanigan is a man 'who knew how to administer the birch' and that, though he only does so as a last resort, 'when forced to do it, he did it in earnest'. And the narrative attributes his success in keeping order in his class in large part to this practice. Still later, some of his students, now grown men, reminisce about the corporal punishment they received from him — 'useful hints applied to a place that shall be nameless'. They heartily forgive Lanigan for 'all the hard treatment' he gave them and conclude that it was for their own good.[28] In another scene, earlier in the novel, Miles Blake is about to whip his son Henry for stealing money from his parents in order to go to that forbidden place of corruption, the theatre. But a well-off Protestant, to whom Miles owes money, intervenes: 'I ask it of you as a particular favor, not to whip Harry. I hate manual correction — it is a barbarous practice.' Miles remembers 'a certain long account standing over against his name in Mr. Thomson's book' and submits.[29] In the novel's terms, this is a serious mistake.

But why does Sadlier pay so much attention to manual correction, and why does she endorse it so heartily, particularly at a historical moment when respectable Irish America was bent on distancing itself from cultural stereotypes of the Irish as violent and of Catholic religious authority as brutal? Richard Brodhead has interpreted mass-circulation writings of the 1850s as contemplating, over and over again, a transition in American culture from one model of education, and the kind of discipline involved, to another. The issue is the acceptability of corporal punishment, and one result, according to him, is that in the 1830s, and 'then even more prominently in the 1840s and early 1850s, the picturing of scenes of physical correction emerges as a major form of imaginative activity in America, and arguing the merits of such discipline becomes a major item on the America public agenda'.[30] While Brodhead acknowledges that one obvious answer to the question of what is at issue in the debates about whipping in antebellum America is slavery, he thinks that in the end this is a correct but partial answer because the question pervades the American imagination so thoroughly, and appears so often without an overt connection to slavery or race. For him, the more complete answer involves the ways in which the American middle class was defining itself at this time. The obsession with and disapproval of whipping is central to 'the theory of socialization that is this middle class's greatest creation, absorption, and self-identifying badge: a theory that might be labeled disciplinary intimacy, or simply discipline through love'. Discipline through love defines itself against its opposite, coercion. It demands 'an extreme personalization of disciplinary authority' rather than relying on persons representing an abstract authority that is separate from and exceeds them. And it requires the 'purposeful sentimentalization of the disciplinary relation: a strategic relocation of authority relations in the realm of emotion'. So authority actually expresses

26 BF, 26, 27, 29, 30. A fair was held at Donnybrook just outside Dublin; notorious for violence and drunkenness, it was closed by Irish authorities in 1855.

27 BF, 31

28 BF, 72, 171, 172

29 BF, 92

30 Richard Brodhead, *Cultures of Letters: Scenes of Reading and Writing in Nineteenth-Century America* (Chicago, IL, 1993), 13

itself as affection. Both these requirements are ways of privatizing authority. Brodhead cites *Uncle Tom's Cabin* as the book which deploys these disciplinary conceptions 'with greatest profundity and force'.[31] Numerous episodes of whipping in Stowe's novel reveal the ineffectiveness of slavery's discipline system, and others illustrate the effectiveness of discipline through love, such as the 'conversion' and education of Topsy.

Sadlier shares Stowe's preoccupation with models of schooling and discipline, and she shares, but also revises, Stowe's rejection of the male-dominated pedagogy of coercion and violence in favour of a female-centred method of love and patient suffering. For example, Sadlier offers a contrast to the violent and ineffective male method of defending Irishness and Catholicism in Mary Blake's 'womanly dislike' of all the fighting Henry does at school. She asks him, 'Does it never come into your head that you'd show more respect for religion by keeping out of brawls, and trying to bear patiently with the troublesome?'[32] And this unmartial attitude is echoed in Father Power's distinction between being willing to die for one's religion, and being willing to live for it. A prediction made earlier in the novel that a boy who begins by fighting for his religion will end up fighting against it comes true for Henry, and his sons grow up with a 'horror of Catholicity, and a great contempt for everything Irish'. 'It is, therefore,' continues the narrator, 'quite probable that they are now to be found in the front ranks of the Know-Nothings.'[33] The wrong kind of violence in the service of defending or maintaining Irish and Catholic identity in youth is not only ineffective, it leads directly to the kind of anti-Irish street violence associated with nativist mobs.

It is also associated with the violence of the New York Irish 'b'hoys' — a term that, as David Roediger observes, was the Irish and urban street pronunciation of 'boy', and denoted a particular type of tough, rowdy, and often dandified, urban white youth.[34] One New Year's Eve, the b'hoys go on a rampage, looting, destroying property, and assaulting people, such as a poor old Irishwoman who runs an apple stand. After they have wrecked her stall and stolen her goods and money, she comments, 'if that's what they call American freedom, I'd rather have the slavery we had at home'. When a shopkeeper fires a gun in self-defence, Henry Blake's former classmate Hugh Dillon, who is among the mob, is killed. For Sadlier, there is a connection between such violence and the martial rhetoric of much of the emerging official and political Irish-American nationalism of the time. Henry Blake goes into politics, trades on his Irishness, and draws his political base from the b'hoys, despite the scorn he feels for them (his Protestant wife reminds him 'If you want to use such fellows you must pay the penalty'). He also gives lip service to the cause of Repeal to secure Irish votes. His hypocritical speech is overly martial in its nationalism; both Henry and his calculating friend, Zachary Thomson, offer to fight and die to free Ireland from British tyranny. Sadlier's narrator asserts that some leaders of the Repeal movement in America were indeed hypocrites, and warns her readers to evaluate public men carefully. When the schools question erupts, 'about the same time that Mr. Henry T. Blake was giving his attention to Repeal', Henry objects to separate schools 'on principle'.[35] Thus Sadlier links militaristic Irish-American hooliganism, some forms of Irish-American nationalism, and nativism as parallel formations dominated by men, by Protestants, and organized around various kinds of coercion, military language, and mob violence. This helps to explain why she compares Mr. Simpson, the Protestant schoolteacher, to Pat of Donnybrook Fair.

---

31 Brodhead, *Cultures of Letters*, 17–18, 19, 35
32 BF, 16, 22
33 BF, 378
34 David Roediger, *The Wages of Whiteness: Race and the Making of the American Working Class*, rev. edn. (London, 1999), 99
35 BF, 248, 249, 251, 261, 262–63

But, on the other hand, Sadlier also casts the process Brodhead traces — the rejection of manual correction in favour of discipline through love — as a Protestant plot. The personalization of the authority involved, and the personalization of Mr. Thomson's intervention — he calls it a 'favor' twice during that scene — help us to locate Sadlier's objection to discipline through love as an objection to what she sees as the excessive privatization of moral authority in American Protestant culture and political discourse. External correction — whipping — is readable in the context of Irish-American pro-slavery sentiment, of course. But it also functions as an antidote to the interiority of Protestant sentimental authority and to the private nature of American political concepts such as pluralism, secularism, individualism, and conscience. The novel explicitly critiques all of these concepts. Again and again, right-thinking characters reject the notion that they should find their ultimate moral authority within themselves, exercise their free will, or assert their individual rights. For example, Edward Flanagan explains to a Protestant that 'Catholics are not accustomed ... to put forth any views on a point of Church discipline. We believe and practice, but never presume to discuss the wise teachings of the Church.' At another point Edward explains the insufficiency of individual conscience as the basis for Christian morality. A Protestant character asks, 'Do you mean to tell me, young man, that conscience is not the inward monitor; the beacon, as it were, that guides to the heavenly port?', and Edward's reply points out that the 'conscience' instilled by different religions demands different duties.[36] Protestant sentimental fiction often relied heavily on conceptions of the 'inner light'. For example, the title of The Lamplighter refers to Trueman Flint, the kindly lamplighter who befriends Gertrude, but it also refers to God, the Great Lamplighter who lit the stars and who is capable of sparking the inner light within unregenerate human souls. At one point Gertrude remarks,

> I know of no religion but that of the heart. Christ died for us all alike, and, since few souls are so sunk in sin that they do not retain some spark of virtue and truth, who shall say in how many a light will at last spring up, by aid of which they may find their way to God?[37]

Sadlier rejects individualism, whether it manifests itself as an insistence on individual rights or as an invocation of the religion of the heart. What all the political and religious formulations the novel criticizes have in common is that they make judgements about the rightness of human actions ultimately dependent upon moral choices that are defined, in some way or another, as private.[38]

As has become clear, in discussing how these discourses of education functioned, we are also talking about citizenship, about civic responsibilities and Catholic participation in the American public sphere. Sadlier is perfectly aware that this is what is at stake in her meditations on education. Her description of the Catholic school insists, 'Many and many a valued citizen did it bring up for the State.' When Miles Blake defends his decision about his children's schooling, claiming that 'men can't be Irishmen and Americans at the same time; they must be either one or the other', Edward Flanagan corrects him: 'I am Irish in heart — Catholic, I hope in faith and practice, and yet I am fully prepared to stand by this great Republic, the land of my birth, even to shedding the last drop of my blood, were that necessary.' Edward is willing to live for his religion (and we see him doing this over and over again), but he is also willing to fight and die for the American state. In order to reconcile her brand of Catholic separatism with American citizenship, Sadlier has recourse to the same violent formulation that she rejected for defending religion. As this uneasy solution suggests, Sadlier's novel is deeply ambivalent about

---

36 BF, 304, 337

37 Maria Susanna Cummins, The Lamplighter (New Brunswick, NJ, 1988 [1854]), 305

38 For an extended discussion of the relationship between nineteenth-century American individualism, privacy, and domestic fiction, see Gillian Brown, Domestic Individualism: Imagining Self in Nineteenth-Century America (Berkeley, CA, 1990).

American discourses of citizenship. When young Henry Blake begins to go wrong, he defies proper parental authority by criticizing his father and putting forth his own competing opinion: 'I guess I've about as good a right to give an opinion as any one else. A'n't I a native-born citizen "of these United States"?'[39]

One of Sadlier's major difficulties, then, was that the tropes of the popular didactic fiction she wanted to write for Irish-American Catholics involved the privatizing gestures she associated with Protestant liberal culture and wanted to resist. Michael Warner has characterized the relationship between political ideology and the forms of popular fiction in terms of a transition from late eighteenth-century republican models of citizenship to nineteenth-century liberal models of nationalism. He argues:

> The modern nation does not have citizens in the same way that the republic does. You can be a member of the nation, attributing its agency to yourself in imaginary identification, without being a freeholder or exercising any agency in the public sphere. Nationalism makes no distinction between such imaginary participation and the active participation of citizens. In republicanism that distinction counted for everything. So the early phase of post-Revolutionary nationalism is marked by a gradual extension of a national imaginary to exactly those social groups that were excluded from citizenship — notably women.[40]

Warner sees two related sets of developments occurring as a result. The first involves the establishment of new kinds of division between public and private, the development of politics into a specialized system entrusted to experts and mediating institutions, and the theorization of the liberal subject as essentially 'private'. The second is that the vocabulary of sentiment begins to dominate the American novel in the nineteenth century.

Lori Merish has analysed this conjunction between new forms of political subjectivity and the popularity of sentimental fiction in illuminating terms. Like a number of critics of sentimental, didactic fiction writing after Tompkins, she argues that the forms of political power or agency available in such fiction are inseparable from submission and dependency:

> Sentimental narratives engender feelings of power as well as submission endemic to liberal political culture; they thus instantiate a particular form of liberal political *subjection*, in which agency and subordination are intertwined ... Sentimental sympathy prescribed forms of paternalism — specifically, of 'benevolent' caretaking and 'willing' dependency — suited to a liberal-capitalist social order that privileged individual autonomy and, especially, private property ownership ... [it] encompassed both a recognition of social hierarchy and a sense of spontaneous, heartfelt assent to power, thus reinventing political hierarchy as psychological norms reproduced within the intimate recesses of the desiring subject.[41]

Obviously, this formulation is related to Brodhead's discipline through love, but it is explicitly a theory of citizenship or political subjectivity, and it highlights the theories of privacy and individualism at the core of a sentimental discourse that is in many respects concerned with human relations and dependency. Merish also observes at various points that liberal political subjection is partly derived

---

39 BF, 15, 55–56, 164
40 Michael Warner, *The Letters of the Republic: Publication and the Public Sphere in Eighteenth-Century America* (Cambridge, MA, and London, 1990), 173
41 Lori Merish, *Sentimental Materialism: Gender, Commodity Culture, and Nineteenth-Century American Literature* (Durham, NC, and London, 2000), 3

from pietistic Protestantism.

Sadlier makes the same connection between the privatizing gestures of sentimental fiction and the individualistic rhetoric of Protestant American political discourse. In response, however, it could be said that *The Blakes and the Flanagans* offers a theory of Catholic political subjection. The novel focuses more on the extended family and Irish Catholic community than on the nuclear family or the autonomous individual. It does involve a theory of authority in which, for example, children submit to their parents out of love, but this subjection is ultimately dependent upon external, even coercive forces — corporal punishment and Church authority. In Sadlier, the privatization of authority is incomplete or partially refused. The novel's rejection of concepts like individualism, freedom of choice, free will, individual rights, and individual conscience enacts a similar insistence on the external, and, more important, still *externalized* authority of the Church. That this formulation has a problematic analogue on the level of the nation — the widely perceived problem of Catholic loyalty to an external power — is evident. It also seems evident that advocating manual correction could be a risky strategy at a time when convent narratives like *Awful Disclosures* were full of exotic scenes of brutal, religiously-inspired physical punishment and abolitionists were keen to expound on the barbarities of whipping. Rather than offering practical advice or a coherent or functional ideology, Sadlier's fiction enacts the difficulties and contradictions Catholic Irish America encountered in trying to craft a culture and community that would be both loyally American and transatlantic, both orthodox and countercultural, respectably middle class and inclusive of the Famine immigrants.

The Pure Woman and the Ghost of the Public: *Bessy Conway*

Like *The Blakes and the Flanagans*, Sadlier's *Bessy Conway; or, The Irish Girl in America* pursues its didactic mission by participating in and revising the traditions of American sentimentalism. And also like *The Blakes and the Flanagans*, *Bessy Conway* challenges sentimental fiction's distinctions between public and private. But there are a number of differences in how these projects are organized, and what contradictions they encounter, in each novel. *The Blakes and the Flanagans* is obsessed with education and citizenship — particularly of men — in part because Sadlier's purpose there was to promote a model of Irish Catholic America that was specifically middle class. *Bessy Conway*, on the other hand, is most interested in regulating female working-class conduct and morality, above all in the sexual realm. *The Blakes and the Flanagans* examined the individual's relation to the new middle class's Irish Catholic American institutions — parochial schools, political and electoral machines, nationalist movements, and so on. *Bessy Conway* does not; instead it emphasizes the individual's relation to the various forms of corruption and temptation that Sadlier, along with her contemporaries, thought of as endemic to urban, working-class life — pathologies that, by the time she wrote the novel, tourists had been going to Five Points in New York to witness for some years. While *The Blakes and the Flanagans* examines education as a matter of methods and institutions, *Bessy Conway* takes up sentimental fiction's model of the civilizing influence of the pious woman and the redemptive nature of feminine love. Generically it moves Sadlier's fiction closer to some of the tropes of melodrama and gothic fiction than the earlier novel; it employs some of the 'hair-breadth scapes by flood and field' that characterized some of the more sensationalist popular fiction of the period, and that she rejected in her Preface to *The Blakes and the Flangans*. And while in *The Blakes and the Flanagans* there is no suspense or mystery, except about how the novel's fundamental propositions will reveal themselves next, *Bessy Conway* is obsessed with mystery and suspense on the level of narrative form and of content, to the extent that it even parodies them.[42]

The novel specifically addresses the massive numbers of young Irishwomen who emigrated and became domestic servants in North America during the mid- and late nineteenth century.[43] The Preface announces that the novel's purpose is 'to point out to Irish Girls in America — especially that numerous class whose lot it is to hire themselves out for work, the true and never-failing path to success in this world, and happiness in the next'.[44] Sadlier describes the urban environment in which this class exists in alarmist and lurid terms:

> Perhaps in the vast extent of the civilized world, there is no class more exposed to evil influences than the Irish Catholic girls who earn a precarious living at service in America. To those who are even superficially acquainted with the workings of that chaotic mass which forms the population of our cities, of the awful depth of corruption weltering below the surface, and the utter forgetfulness of things spiritual, it is a matter of surprise that so many of the simple-hearted peasant girls of Ireland retain their home-virtues and follow the teachings of religion in these great Babylons of the west.

The threat to such girls, uniquely endangered as they were, was doubly important because of the influence women exerted in the domestic sphere: 'Every woman has a mission, either for good or evil; and, unhappily for society, the lax, and the foolish, and the unprincipled will find husbands as well as the good and virtuous. The sphere of influence thus extended, who can calculate the results, whether good or ill?'[45]

The beginning of the novel explicitly casts Bessy as an instrument of divine providence, a woman who accomplishes God's purposes in the world. The novel opens, temporally, where it ends — on the prosperous farm of Bessy's family in Ireland, where the Conways have weathered 'the dark days of famine and pestilence' successfully and without serious permanent loss, as a result of Denis Conway's 'cheerful and patient reliance on Divine Providence' — divine providence, that is, in the person of his daughter Bessy. How and why Bessy manages to embody divine providence is announced as the subject of the novel:

> But how did Providence bring all this about? I hear some of my readers ask, and this is just what I am going to tell. Visible agents are always employed to carry out the divine economy in regard to human affairs. Now who was Denis Conway's Providence? ... Who but his own daughter Bessy.[46]

Then the novel backtracks to the time when Bessy, who wants to 'see the world', leaves her happy home to become a domestic servant in America. With her on the boat are several characters who will figure in her story; the most important are a hunchback named Paul Brannigan, and Master Henry Herbert, the

---

42   For example, in one sequence a mysterious stranger on board the ship has aroused much curiosity among the passengers, most of whom are not Irish. The mystery is solved, in disappointing fashion, for the ignorant observers: the mysterious stranger turns out to be a Catholic priest. Mary Anne Sadlier, *Bessy Conway; or, The Irish Girl in America* (New York, 1904 [1861]), 58–59; hereafter cited as BC.

43   On Irish female immigration and domestic service, see Egan, '"White", If "Not Quite"'; Kenny, *American Irish*, chs. 3–4; Hasia Diner, *Erin's Daughters in America: Irish Immigrant Women in the Nineteenth Century* (Baltimore, MD, and London, 1983); Diane Hotten-Somers, 'Relinquishing and Reclaiming Independence: Irish Domestic Servants, American Middle-Class Mistresses, and Assimilation, 1850–1920', *Éire-Ireland*, 36, 1–2 (2001), 185–201; Janet Nolan, *Ourselves Alone: Women's Emigration from Ireland, 1885–1920* (Lexington, KY, 1989).

44   BC, iii

45   BC, iii, iv

46   BC, 6

ne'er-do-well son of the local ne'er-do-well landowner. Bessy keeps her faith in America, and resists the many dangers and temptations the New World contains — secularism, sexual seduction or assault, drink, fine clothes, and inappropriate notions of her individual rights. As a result, she prospers, and, at the end of the novel, she returns home seven years later, during 'the terrible year of the Famine', just in time to use the money she has earned to save her family from an eviction already in progress.[47] The novel details, though in fairly restrained terms, the effects of the corrupting urban environment on other characters. But Bessy, rather than struggling with various temptations, does not seem to be particularly tempted in the first place, though it is clear that she has a soft spot in her heart for Henry. In other words, she does not really undergo a process of education, though there are scenes in the novel that are described as 'lessons' for her; she moves through a corrupting environment, relying on an already existing and complete moral and religious compass.

Sadlier focuses much of the novel's meditation on corruption and subsequent redemption on Henry. When the story opens, he wants to marry Bessy, but is not an acceptable suitor because he is a Protestant. Rejected by Bessy, who is described repeatedly as the sole pure and civilizing influence in his life, as 'the one link that binds me still to virtue', he is also incessantly haunted by a mysterious guilty secret. For example, in one scene he soliloquizes, 'There is but one being in the world whom I love, ... but one who has power over my heart ... but ... my wayward fate — or my evil genius — flings its dark shadow between us two.'[48] Once in America, he continues to suffer rebuffs from the conscientious Bessy, and gives himself over to various forms of debauchery. In contrast to the relatively unthinking characters in *The Blakes and the Flanagans* who lose their faith and are only occasionally troubled by their consciences, Henry is a gothic tortured soul; the memory of his unnamed crime, his sense that he is 'in the hands of an angry God', and his alienation from what he knows is the only humanizing and mediating female figure in his life all combine to render him a figure in the tradition of Melmoth the Wanderer or, in a somewhat different register, Simon Legree. He is repeatedly described as pale, haunted, lurid, ghastly, and corpse-like. For example, during the crossing, the ship encounters a storm — and the storm appears repeatedly as metaphor for both Henry's tempestuous and sinful existence and his ideas of God's wrath, as in phrases referring to his 'stormy passions'. Refusing to go below, Henry stands on the deck:

In truth he was a wild unearthly figure, as he stood there in the black starless night, his uncovered head dripping with the briny spray. His face was pale as a sheeted corpse, and his eyes were wild and haggard, as the fast-flashing lightning shone on his unsheltered form. His thoughts were of death — death and judgment, but not of repentance. Fear and despair were in his soul, for he thought the hour of vengeance was at hand and the arm of God raised to smite him.

When he is overcome by the storm on the deck, Bessy and Paul rescue him together, prefiguring the larger plot of the novel.[49]

Henry's dark secret — the most important one — is revealed in a dramatic public scene by Paul late in the novel. It is that he and some friends used to visit the ruined abbey in Ardfinnan and gamble with dice and cards, using a pile of dead monks' bones for a table. This sacrilegious act, with its gestures towards selling his soul to the devil, has already called down divine retribution; Henry is the only one of the company still left alive. And of course the revelation of the secret causes a horrified Bessy to demand that Henry never speak to her again. Immediately after this, the novel leaves America to acquaint us with the Conway's plight in Ireland, and recounts how Bessy saves them. But Henry turns up in Ireland

47 BC, 263
48 BC, 144, 170
49 BC, 42, 310

again, and Bessy encounters him, haunting the abbey once more, but this time he is doing penance, having been converted to Catholicism. He tells Bessy: 'I have been guilty before God and the world, but not before you — ... I have loved you, God only knows how well, — you have been my star of hope — my rock of safety amidst the raging billows of this sinful world.' All of Bessy's horror at his past conduct vanishes, paving the way for a happy resolution:

> Now that Herbert was converted from his evil ways, she cared not who saw them together, for in her heart she was proud of his affection. And well she might, for with his fortune and personal advantages there were few ladies in the country that would not have been flattered by those attentions so long and so devotedly bestowed on her.

And Bessy agrees to marry him. Unlike his parents (who have died), Henry becomes 'an example to the surrounding gentry, and was generally acknowledged to be one of the best landlords in the county Tipperary. And Bessy was the happiest of wives.'[50] Thus the sphere of Bessy's good influence grows incalculably wide, and the novel ends on a note of domestic and political harmony reminiscent of Maria Edgeworth's *The Absentee* (1812).

It might seem at this point that Sadlier has forgotten her objections to the private Protestant sentimental theory of discipline — or salvation — through love, and entirely personalized authority. But this is not the case. Although Henry's conversion is obviously in some sense due to Bessy's womanly influence — and throughout the novel his continued devotion to her embodies his potential for regeneration, the spark of an inner light that could still lead him to God — womanly influence alone is not sufficient to make him realize that potential. The actual, or perhaps, supplemental (in a Derridean sense), agent of his conversion is Paul Brannigan. After Bessy has left America, at the low point in his former life, Henry is knifed by some companions in crime and left in the street. He is rescued and taken to a Catholic hospital, where Paul, who has long been his enemy, visits him daily and effects his salvation.

Paul is, in many ways, the most intriguing figure in the novel. The text harps constantly on his physical deformities, his dwarf-like stature, his hunched back, his 'discordant laugh' and his twisted visage. For most of the novel, he literally haunts Henry, repeatedly popping up at his elbow at dramatic moments to utter frightening reminders of Henry's fearful guilty secret. In the scene in which Henry stands on the deck of the ship during the storm, for example, Paul appears and speaks to him, and at first Henry wonders in confusion 'was that an echo from within or without? Was that voice from heaven, or earth, or hell?' As it turns out, Paul is not a 'misbegotten fiend' or 'devil' but a sincere Catholic whose piety equals, and parallels, Bessy's.[51] He adopts as his mother an old woman whose son has died, he teaches Sunday school lessons to poor newsboys in the park, and his frequent tears provide an index to his moral worth. His truly gothic persecution of Henry turns out to have been for Henry's own good. Henry's final plunge into dissipation was an attempt to spite Bessy: 'I thought — forgive me, Bessy! that in devoting myself to destruction, I was planting a poisoned arrow in the heart that had so coldly cast me off.' When Henry recounts the story of his conversion, he recalls that, after hearing Paul speak to him in the hospital, 'like a flash of lightning, the fear of God's judgments darted through my soul'. Paul combines nurturing feminine love with a more threatening vision of an angry God. He is 'the good Samaritan who poured oil into my wounds and balm into my heart. He spoke to me of the eternal truths — of death, judgment, heaven and hell.'[52]

50 BC, 306, 314–15
51 BC, 42–43, 99
52 BC, 308–10

Clearly on one level Paul can be read as the embodiment of Henry's twisted and stunted conscience, a conscience that nevertheless remains active and finally converts him. But such a reading misses another function of Paul's that is arguably more important in the novel. The text is preoccupied with various forms of orality—gossip, rumour, story-telling, eavesdropping, and reputation. It repeatedly organizes itself around a dialectic between the concealing and revealing of information and misinformation. In addition to Henry's dark secret, numerous smaller mysteries and secrets populate the text: who is the mysterious man in black on board the ship? How did Dolly's son Phillip die? What crimes did Henry's father commit to get his estate? Even Dolly's ability to discern that an American-born priest is not from Ireland is phrased in terms of an occult knowledge, as another priest asks her, 'What marks and tokens [do] you have on a priest?' Above all, however, the novel's preoccupation with secrets, rumours, and oral culture centres around Paul. When he is first introduced into the text, he is telling tall tales on board the ship. When he reveals Henry's secret to the assembled crowd, he locks the door and begins, 'I'm going to tell a story, and I don't want to be disturbed ... I used to be a great hand at telling stories.' 'I believe,' he continues a few minutes later, 'it's a ghost story.'[53] He is a weird, composite figure: a traditional Irish story-teller, the holder and revealer of secret knowledge, a busy-body who keeps the other characters under constant surveillance, and even a kind of urban hedge-schoolmaster.

Bessy's biggest problem is that her reputation will suffer if Henry persists in pursuing her, and many minor incidents revolve around this threat or around rumours of one kind or another. In one sequence, Bessy has a confrontation with a fellow servant who has neglected to go to Mass. In retaliation the servant taunts Bessy for having a male follower. Bessy thinks in consternation, 'Was Herbert still keeping her in mind, then, and haunting like a ghost on her account the house which he might not enter?' On the next page she has a conversation with Paul in which Henry's name comes up, and afterwards Bessy walks through the street, musing tearfully, 'It's no wonder I was afeard of remarks bein' passed, for I see I can't escape people's tongues as long as himself and me are in the same city.' Right on cue, Henry turns up in person and asks her what is wrong. Bessy 'feared to raise her eyes or give any sign of recognition, for she knew it was Henry Herbert that spoke, and she began to have an instinctive notion that prying eyes were ever upon her, and ears ever open to find pretence for insinuation'.[54] Bessy's body is never really in danger of being violated by Henry, but her public reputation is. This produces her gothic paranoia about being haunted, both by him and by the eyes, ears, and tongues of community opinion.

These eyes, ears, and tongues belong, above all, to Paul. He is a figure for the kinds of community life, standards, and consequences organized around oral forms of circulation and publicity. Scholars are generally accustomed to reading gothic tropes as either externalizing private or psychological phenomena (as in much psychoanalytic work on the gothic) or embodying collective guilt or anxiety (as in many readings of the Anglo-Irish gothic). In contrast, *Bessy Conway* offers a different kind of gothic. The purpose of the novel's gothic trappings — descriptions of Paul as demonic and physically misshapen, Henry's sense of his own gothic damnation, Bessy's fears of being haunted, and the way coincidence functions in the novel — is to figure the public and community life of working-class Irish immigrants, and the disciplinary mechanisms their orally based culture employs against those who transgress its norms. This helps to explain the weird combination that structures Paul's character — gothic, misshapen imp, dwarf, devil, and powerful embodiment, proponent, and policeman of the novel's most cherished values. It also helps to explain the fact that perhaps the novel's most dramatic scene is the one in which Paul tells the story of Henry's secret, not just to Bessy, but to a large crowd of people, including Bessy. Rejection by Bessy and shaming by Paul, the private discipline of love and the

53 BC, 130, 243–45
54 BC, 82–84

public discipline of an oral, gothic community or culture, are the two inseparable factors in Henry's conversion. To return to Sadlier's revision of the sentimental trope of the influence of the pure and pious woman, Bessy, like Paul, is the agent, rather than the embodiment, of the divine, and its authority exceeds her and is separable from her. In *Bessy Conway* we see Sadlier rewriting sentimental fiction's privatizing gestures, this time not in terms of institutions, educational methods, print, and a middle-class world, but in terms of oral culture and community, gothic tropes, and the potential horrors of urban and working-class corruption.

In *Elinor Preston*, Sadlier also figures a semi-public sphere as a realm in which communal disapproval and discipline are brought to bear on the errant individual subject. Early in the novel, a family friend plays a joke on Elinor's haughty but lovable, unmarried Aunt Kate. Aunt Kate's foibles are 'family pride' and a willingness to believe that, old as she is, she might be an object of interest to a suitor. She and a prospective suitor are misled and embarrassed; Aunt Kate is so humiliated that she has to retreat to her room and lie down to 'quiet her nerves'. This happens in front of a party including family members and others. Even Elinor's saintly mother, who tries to protect her sister-in-law from the worst of the ridicule that ensues, interprets and enjoys the incident as a joke.[55] Such joking would be anathema to writers like Stowe, Warner, and Cummins. For them, it could only reveal the depravity of the jokers and display the goodness of the protagonists who refuse to countenance them. There is a similar figure in *The Lamplighter*, for example, named Patty Pace, whom Gerty protects from the malicious humour of other characters. In Sadlier's novel, however, this form of humour indicates the public exercise of a communal sense that Aunt Kate's pride needs to be exposed and taken down a peg, and no member of the family or community is immune from its appeal. It illustrates something that Conrad Arensberg would observe later about folk humour in the Irish countryside, that humour is the 'velvet glove that clothes the iron hand' of social control.[56]

A final indication that Sadlier revises sentimental fiction's forms of privacy lies in her treatment of writing itself. Didactic American fiction placed a high value on literacy, reading, and writing. In *The Wide, Wide World*, for example, Eleanor Montgomery's mother gives her a parting gift of a writing desk and writing implements. And while these novels are uncomfortable with their status as novels, they are full of scenes in which 'improving reading' is a good thing, and in which communication by letter reinforces the private, unmediated bonds between worthy people. Reading and writing are not mediating technologies in these novels; they are the means of extending the private self and connecting it to other selves. Sadlier's fiction, in contrast, is replete with scenes that propose the semi-public and mediating nature of writing. In *Bessy Conway*, Bessy sits down to write a letter home, and her task is awkward, unfamiliar, and daunting:

> It was no trifle of a job for Bessy Conway to indite such a letter as she wished to send home ... now when she found herself actually sitting down to the performance of that solemn act, the undertaking loomed up before her in awful magnitude ... Had it been to any one else she thought she would never have courage to begin, but as memory brought back the fireside at home, and the group of ever-loved, never-forgotten faces, and the tears that would fall from many eyes at the reading of 'Bessy's letter,' all her fears vanished, and she set about her task with the greatest alacrity ...[57]

---

55   EP, 23, 38
56   Conrad Arensberg, *The Irish Countryman* (New York, 1937), 106
57   BC, 132

As Bessy predicts, when the letter arrives in Ireland, it is a public event; the priest is called in to read it, and it is passed around from one reader to the next in the Irish tradition of the 'American letter'. In *The Blakes and the Flanagans*, books indicate the sectarian nature of public school education. As previously mentioned, the Blakes' daughter Eliza does well at the ward school, and receives an anti-Catholic history book as a prize; at the Catholic school the prize for achievement is an appropriately Catholic *Lives of the Saints*. And in *Elinor Preston*, a well-meaning but proselytizing Protestant gives Elinor a copy of John Bunyan's *Pilgrim's Progress*, which she promptly burns in an '*auto-da-fé*'.[58] Protestant and Catholic didactic novels thus belong to different 'cultures of letters,' to use Brodhead's helpful phrase. They are written for different audiences, with different didactic aims, and have different ideas about the status of writing itself. For Sadlier, reading and writing are public in two senses: they are explicitly mediated and mediating technologies, and they reveal the often sectarian nature of forms of publicity offered by print culture.

In pursuing her efforts to imagine various kinds of civic or public space for American Catholicism, to counter anti-Irish and anti-Catholic prejudice, to show the Famine immigrants how to prosper in the New World, Sadlier could have invoked the principles that structured contemporary formulations of the public: individualism and privacy. And her attempts to help consolidate American Catholicism as the religious system of the respectable do constitute a disciplinary project that encouraged Irish assimilation into American capitalism and political culture. At the same time, however, this project is deeply countercultural, based on concepts and mechanisms that are inimical to American capitalism and political culture and prevent her from embracing individualism and privacy. She took up the fictional genre that was most popular in her day, and most committed to its work in and for the public, and found herself rejecting or revising some of its most distinctive literary and ideological features. Her generic engagements and revisions enable, and are inseparable from, her critiques of American political discourses and the complexities of trying to produce popular fiction that would 'raise the tone of the community' in mid-nineteenth-century Irish Catholic America.

58 EP, 268

Tradition and Misalliance: J. S. Le Fanu

Terms like heritage and tradition have often functioned as problems, absences, or crippling legacies in discussions of Anglo-Irish culture.[1] In Joseph Sheridan Le Fanu's 1864 gothic novel, *Uncle Silas*, the heroine, the beautiful heiress Maud Ruthyn, promises her exacting and aristocratic father, Austin, that she is willing to 'make some sacrifice' in order to restore the lost honour of their family name and tradition.[2] Her father exhorts her to remember that 'the character and influence of an ancient family is a peculiar heritage — sacred but destructible; and woe to him who either destroys or suffers it to perish!'[3] Austin Ruthyn's speech points out two important features of nineteenth-century Anglo-Irish literature: its tendency to figure Anglo-Irish tradition — political and cultural — as an aristocratic dynasty, and its ambivalent characterization of that tradition as both sacred and fragile. His daughter Maud, the silent recipient of his injunctions and the willing sacrifice to the family honour, indicates a related characteristic of Anglo-Irish literature: its persistent habit of encoding its discussions of tradition in representations of gender and sexual issues. *Uncle Silas*, in particular, structures its representations of Anglo-Irish political anxieties as anxieties about the construction of femininity and the regulation of female sexuality.

Anglo-Irish literature, as distinct from Irish literature written in English, can be defined as the literary production of the social and political caste whose domination of Ireland under British rule was known as the Protestant Ascendancy. The Anglo-Irish were a local ruling class whose pretensions to aristocracy belied their profoundly middle-class character, and whose imaginative construction of an authoritative, aristocratic political and cultural tradition belied their dependence on English centres of power for their strength and legitimacy in Ireland. Like all traditions, the Anglo-Irish tradition was an invented tradition whose asserted unity and stability over time and across groups of people sought to

---

1 For example, Robert Welch remarks that 'to speak of tradition in nineteenth-century Irish literature is to be conscious of an absence'; see his 'Constitution, Language and Tradition in Nineteenth-Century Irish Poetry', in Terence Brown and Nicholas Grene, eds., *Tradition and Influence in Anglo-Irish Poetry* (London, 1989), 7. G. J. Watson, *Irish Identity and the Literary Revival: Synge, Yeats, Joyce, and O'Casey* (New York, 1979), 20, claims that in Irish literature 'always lurking somewhere near the surface is a painful sense of a lost identity, a broken tradition, and the knowledge that an alien identity has been, however reluctantly, more than half embraced'.

2 Joseph Sheridan Le Fanu, *Uncle Silas: A Tale of Bartram-Haugh*, ed. W. J. McCormack with Andrew Swarbrick (New York, 1981 [1864]), 102; hereafter cited as US

3 US, 104

mask change and fragmentation.[4] What was unusual about the Anglo-Irish was the degree to which change and fragmentation themselves became the consistent, identifiable characteristics of their invented political and cultural tradition. Because of their hybrid cultural status and tenuous political position, the Ascendancy imagined an Anglo-Irish tradition that was legitimating and empowering, but simultaneously broken, betrayed, and corrupt. Many of the features specific to Anglo-Irish literature and culture (and illustrated in *Uncle Silas*) are the results of this ambivalent structure.

Le Fanu's life and family background typify, in many ways, the predicament of the Anglo-Irish in the mid-nineteenth century. He was born in 1814 into a middle-class professional (rather than landowning) family. Le Fanu's father was a Protestant minister whose fortunes declined with Catholic Emancipation and growing resistance to tithes. Eleven years of Le Fanu's childhood were spent living in Phoenix Park, at the military school where his father was chaplain and where Le Fanu observed constant displays of British military and imperial power that were spectacular yet clearly symbolic and ritualized. The parades, ceremonies, and symbols that dominated Dublin's military life were the trappings of military force rather than its instruments; they suggested power, but power centred elsewhere.[5] In 1826 Le Fanu's father became the rector at Abington, in Limerick, and there the family became the target of popular resentment and hostility during the disturbances over tithes in the early 1830s. Le Fanu was trained as a lawyer but became interested in writing, and managed to make a relatively meagre but respectable living at it. He bought the *Dublin University Magazine* in 1861 and acquired a partnership interest in the *Dublin Evening Mail*. While he could and did serialize his novels in the *Dublin University Magazine* thereafter, Le Fanu remained financially dependent on selling them to his London publisher.[6]

These experiences — living close to a military presence that was more show than substance; being not merely isolated from but openly resented, howled at, and even stoned by the native Irish at Abington; and remaining dependent on his London publisher and the English literary marketplace for his living — all gave Le Fanu an acute sense of the tenuous political and cultural position of the Anglo-Irish. Le Fanu's response to this position was a series of political interests and associations, all of them dedicated to preserving the Anglo-Irish as a distinct and superior caste. As W. J. McCormack puts it:

> Le Fanu's politics had swung remarkably during his early years, from violent denunciations of the Liberator to a covert and short-lived endorsement of Repeal, from practical cooperation with Young Irelanders to unsuccessful canvassing for a Tory nomination. There was a consistent thread running through these widely separated corners of the fabric, which might be described variously as opposition to politicized Catholicism or attempts to redefine grounds for Protestant supremacism.

By the time he wrote *Uncle Silas* Le Fanu was a committed conservative with an intense interest in Irish politics, and was the only contemporary Irish writer of note who was actively involved in the Dublin political and intellectual scene.[7]

Despite the fact that the novel in its final form is set in England, Le Fanu's critics have generally agreed on its underlying 'Irishness'. McCormack, whose literary biography of Le Fanu is the best and most thorough examination of his work to date, claims that 'more than any other of the novels of "an English setting and of modern times" *Uncle Silas* indirectly reveals an Anglo-Irish provenance'.[8] In her

---

4   The phrase 'the invention of tradition' is associated with Eric Hobsbawm's work, especially Eric Hobsbawm and Terence Ranger, eds., *The Invention of Tradition* (New York, 1983). Benedict Anderson, *Imagined Communities: Reflections on the Origin and Spread of Nationalism*, rev. edn. (London and New York, 1991) is also relevant here.

5   See W. J. McCormack's *Sheridan Le Fanu and Victorian Ireland* (Oxford, 1980), ch. 1, esp. 15–16.

6   See McCormack, *Sheridan Le Fanu*, 37–71, 200.

7   McCormack, *Sheridan Le Fanu*, 196, 209

8   McCormack, *Sheridan Le Fanu*, 204

Introduction to the 1947 edition of the novel, Elizabeth Bowen recorded her impression that Uncle Silas is 'an Irish story transposed to an English setting', and this is quite literally true.[9] Uncle Silas is based on a short story that Le Fanu originally published in 1833 under the title 'Passage in the Secret History of an Irish Countess'. It was reprinted in 1851, with some minor changes, as 'The Murdered Cousin'. In the original short stories, which are set in Ireland, Le Fanu was explicit about the Irish referents of his tale about a noble family degenerating into such displays of vice and crime as gambling, attempts to force the narrator into marriage, and murder. The framing narrator of 'Passage in the Secret History of an Irish Countess', a Catholic priest named Father Purcell, testifies to the historical accuracy of the narrative: 'To those who know anything of the history of Irish families, as they were less than a century ago, the facts which immediately follow will at once suggest the names of the principal actors.'[10] The narrator of 'The Murdered Cousin' characterizes the text as a 'story of the Irish peerage'.[11]

Since the major market for Anglo-Irish literary production was England, Anglo-Irish writers like Le Fanu had to accommodate British reading tastes, which preferred romance to politics, especially where the Irish were concerned, and which often preferred not to read about the Irish at all. Indeed, one distinguishing feature of Anglo-Irish literature has always been its economic dependence on an English market whose demands often dictated that Anglo-Irish writers present Irish political concerns and questions in indirect and encoded form. During the 1860s, the Fenian threat made Irish settings and themes particularly unpalatable to the English reading public, and in 1863 Le Fanu's London publisher demanded that future novels deal with English settings and modern times.[12] Accordingly, when Le Fanu expanded his story into Uncle Silas he abandoned the Irish scene and set the novel in England. He also added the sexual corruption of a cross-class marriage to the list of Silas's sins, and, further, made Silas's misalliance with a Welsh barmaid his original sin, the one that initiates his family's decline and functions as a symbol for his corruption in general. The barmaid's lower-class origins and Welsh ancestry maintain the connection, established explicitly in the short stories, between Celtic nature or influence and the family's descent into debauchery and decay. 'She drank,' comments Maud's cousin, Monica Knollys; 'I am told that Welsh women often do.'[13]

While he suppressed the overtly 'Irish' aspects of the story by changing the setting and dropping references to the lamentable state of the Irish peerage, Le Fanu enlarged upon the text's indirectly or structurally Irish characteristics through its emphasis on sexual corruption and its preoccupation with Maud's femininity. To work out why genealogical decay, the sexual corruption of marital misalliance, and a preoccupation with the nature and construction of femininity indicate the text's specifically Anglo-Irish origins and concerns, the relationship between the Protestant Ascendancy and English imperialist culture needs to be examined.

Assimilation, Sexuality, and the Anglo-Irish

Anglo-Irish discourses about their uncertain political and cultural status were intimately bound up with representations of gender and sexuality as a result of the structure of contemporary British imperialism. During the nineteenth century, British rule of Ireland underwent two related changes that crucially

9   Introduction to Uncle Silas: A Tale of Bartram-Haugh, ed. Elizabeth Bowen (London, 1947), 8
10 J. S. Le Fanu, 'Passage in the Secret History of an Irish Countess', in The Purcell Papers, 3 vols. (London, 1880), vol. 2, 2
11 J. S. Le Fanu, 'The Murdered Cousin', in E. F. Bleiler, ed., Ghost Stories and Mysteries (New York, 1975), 216
12 McCormack, Sheridan Le Fanu, 140. Also see Maurice Colgan, 'Exotics or Provincials? Anglo-Irish Writers and the English Problem', in Wolfgang Zach and Heinz Kosok, eds., Literary Interrelations: Ireland, England, and the World, vol. 3, National Images and Stereotypes (Tübingen, 1987), 36.
13 US, 147

affected Anglo-Irish attitudes and anxieties. First, the number and complexity of agencies, institutions, and laws used to administer Ireland increased steadily over the course of the nineteenth century, and second, during that period British domination shifted from a reliance on military and legal coercion to an increasing reliance on integrating the native Irish into the state apparatus.[14] Increasing agitation for Catholic Emancipation was a major cause of this shift, and the granting of Emancipation in 1829 was an important means of institutionalizing it. Political integration demanded, or was thought to demand, cultural and linguistic assimilation; the establishment of the national schools in Ireland, in which students were forbidden to speak Irish and were taught English history and literature exclusively, followed hard upon the heels of this last Catholic Relief Act. The Irish were to assimilate themselves to the English model of good citizens and responsible economic, political, and sexual actors. Imperial discourses usually characterized such assimilation as a progress from barbarism to civilization. As a result, more and more aspects of Irish life and character were targeted for government observation and regulation, including Irish sexual and reproductive behaviour; the year in which Le Fanu's novel was first published in its final form, 1864, was also the first year in which government statutes required that all Irish births be registered.[15]

While mid-nineteenth-century British imperialist thought was characterized by new practical and ideological emphases on assimilating the native Irish into the cultural and political structures of Britain, it was also characterized by profound anxieties about assimilation in its more threatening guises. The spectres that haunted the colonial, and especially the Anglo-Irish, imagination were racial assimilation that, it was feared, would sap the strength and purity of England, and assimilation as the descent of the British to the political and social level of the barbarous Irish. In Ireland such anxieties did not merely express colonial fears of 'going native'; they represented an acute awareness that the shape of the relationship between the Protestant Ascendancy and the Catholic Irish was in fact changing, albeit slowly. The history of the Anglo-Irish in the nineteenth century is one of a gradual diminution of wealth and power. Colonial discourses alternately allegorized Anglo-Irish relations as a family romance and expressed fear of just such a romance between Saxon and Celt on a literal level. Assimilationist thought was both a basis for policy and a response to already existing political and social trends, expressing both the will to power of British imperialism and its fears of impotence and decay.

Matthew Arnold's 'On the Study of Celtic Literature' demonstrates the central ambivalences of contemporary assimilationist thought, ambivalences that appear most strikingly in Anglo-Irish literature. It also illustrates that these ambivalences were inseparable from questions of gender and sexuality. Published in 1866, two years after Uncle Silas, Arnold's text would become a founding document of the Celtic movement's cultural nationalism in the last two decades of the nineteenth century. At the time of publication, however, Arnold intended the lectures as contributions to constructive unionism.[16] He proposed that the English should strengthen their imperial power by assimilating the Irish more thoroughly into the political and cultural structures of Britain. Merely keeping order was not enough; the English needed to integrate the Irish into the state by giving them a fair and rational system of government and by allowing them a certain amount of local control over that system. Arnold constructed

14 F. S. L. Lyons, Ireland since the Famine (London, 1971), esp. pt. 1. Lyons documents the increasing volume and complexity of regulatory discourses and institutions in Ireland, arguing that in many respects Ireland functioned as a kind of 'social laboratory' (65) for the English, who often tried out new rules and procedures in Ireland before introducing them into England.

15 Lyons, Ireland since the Famine, 68

16 On Arnold's construction of the Celtic element in literature, see John V. Kelleher, 'Matthew Arnold and the Celtic Revival', in Harry Levin, ed., Perspectives of Criticism (Cambridge, MA, 1950), 197–221; Rachel Bromwich, Matthew Arnold and Celtic Literature: A Retrospect, 1865–1965 (Oxford, 1965); and Maurice Riordan, 'Matthew Arnold and the Irish Revival', in Literary Interrelations, vol. 3, National Images and Stereotypes, 145–52.

a version of Celtic nature that was inferior but complementary to the English character: the Celt was a flawed genius, incapable of self-government, whose brilliant but unstable nature had much to offer the more plodding and rational Saxon. Arnold's version of English imperial hegemony was based on exploiting and cultivating sympathy and natural affinity rather than on force, demanding that Anglo-Saxon and Celt blend their complementary natures into a more perfect whole. This in turn would foster a peaceful political union with 'its parts blended together in a common national feeling'.[17]

Arnold's positive and sympathetic (but ultimately damning) characterization of the Celt, and his claim that the Saxon would benefit from embracing, within limits, the Celtic spirit, were among the most radical aspects of Arnold's argument. They also revealed the central contradictions and ambivalences of assimilationist thought with striking clarity. Two points are of particular interest here. First, much of Arnold's essay was concerned with outlining the Celtic element in English literature and with revealing the deep affinities and hidden kinships between the Irish and the English. Arnold advocated assimilation by claiming that it was already at least partially achieved. The assertion that the English had already assimilated some of the Celtic spirit led him to the fear that they might be debilitated by their Celticism. 'Perhaps, if we are doomed to perish,' Arnold wrote, 'we shall perish by our Celtism ... and yet those very Celts, by our affinity with whom we are perishing, will be hating and upbraiding us all the time.'[18] The same affinities that Arnold hoped would strengthen British imperial power could also prove its undoing; the British effort to civilize the Celt could instigate or hasten the Saxon's descent into barbarism.

Second, Arnold explicitly connected the Celt's disabilities and 'habitual want of success' to femininity, a femininity marked by nervousness, inconsistency, and lack of balance: 'no doubt the sensibility of the Celtic nature, its nervous exaltation, have something feminine in them, and the Celt is thus peculiarly disposed to feel the spell of the feminine idiosyncrasy; he has an affinity to it; he is not far from its secret'.[19] Arnold was by no means alone in equating femininity and Celtic nature in terms that related both to nervous disorders. Ernest Renan's La Poésie des races celtiques, upon which Arnold drew heavily in 'On the Study of Celtic Literature', had made the same connections in 1854:

> If it be permitted us to assign sex to nations as to individuals, we should have to say without hesitance that the Celtic race ... is an essentially feminine race. No human family, I believe, has carried so much mystery into love. No other has conceived with more delicacy the ideal of woman, or been more fully dominated by it. It is a sort of intoxication, a madness, a vertigo.[20]

What Julian Moynahan has called the 'confusion in the mid-Victorian mind ... between ideas of Celtic nature and of woman's nature' attributed a debilitating mental or nervous instability to both, and this structure of thought persisted beyond the turn of the century.[21] The Celt's femininity marked both his

17 'The Incompatibles', in English Literature and Irish Politics, vol. 9 of The Complete Prose Works of Matthew Arnold, ed. R. H. Super (Ann Arbor, MI, 1973), 242. David Lloyd's Introduction to his Nationalism and Minor Literature: James Clarence Mangan and the Emergence of Irish Cultural Nationalism (Berkeley, CA, 1987), 6–13, contains an excellent discussion of Arnold's assimilative ideology.

18 Matthew Arnold, 'On the Study of Celtic Literature', in Lectures and Essays in Criticism, vol. 3 of The Complete Prose Works of Matthew Arnold, ed. R. H. Super and Sr. Thomas Marion Hoctor (Ann Arbor, MI, 1962), 382

19 Arnold, 'Celtic Literature', 344, 347

20 Ernest Renan, The Poetry of the Celtic Races and Other Studies, trans. William G. Hutchinson (London, 1896), 8

21 Julian Moynahan, 'Lawrence, Woman, and the Celtic Fringe', in Anne Smith, ed., Lawrence and Women, (London, 1978), 127. L. P. Curtis, Anglo-Saxons and Celts: A Study of Anti-Irish Prejudice in Victorian England (Bridgeport, CT, 1968), 51, claims that 'of the many pejorative adjectives applied by educated Englishmen to the Irish perhaps the most damaging, certainly the most persistent, were those which had to do with their alleged unreliability, emotional instability, mental disequilibrium, or dualistic temperament'. Curtis also comments (61) that 'Irish femininity was also a persistent theme', and observes

inferiority and his naturally complementary relationship to the masculine Saxon. Arnold's insistence on the existence of (potentially threatening) natural affinities between the Irish and the English and his attribution of a near-hysterical femininity to the Celt appear in Anglo-Irish literature with striking regularity. Since assimilation was often figured as a reconciliation through marriage, and since contemporary theories of the racial difference between Saxon and Celt represented it as, in part, a gender difference, it is not surprising that Anglo-Irish texts interrogated the prevailing political structures and issues through representations of romance, sexuality, and gender. Indeed, for many, as for Le Fanu, the economic constraints under which they wrote made it imperative. Sympathetic unionists had long advocated assimilation as the route to a harmonious empire, and had found marriage between the feminine Celt and masculine Saxon the most inviting and profitable figure for such assimilation. Sydney Owenson's The Wild Irish Girl (1806) is perhaps the best known of these imperial romances.

But Owenson's book was written before Catholic Emancipation and the rise of a Catholic middle class made integration inevitable on a less romantic and more threatening level. As the nineteenth century progressed, and governmental policy and rhetoric increasingly emphasized integration in a number of concrete ways, Anglo-Irish anxieties about their own weakness and tenuous hold on power focused more and more on the dangers of assimilation. For the Anglo-Irish imagination, assimilation did not usually signal a harmonious reconciliation with the native Irish; more often it meant their extinction through the absorptive powers of the Gael. The terms in which the prevailing discourses on assimilation cast the possibilities for maintaining British imperial power in Ireland spelled the demise of the Anglo-Irish as a distinct group. For the Anglo-Irish, to stay in power was also to become extinct. Because of this contradiction, Anglo-Irish writers produced a different version of the imperial romance of reconciliation, a gothic version expressing Arnold's fears of the English perishing through their affinities with Celts and his ascription of a nervous and unbalanced femininity to the Irish. Such texts represented sexuality as the agent of corruption and immolation rather than healthy assimilation, and revealed apparent political and dynastic strength as emptiness and weakness.

While financial necessity demanded that, in expanding and revising, Le Fanu shape the novel to accommodate the British reading public's taste for romantic and sensational thrillers, Uncle Silas also belongs properly to an Anglo-Irish tradition of 'Big House gothics'. From Maria Edgeworth to Yeats to J. G. Farrell, writers in this tradition have lamented or chastised the internal corruption of the Anglo-Irish and have figured the political and cultural decline of the Ascendancy as the genealogical decay of a family dynasty in a gothic setting. Such texts represent the Anglo-Irish less as victims of British indifference or Irish resentment than as victims of their own vices and debilities. Throughout the nineteenth century the Anglo-Irish were criticized for absenteeism, provincialism, greed, profligacy, and a host of other irresponsible behaviours. In 1849 Thomas Carlyle saw Ireland as symptomatic of a general aristocratic decline, exclaiming, 'Alas, when will there any real aristocracy arise (here or elsewhere) to need a Capitol for residing in!'[22] Standish O'Grady's famous description of the Anglo-Irish 'rotting from the land in the most dismal farce-tragedy of all time, without one brave deed, without one brave word', was nothing new; it formed part of a tradition, well established by the 1860s, of characterizing the Anglo-Irish as an aristocracy in decline due to their own internal weaknesses.[23]

that 'the relevance of such attributions to English policy in Ireland lies in the assumed connections between femininity and unfitness for self-government'. On the mid-nineteenth century's anxieties about women's mental instability and sexual corruption, see Bram Dijkstra, Idols of Perversity: Fantasies of Feminine Evil in Fin-de-Siècle Culture (New York, 1986); and Elaine Showalter, The Female Malady: Women, Madness, and English Culture, 1830–1980 (New York, 1985).

22 Thomas Carlyle, Reminiscences of My Irish Journey in 1849, ed. J. A. Froude (London, 1882), 55
23 Standish O'Grady, 'The Great Enchantment', in Selected Essays and Passages, ed. Ernest A. Boyd (Dublin, n.d.), 180

Paramount among the perceived internal weaknesses of the Anglo-Irish was their susceptibility to the wrong kinds of assimilation with the Celtic Irish. In the absence of a specifically Irish setting, Le Fanu introduced the sexual corruption of Silas's mismatch with a lower-class Celt to suggest the novel's connections with the threatened Ascendancy. In addition, he emphasized issues of genealogical continuity and dynastic decline to indicate a particularly Anglo-Irish decay. While he was giving Uncle Silas its final form, Le Fanu was engaged in two separate correspondences about his own family genealogy, and the names Austin, Ruthyn, and Silas, none of which appear in the short stories, can be found among Le Fanu's own Anglo-Irish relatives.[24]

Silas's son from this marriage, Dudley, a coarse, brutal villain whom Maud finds repulsive, incarnates the family's degradation. Ironically, Silas describes Dudley as the culmination of precisely those hereditary qualities that Silas's marriage has imperilled in the Ruthyn family. He tells Maud that 'Dudley is the material of a perfect English gentleman' and 'a Ruthyn, the best blood in England — the last man of the race'. This parodic combination of asserted cultural and genealogical purity with obvious barbarism and corruption is not merely an ironic comment on the disparity between what Silas imagines Dudley to be and what he is. It points to Anglo-Irish fears that the well-bred English or Anglo-Irish gentleman might, on some level, be indistinguishable from the debauched barbarian; fears that, as Matthew Arnold argued, deep affinities between Celt and Saxon were already established and partial assimilation was a natural fact. Silas's plan to persuade Maud to marry Dudley is frustrated when Dudley's lower-class wife appears to claim him. Silas comments angrily that Dudley has found 'a very suitable and vulgar young woman.'[25] Dudley's marriage is both an appropriate index to the family's decay, which renders a Ruthyn a 'suitable' match for a 'vulgar young woman,' and a treacherous repetition of the original misalliance. Such repetition gestures toward the inherent and inevitable nature of the genealogical decline it represents.

Since most nineteenth-century Anglo-Irish gothic stories were narratives of internal corruption and decline, they usually revolved around collapsing the distinction between the corrupt house and the apparently pure lineage. Much gothic fiction of the period begins by positing an external threat, only to reveal the internal origin of the horror.[26] Silas, whose side of the family spirals lower and lower on the social and moral scale through repeated misalliances, and his brother Austin, proud of his pure blood and intent on rehabilitating the dynastic line, are in fact true blood brothers, twin manifestations of the same Anglo-Irish tradition, a tradition whose distinguishing feature was that it was imagined as simultaneously empowering and enfeebling.

Le Fanu charted the collapse of the distinction between the pure and the corrupt via his interest in Emanuel Swedenborg; W. J. McCormack has argued convincingly that Le Fanu gave Uncle Silas a Swedenborgian structure. In Swedenborg the soul relives its actions after death, and their true moral significance in the world is revealed. Uncle Silas is structured around a series of parallels between Austin and Silas, Knowl and Bartram-Haugh (their respective manor houses), and the events that occur at each location. In effect, everything appears or happens twice, and, McCormack argues, Bartram-Haugh is the postmortem re-creation of Knowl in the Swedenborgian sense.[27] While the events of the narrative progress toward a happy ending in which Maud escapes from Silas and Dudley and preserves the purity

---

24 McCormack, Sheridan Le Fanu, 2, 205–06
25 US, 248–49, 325, 331
26 In her Freudian/Lacanian study of fantastic literature, Rosemary Jackson argues that as society became increasingly secularized during the nineteenth century, gothic fiction came to embody the internal and personal origin of horror, rather than external and supernatural sources; see Fantasy: The Literature of Subversion (London and New York, 1981), 55.
27 McCormack, Sheridan Le Fanu, 148–94

of her name and lineage, the text renders this progress meaningless by revealing the deep identity between Bartram-Haugh and Knowl. Maud's journey from Knowl to Bartram-Haugh is not a transition from one location to the other or from purity, innocence, and safety to corruption and danger. Rather, it marks a process of revelation. This process has its parallel in Maud's circular journey away from Bartram-Haugh, under her Uncle Silas's assurance that she is on her way to France, only to find herself even more securely imprisoned in Bartram-Haugh. The barbarous crime and decay rampant in Silas's rotting mansion form the inverted mirror image of Austin's cultured preoccupation with family name and lineage.

Austin's role as a local landowner also suggests hidden kinships between his purity and Silas's corruption, which prepare the ground for more explicit and thorough assimilation. Maud extravagantly praises her father's deportment as a responsible member of the gentry:

> Considering how entirely he secluded himself, my father was, as many people living remember, wonderfully popular in his county. He was neighbourly in everything except in seeing company and mixing in society. He had magnificent shooting, of which he was extremely liberal. He kept a pack of hounds at Dollerton, with which all his side of the county hunted through the season. He never refused any claim upon his purse which had the slightest show of reason. He subscribed to every fund, social, charitable, sporting, agricultural, no matter what, provided the honest people of his county took an interest in it, and always with a princely hand; and although he shut himself up, no one could say that he was inaccessible, for he devoted hours daily to answering letters, and his cheque-book contributed largely in those replies. He had taken his turn long ago as High Sheriff; so there was an end of that claim before his oddity and shyness had quite secluded him. He refused the Lord-Lieutenancy of his county; he declined every post of personal distinction connected with it. He could write an able as well as a genial letter when he pleased; and his appearances at public meetings, dinners, and so forth were made in this epistolary fashion, and when occasion presented, by magnificent contributions from his purse.[28]

Maud's exaggerated language describes her father as everything that most Irish landlords were not. Austin's 'wonderfully popular' status and 'neighbourly' behaviour indicate a close and benevolent relationship with the community, contrasting sharply with the usual descriptions of the Anglo-Irish as isolated and scornful of their local communities. His hyperbolic willingness to subscribe to 'every fund, social, charitable, sporting, agricultural, no matter what' contrasts with the often criticized landlords who refused to spend money locally and drained Irish capital into English banks and estates. It also contrasts with Silas, who has been cutting down trees and using them for coal or selling the bark, wasting the resources of his estate because he is strapped for cash.[29]

While Austin is the embodiment of the ideal landlord, what is missing is, literally, his body. Maud's description figures him as a kind of resident absentee in his own neighbourhood. He is both neighbourly and isolated, a voluntary recluse. He makes repeated contact with the local community, but this contact is always mediated, never direct; his physical presence, even at public meetings and dinners, is supplanted by letters and monetary contributions. The complete absence of his physical presence suggests his connections with the irresponsible absentees so often represented in nineteenth-century Anglo-Irish literature, with the kind of destructive proprietorship Silas represents, and with the experience of Le Fanu's family, who left Abington in 1832, at a financial loss, to move to Dublin

28 US, 130–31
29 US, 263

temporarily while the tithe war and local hostility to the Le Fanus were at their height (they returned to Abington in 1835).[30] Austin's political and economic clout are present only in their effects; like Anglo-Irish hegemony in Ireland, they lack a local centre of power. The very terms in which Maud represents Austin's power also reveal the chimerical nature of that power.

The Celtic Hysteric

A number of critics have argued that the political unconscious of Anglo-Irish literature has a particularly gothic structure.[31] Uncle Silas's preoccupation with dynastic families, its description of the power of such families as present more in its effects than in its physical manifestations, and the novel's dismantling of the boundaries between the pure and the corrupt are all characteristics that inform critical evaluations of the text as an Anglo-Irish gothic. Elizabeth Bowen invokes the isolation of the Ascendancy and an obsession with bloodlines as evidence of the text's Irishness, citing the 'hermetic solitude' of the Ascendancy country house and the 'demonic power of the family myth' as evidence.[32] In his biography of Le Fanu, McCormack lists an atmosphere of 'a sinister vacancy from which authority has withdrawn' and Le Fanu's interest in dynasties as markers of his Anglo-Irish origins and concerns.[33]

Such assessments have become part of a standard formulation of Anglo-Irish gothic.[34] The symbolic geography of the contrast between the solitary Big House and the surrounding villages has offered an exemplary image of an Ascendancy culture whose distinctive characteristics derive from its dependence on an absent centre of power and its alienation from those it rules close at hand. So the disintegration, through its own internal weaknesses, of the territorial dominance and dynastic continuity symbolized by the Big House has proved a resonant and recurring figure through which Anglo-Irish texts could articulate their sense of tradition as fractured and corrupt, something that was betrayed in the precise moment and act of its handing down.

The role of gender and sexuality in this gothic sense of tradition has been much less extensively discussed. While an approach to the gothic that is material and political rather than psychological is at least as old as the Marquis de Sade, such criticism has usually paid insufficient attention to the specifically sexual nature of many of the gothic's most characteristic obsessions; critics who discuss

30 McCormack, Sheridan Le Fanu, 40
31 Julian Moynahan argues that in Ireland 'Gothic literature often carries a heavily political or meta-political charge'; see his 'The Politics of Anglo-Irish Gothic: Maturin, Le Fanu and "The Return of the Repressed"', in Heinz Kosok, ed., Studies in Anglo-Irish Literature (Bonn, 1982), 44. Patrick Rafroidi, Irish Literature in English, vol. 1, The Romantic Period [1789–1850], (Gerrards Cross, 1980), 64, notes that in Ireland the haunted gothic house had a 'resonance … that had long ceased to impress in the neighbouring island'. Mary E. F. Fitzgerald, 'The Unveiling of Power: Nineteenth-Century Gothic Fiction in Ireland, England and America', in Literary Interrelations, vol. 2, Comparison and Impact, 15, observes that 'the more mythologised the power structures of a society, the more productive gothic seems as a means of exploring them', and she argues that Ireland, in which power was both brutally exercised, and exercised from a distance, by agents who were visibly absent (like absentee landlords), produced gothic fiction distinguished by power that is present in its effects but is always located elsewhere.
32 Bowen, Introduction, Uncle Silas, 8
33 McCormack, Sheridan Le Fanu, 207
34 This characterization of the political world of Anglo-Irish gothic has found its way into several influential surveys. A. Norman Jeffares, Anglo-Irish Literature (New York, 1982), 132, concludes that Le Fanu's 'experience of agrarian and sectarian strife in the Limerick countryside underlay the sensational, the Gothic atmosphere of his major novels'; and Seamus Deane, A Short History of Irish Literature (London, 1986), 100, asserts that 'Irish Gothic establishes the abiding presence in the latter part of the century of the dilapidated Ascendancy house, in which the former masters are increasingly isolated from the surrounding tenantry and reduced, politically and economically, to a state of psychic exhaustion.'

the distinctive sexual aspects of the gothic tend to adopt a psychoanalytic approach.[35] It is important to reveal the political referents and structures of the Anglo-Irish gothic by attending to, rather than evading, the central role that sexuality, especially female sexuality, plays in gothic fiction. Given the prevailing emphasis on assimilation in imperial discourses on Ireland, the widespread tendency of writers and politicians to figure assimilation (whether beneficial or threatening) as a sexual romance, and the period's association of Celtic and feminine nature, it seems inevitable that representations of gender and sexuality would play a crucial role in Anglo-Irish writing about the problematic political and cultural status of the Ascendancy. In Uncle Silas, as in 'On the Study of Celtic Literature', femininity, nervous disorders, and a debilitating Celticism are equivalent.

Maud's relation to the Ascendancy tradition represented by her father is fractured, obscured, and alienated to such an extent that, in a sense, her true heritage is to be denied a heritage. Her Uncle Silas's plot to kill her and inherit her money is merely the most melodramatic element in the text suggesting the tenuous and threatened nature of Maud's inheritance. There are other indications that Maud is estranged from her family tradition as well. The dominant emotions Austin Ruthyn evokes in his daughter are awe, fear, and anxious curiosity, and while her father is preoccupied with the reputation and purity of his ancient lineage, Maud confesses her ignorance of their 'family lore' on the novel's first page. Throughout the first half of the text, Maud remains ignorant of the nature of the sacrifice that she has pledged to make. And of course much of the plot revolves around Maud's gradual discovery of her uncle's true nature. Maud's peculiar heritage places her in relation to a stern and threatening dynastic tradition, all the more threatening because the palpable oppressiveness of its presence is matched by the impalpable mysteries surrounding its precise nature and content.

Maud's incomplete relation to and ignorance of her heritage are part of her gendered unfitness for the task entrusted to her. 'Pity she's a girl, and so young,' laments her father, as he decides to perpetuate her ignorance about the sacrifice he demands of her. Austin reasons that as women are easily frightened and unreliable, he must secure Maud's co-operation without telling her what that co-operation involves, musing, 'They are easily frightened — ay, they are ... I had better do it another way — another way; yes — and she'll not suspect — she'll not suppose.' Maud's femininity makes her potentially inadequate as the agent of traditional and genealogical continuity, and she shares her father's view of nervous young women. The attitude of the adult, married Maud who narrates the story towards the seventeen-year-old Maud who experienced it is illustrated by such comments as 'I was but a hysterical girl.' Maud has what she terms a 'peculiar temperament' to match her peculiar heritage, and her narrative comments incessantly on her weaknesses of character and on the state of her nerves: the text applies the adjective 'nervous' to Maud with a frequency that borders on the obsessive, she is often on the verge of hysteria, and occasionally is actually hysterical.[36] The self-accusatory narrative of a self-confessed hysteric has precisely the structure of the Anglo-Irish gothic. The Anglo-Irish gothic's preoccupation with unreliable, alienated, and empty centres of political power, and its focus on internal sexual corruption, find their corollary in Maud's emphasis on her helplessness, self-doubt, and emotional instability. Both invoke the contemporary definitions of femininity that allied it to nervous weakness and disease.

---

35 See, for example, Kenneth W. Graham, ed., Gothic Fictions: Prohibition/Transgression (New York, 1989) and Victor Sage, Horror Fiction in the Protestant Tradition (London, 1988). On the other hand, Juliann Fleenor, who draws a parallel between women and minority writers as marginalized from the literary mainstream, argues that the gothic is a congenial form through which to express a writer's separation from her culture; see the Introduction to her The Female Gothic (London, 1983), 8. She links (15) gothic description of architecture and setting with the intersection of public and private, political and sexual, in the heroine's body because the gothic 'uses traditional spatial symbolism of the ruined castle or an enclosed room to symbolize both the culture and the heroine'.

36 US, 5, 6, 107, 298

Maud's other striking feature as a narrator is her penchant for disparaging her own sex. Never was a heroine so critical of women as a category or so uncomfortable with her own femininity. Maud observes at various moments in the text that 'the female heart' is characterized by 'an ineradicable jealousy', that women have little capacity for logical argument, that women are by nature 'factionists' rather than impartial judges, that 'women [have] preferred hatred to indifference, and the reputation of witchcraft, with all its penalties, to absolute insignificance', and that 'man's estimate of woman is higher than woman's own'.[37] While Maud works to honour her father's request and rehabilitate the family name and lineage, her femininity and sexuality mark her internal corruption and constantly threaten to betray her.

The most dangerous element in Maud's femininity is her sexual vulnerability; the novel establishes Maud's desires and sexual behaviour as particular points of danger requiring vigilant regulation. After failing to discourage an admirer adequately, Maud comments:

> Now, it was very odd of me, I must confess, to talk in this way, and to receive all those tender allusions from a gentleman about whom I had spoken and felt so sharply only the evening before. But Bartram was abominably lonely. A civilised person was a valuable waif or stray in that region of the picturesque and the brutal; and to my lady reader especially, because she will probably be hardest upon me, I put it — can you not recollect any such folly in your own past life? Can you not in as many minutes call to mind at least six similar inconsistencies of your own practising? For my part, I really can't see the advantage of being the weaker sex if we are always to be as strong as our masculine neighbours.[38]

Maud figures her femininity as a potentially dangerous set of sexual weaknesses and instabilities. Trapped in and tainted by 'that region of the picturesque and the brutal' — an excellent description of colonial England's characterization of Ireland — Maud succumbs to the temptation of indulging in a slightly uncivilized, if minor, sexual transgression. The exciting cause and potential victim of her transgression is the 'civilized' suitor. Her appeal to the female reader on the basis of a shared corruption suggests that it is simply the nature of feminine desire to resist and elude control, to be inconsistent and corrupt. Her assertion that if one is going to be designated the weaker sex, one might as well behave like the weaker sex indicates one of the potentially worrisome aspects of assimilationist ideology; part of the corruption attributed to Celts and women was that they *wanted* to be corrupt, and might refuse to try to emulate their more masculine and English neighbours. Like her family heritage, Maud's femininity is not only potentially debilitating, it is also mysterious, and its depths of deceit and desire are only partially clear to Maud herself, as when she wonders, 'What girl was ever quite frank about her likings? I don't think I was more of a cheat than others; but I never could tell of myself.'[39] Maud's femininity is an internal corruption, a link with the barbarous of which she has imperfect knowledge and unstable control. It demands a régime of observation and regulation that Maud is only intermittently willing and able to sustain.

In the world of *Uncle Silas* the unregulated, uneducated female character is an unreliable, potentially disruptive thing. This is also illustrated by Silas's daughter, Milly, and Milly's education at Maud's hands reinforces the novel's sense of female social and sexual identity as something that must be carefully constructed to avoid chaos. Milly has the natural aptitude to become a lady but has 'no more education than a dairy-maid', and Maud is eager to restore her to her proper class station. Silas calls Milly 'a very

37 US, 25, 61 129, 167, 373
38 US, 295
39 US, 286

finished Miss Hoyden' and attributes her wildness of character 'to that line of circumvallation which has, ever since [her] birth, intercepted all civilisation on its way to Bartram'. Maud resolves to 'effect some civilising changes' in Milly's language and demeanour, and regards an instance of temporary intransigence as a 'relapse into barbarism'.[40] The language of civilization and barbarism here and in Maud's confession about her admirer is the language nineteenth-century imperial discourses used to describe cultural differences between English and Irish and to call for integration of the Irish barbarians into English civilization.[41] Bartram-Haugh's isolation from 'all civilisation', Milly's relapse, and Maud's temporary weakness all inscribe a different and sinister possibility: that the civilized Anglo-Irish will succumb to the barbarous Irish.

The threatening figure of Madame de la Rougierre, Maud's evil governess, who is in league with Silas and whose French origins signify a corrupting continental influence, also emphasizes the importance of a girl's education, further dramatizing the danger that assimilation can work in reverse, from Saxon to Celt. At one point she threatens Maud mockingly, 'Do you not perceive, dearest cheaile, how much education you still need?'[42] While Maud works to civilize her barbaric cousin and to complete her own assimilation into her father's tradition, her nervous weaknesses and sexual lapses indicate her vulnerability to the assimilation-as-regression that her governess represents. Maud's femininity, which encompasses her nervous instability and her alienated relation to her family heritage as well as the specifically feminine weaknesses she attributes to her sex, emerges as a major threat to the character and influence of the ancient family whose rehabilitation her father urges her to undertake.

Much current feminist criticism of the gothic as a genre stresses its engagement with what Claire Kahane calls 'the problematics of femininity'.[43] The typical gothic novel narrates the education of the heroine's desires; the dangers she confronts are in some respect sexual ones, and the text concludes with her marriage and reintegration into society. In Uncle Silas Maud's apparent escape from the decay represented by Bartram-Haugh to the health represented by Knowl assumes the shape of her confrontation with the problematics of femininity. She wrestles with and conquers her hysterical tendencies, negotiates the sexual dangers represented by Captain Oakley and Dudley Ruthyn, makes an appropriate match with Lord Ilbury (one of the trustees of her estate), and bears him a son. She achieves a socially acceptable femininity and is reintegrated into civilized society. She rejects forbidden sexualities and alliances, and chooses a permissible one that will ensure proper genealogical continuity. As Maud remarks in the novel's conclusion, 'the shy, useless girl you have known is now a mother'.[44]

Maud's escape may be characterized as 'apparent' because while her flight from her Uncle Silas (who wanted to defraud her of her heritage) and her marriage to Ilbury (whose position as a trustee signifies his guardianship of her rightful heritage) seem to suggest that she accomplishes her father's will, the novel's Swedenborgian structure links these alternatives as the two conflicting and inseparable faces of Anglo-Irish tradition. The novel's Swedenborgian linking of Knowl and Bartram-Haugh suggests the internal corruption of Anglo-Irish tradition, and Maud's journey from the former to the latter and back again casts her as the physical embodiment of that link. Maud's successful negotiation of sexual

40 US, 197, 216, 240
41 On the history of the language of civilization and barbarism in British political discourses on Ireland, see Seamus Deane, *Civilians and Barbarians* (Derry, 1983).
42 US, 355
43 See Claire Kahane, 'The Gothic Mirror', in Shirley Nelson Garner, Claire Kahane, and Madelon Sprengnether, eds., *The (M)other Tongue: Essays in Feminist Psychoanalytic Interpretation* (Ithaca, NY, 1985), 336, where she suggests that the central mystery of the gothic revolves around the problems of femininity and maternity: 'What I see repeatedly locked into the forbidden center of the Gothic which draws me inward is the spectral presence of a dead-undead mother, archaic and all-encompassing, a ghost signifying the problematics of femininity which the heroine must confront.'
44 US, 424

threats, her role in civilizing Milly, and her advantageous marriage, all suggest her affiliations with the version of Anglo-Irish tradition embodied by her father and Knowl. But her dangerous and unstable femininity also connects her with Celts, corruption, and misalliance — Silas's Welsh barmaid, Dudley's lower-class wife — and marks her internal, already established vulnerability to the degradation Dudley represents. Maud's femininity is structured as an inherently treacherous relation to her dynastic tradition; it provides a framework for the novel's depiction of Anglo-Irish tradition as fallen, broken, and betrayed from within through their alienated separation from English traditions and or their intimate proximity to Irish ones. While on one level Maud successfully assimilates herself to the proper English civilization represented by Ilbury, on another level the text suggests the inevitability of her surrender to the kind of Celtic assimilation that Anglo-Irish writers found so threatening.

Fears about the fate of the Ascendancy haunted Le Fanu's imagination, and the original short story took these fears to their logical conclusion. Unlike *Uncle Silas*, 'Passage in the Secret History of an Irish Countess' does not have a happy ending: although the heroine escapes from her uncle, she does not preserve her sacred but destructible heritage, and her life following the events she narrates is 'long and sorrowful'.[45] Father Purcell's narrative emphasizes her role in the destruction of not one but two Irish dynasties. 'Strange!' he muses, 'two powerful and wealthy families, that in which she was born, and that into which she had married, have ceased to be — they are utterly extinct.'[46] But the British readers who preferred English settings also preferred happy endings, so once again Le Fanu suppressed an aspect of the original story that gave it a specifically Anglo-Irish provenance.

The necessity for negotiating between the Irish origins of *Uncle Silas* and the demands of the English literary market encouraged Le Fanu to encode the text's political concerns in the languages of sexuality, femininity, barbarism, and civilization, which characterized colonial discourses on the benefits and/ or dangers of assimilating the Irish more thoroughly into England. The novel's preoccupation with Maud's femininity, its covert association of dangerous femininity with a specifically Irish corruption, its emphasis on the process of constructing a more stable female character through education or civilization, and its representation of sexual misalliance as the exemplary betrayal of tradition, all constitute its distinct Anglo-Irishness and subtly distinguish it from the English sensational thrillers of the period with which it competed. *Uncle Silas* is a text about the unique uncertainties of Anglo-Irish culture in so far as it both claims *and* refuses to resolve the problematics of femininity that constitute Maud's peculiar heritage.

---

45 Le Fanu, 'Passage in the Secret History of an Irish Countess', 102
46 'Passage', 2

'Goodbye Ireland I'm going to Gort': James Joyce

This locality is more *around* temporality than *about* historicity: a form of living that is more complex than 'community'; more symbolic than 'society'; more connotative than 'country'; less patriotic than *patrie*; more rhetorical than the reason of state; more mythological than ideology; less homogeneous than hegemony; less centred than the citizen; more collective than 'the subject'; more psychic than civility; more hybrid in the articulation of cultural differences and identifications — gender, race or class — than can be represented in any hierarchical or binary structuring of social antagonism.

Homi Bhabha, 'DissemiNation'[1]

A nation is the same people living in the same place ... Or also living in different places.

James Joyce, *Ulysses*[2]

Irish studies shares with postcolonial studies an interest in the multifarious transactions between material and symbolic geographies that enable a wide range of discourses. The epigraphs above organize the problematic of defining or narrating the nation around the confusions and complexities of place that arise from such transactions. Homi Bhabha claims that the nation is 'a ubiquitous and obscure form of living the *locality* of culture' that can only be defined through a potentially endless recitation of what it is distinct from, yet related to.[3] Leopold Bloom appeals to an apparent tautology whose central comparative term is missing — the 'same people' — and whose spatial elements appear to cancel each other out: 'the same place' or 'different places'. There is a long tradition in Joyce scholarship of delineating Joycean geographies and more recent critics have offered various fruitful approaches to the issues surrounding the nation in Joyce's works.[4] But it is also the case that Joyce takes up the issue of narrating the Irish nation

---

1 Homi Bhabha, 'DissemiNation: Time, Narrative, and the Margins of the Modern Nation', in Homi Bhabha, ed., *Nation and Narration* (New York and London, 1990), 292
2 James Joyce, *Ulysses* (New York, 1986 [1922]), 12.1422–28; hereafter cited as U
3 Bhabha, 'DissemiNation', 292
4 On Joycean geographies, see, for example Michael Seidel, *Epic Geography: James Joyce's 'Ulysses'* (Princeton, NJ, 1976); on the nation in Joyce's works, see Vincent J. Cheng, *Joyce, Race, and Empire* (Cambridge, 1995), Enda Duffy, *The Subaltern 'Ulysses'* (Minneapolis, MN, 1994); Emer Nolan, *James Joyce and Nationalism* (London, 1995); Declan Kiberd, *Inventing Ireland* (Cambridge, MA, 1996).

in a kind of geographical representation that has received scant attention from either critical tradition. These works foreground spatial scale — the local, regional, international — which are sometimes thought to represent alternatives to the category and/or ideology of the nation.[5] And it is precisely through these alternative scales, and the opportunities and obstacles they pose for imagining the scale of the national, that, in contrast, Joyce's engagement with the problematic of the nation appears most vividly.

Although the focus here is on 'The Dead' and A Portrait of the Artist as a Young Man, this particular geographical approach to narrating the nation appears in Ulysses and Finnegans Wake as well. For example, in 'Cyclops', just after Bloom utters his definition and the Citizen challenges his right to be included in any conception of the Irish nation, Joe's handkerchief swells into an 'intricately embroidered ancient Irish facecloth'.[6] The cloth parodies (among other things) a nationalist geography of Ireland. It is inscribed with a diverse collection of places, some of which would be natural fodder for nationalist sentimentalizing, like the lakes of Killarney and Croagh Patrick. Others remind us of how colonialism shaped Ireland, like the three birthplaces of the first Duke of Wellington and Tullamore jail. The absurdity of still other places undercuts any dream of an Irish nation that claims to encompass them, like Fingal's Cave, which is actually in Scotland, and Kilballymacshonakill, which is not a place at all. One could read the cloth as an illustration of Joyce's much-quoted claim in 'Ireland, Island of Saints and Sages' that 'our civilization is a vast fabric, in which the most diverse elements are mingled'.[7] But if the cloth represents the hybridity of the Irish nation, it also indicates how persistently and thoroughly Joyce thought through national issues in spatial and geographical terms.

The geographical imagination at work here conducts a critique of naïve nationalist equations of the nation with its physical territory that points in two related directions. On the one hand, the imagined community of the nation is far too complex and dispersed to be metaphorized as a space, with its suggestions of contiguity, wholeness, and fixed boundaries. On the other, the actual physical spaces over which nation-states exercise sovereignty are far too complicated to be analysed solely through reference to that sovereignty, as integrated and natural national territories. One thing that is lacking in both cases is an appreciation of the importance of, and the relations among, different spatial scales. The nameless narrator of 'Cyclops', who displays equal scorn for the conceptions of the nation offered by Bloom and the Citizen, brings up this issue when he announces his intention to step outside to urinate: 'Goodbye Ireland I'm going to Gort'.[8] The usual form of this colloquial phrase is 'Goodbye Dublin I'm going to Gort.'[9] The narrator's humorous revision of it, which suggests that Gort somehow is not 'in' Ireland, is in keeping with the parody of nationalist geography on Joe's handkerchief. Gort lies in County Galway, near Augusta Gregory's Coole, and the phrase represents one of Joyce's many assertions that the idealized West of Ireland offered by the cultural nationalism in which she was a central figure is not to be found anywhere in the real Ireland. It also crosses geographical movement westward, between two comparable material locations, with two other kinds of movement, from the scale of the national to a more local scale, and from the material to the metaphorical. Joyce's rendition of the problematics of narrating the nation repeatedly organizes itself around this combination.

While the epigraph from Bhabha's influential essay appears to insist on the specificity of locality, the essay itself displays the tendency common to much postcolonial and poststructuralist work

5   For a recent collection of essays in geography in which investigations of regional particularity or international connection in Ireland often present themselves as critiques of the national, see Brian Graham, ed., In Search of Ireland: A Cultural Geography (London, 1997).
6   U, 12.1438–39
7   James Joyce, Critical Writings, ed. Ellsworth Maason and Richard Ellmann (New York, 1959), 165; hereafter cited as CW
8   U, 12.1561
9   Don Gifford, Ulysses Annotated (Berkeley, CA, 1988), 366

to employ many spatial metaphors but to treat the materiality of space as fairly transparent and unproblematic. Bhabha approaches the complexity of the nation, metaphorized consistently, though not exclusively, as the 'space of the nation', through time, most notably in his widely cited articulation of the contradictory 'double-time' of the nation. Bhabha wants to show that 'the space of the modern nation-people is never simply horizontal', to investigate its 'irredeemably plural modern space', and his theoretical vocabulary of terms like 'enunciatory position', 'space of cultural signification', and the 'site of writing' relies heavily on spatial metaphors.[10] At the same time, the essay often characterizes the conceptions of the nation it critiques as forms of spatial thinking that naïvely equate people, territory, and nation. The crude, and crudely spatial, conception of the nation is disarticulated through an analysis of the complexities of temporality. Thus while narrating the nation is rendered wonderfully, helpfully problematic, the materiality of national space and the category of space itself remain fairly inert, naturalized, and abstract.

Neil Smith's *Uneven Development* offers a useful counter-example that approaches the complex materiality of space through scale. For Smith, space is 'deep space', which is 'the space of everyday life in all its scales from the global to the local … quintessentially social space'. He argues that geographical space, including nature itself, is produced in a particular way under capitalism; uneven development is the 'geographical expression of the contradictions of capital'. Uneven development is organized through the 'continual determination and internal differentiation of spatial scale'. Each scale — the urban, the nation-state, and the global — is determined as 'an integrated space-economy', a geographical unit that represents an identifiable and separate scale of social activity.[11] At the same time, it is also subject to internal differentiation and shaped by its relation to larger scales, factors which both enable and threaten each scale's drive towards realizing itself as 'absolute space'. This contradictory structure in which the drive towards equalization and the drive towards differentiation confront each other at various scales is the central feature of the production of space under capitalism, and the contradictions of capitalism appear in the problematic doubleness assigned to scale.

Bhabha's and Smith's approaches are complementary. Together they suggest ways of examining relationships that are at the centre of the problematic of the nation; relationships between material and metaphorical space, and between capitalist modernity and the modernity of the nation. A number of scholars have argued that Ireland's entry into a specifically colonial modernity was especially traumatic and uneven.[12] However 'belated' Joyce might find the Irish, colonial Ireland was not simply backward or underdeveloped in relation to Britain, whatever one might mean by that.[13] Instead, through colonial intervention, it became a disorienting mixture of the archaic and the modern. The beginnings of the economic and social transformations of the nineteenth century — the extermination of the cottier class, the rise of the strong farmer, the establishment of high rates of celibacy and late marriage age, the haemorrhage of emigration — preceded the Great Famine of the 1840s. But they were greatly accelerated by it, and the Famine constituted, among other things, a sudden, disastrous, and incomplete transition to modernity, especially in agricultural production and the social organization of rural life. If the relative indifference and ineptness with which the British handled the catastrophe of the Famine provided one source of the juxtaposition between the archaic and the modern, a highly modernized state apparatus and a willingness to intervene in Irish society provided another. Historians have often argued that Britain treated Ireland as a 'social laboratory in which Englishmen were prepared

10 Bhabha, 'DissemiNation', 293–303

11 Neil Smith, *Uneven Development: Nature, Capital and the Production of Space* (Oxford, 1984), 135–36, 152, 160–61

12 Michael Hechter, *Internal Colonialism: The Celtic Fringe in British National Development* (Berkeley, 1975); Luke Gibbons, *Transformations in Irish Culture* (Cork, 1996); Terry Eagleton, *Heathcliff and the Great Hunger: Studies in Irish Culture* (London, 1995), 273–319

13 *CW*, 70

to conduct experiments in government which contemporary opinion at home was not prepared to tolerate'.[14] Ireland had a national school system before England did, and, as Terry Eagleton observes, by 1850, Ireland had one of the 'most commercially advanced agricultures in the world, and was fast developing one of the world's densest railway systems'.[15]

Thus the uneven development that expresses the contradictions of European capitalist modernity was especially acute in Ireland. Some of Benedict Anderson's work since *Imagined Communities* offers a way of tying the material geography of uneven development to the rise of specifically national forms of consciousness and culture. Anderson metaphorizes the displacements of modernity — geographical and otherwise — as forms of exile. He argues that in the nineteenth century the migration of populations, the standardization of print languages, and the establishment of national school systems represented forms of exile from local origins and affiliations, and that nationalism constituted a compensatory 'project for coming home from exile'. It was 'the essential nexus of long-distance transportation and print capitalist communications', a nexus that was well developed in largely pre-industrial Ireland, rather than industrialization *per se*, that first prepared the ground for the rise of nationalism. For Anderson's exile, geographical movement (and the other displacements for which it stands in) provokes a nostalgia for a local scale that is eased when the individual transfers some of his or her energies and affections upwards, to the scale of the national: 'It was beginning to become possible to see "English fields" in England — from the window of a railway carriage.'[16]

Anderson's theory fits well with the long-standing observation of historians that modern Irish nationalism took hold first in the modernizing, relatively prosperous agricultural regions and small towns that experienced these changes earlier than the poor and underdeveloped Gaeltacht.[17] However, because Ireland's modernization was inextricably bound up with the uneven development of colonialist, highly modernized communications and transportation systems, and the sorts of exile they generated, it occurred in conjunction with archaic or residual social, economic, and cultural formations. In addition, emigration, the decline of the Irish language and the imperial origin of national schools were traumatic, much discussed, and specifically colonial issues. And the nationalisms that emerged were revolutionary rather than state nationalisms. Both materially and symbolically, the specifically colonial nature of Ireland's capitalist modernity helped produce a national imaginary related to but distinct from European statist nationalism.

In nineteenth-century Ireland, the transfer of loyalties to a national scale was an uncertain and incomplete process, and other supposedly regressive responses to the exilic dislocations of modernity were available. For example, part of Daniel O'Connell's unprecedented success in mobilizing and nationalizing the Irish masses was due to his genius for tapping into specifically local grievances and loyalties and tying them to a nationalist project. At the same time, however, he worked hard to discourage the agrarian disturbances and secret societies whose motives and targets were regional rather than national, and which were an attempt to enforce the traditional social and economic structures and values that were being destroyed by agricultural modernization.[18] The notion of a 'transfer' is itself somewhat misleading; local issues and affiliations operated simultaneously within a wider national framework without necessarily ceasing to be (problematically) local.[19] With this caveat, Smith's attention to the complex materiality of geographical space and Anderson's metaphorical use

---

14 F. S. L. Lyons, *Ireland since the Famine* (London, 1971), 74

15 Eagleton, *Heathcliff and the Great Hunger*, 274

16 Benedict Anderson, *The Spectre of Comparisons: Nationalism, Southeast Asia and the World* (London and New York, 1998), 62–65

17 George Boyce, *Nationalism in Ireland* (London, 1991)

18 Oliver MacDonagh, *Hereditary Bondsman: Daniel O'Connell, 1775–1829* (London, 1988), and *The Emancipist: Daniel O'Connell, 1830–47* (New York, 1989)

19 Luke Gibbons, 'Identity Without a Centre: Allegory, History and Irish Nationalism', in Gibbons, *Transformations*, 134–48

of geographical movement demonstrate, in very different ways, that the national is to be grasped most fully in its relation to other scales, rather than in opposition to them. Both differ from the standard observations that some nationalists are more cosmopolitan or more respectful of regional and local difference than others because they insist that these other scales are structurally, simultaneously, both necessary and inimical to the national.

Seamus Deane has acutely observed that Joyce's civilization was 'the civilization of Catholic Dublin, related to but distinct from that of Catholic Ireland', and much current Joyce scholarship understandably focuses on Joyce's Dublin as exemplary of Ireland's uneven development or the relationship between the national and more local scales.[20] Any facile equation of urban life, progress and modernity is impossible to sustain in light of the bad housing, poor health facilities and general decline endured by Dublin as part of the United Kingdom.[21] But Dublin's incomplete and uneven colonial modernity had a counterpart in what we might call the perverse modernity of the Irish countryside. Rural villages in post-Famine Ireland were not modern anonymous collectivities. But they were also not the kind of totalizable, knowable, face-to-face communities that some scholars associate with pre-capitalist forms of social life. The main reasons for this were Ireland's uniquely high rate of emigration, driven in part by agricultural modernization, mostly (during this period) to the United States, and the specific cultural meanings attached to emigration in Irish culture. Every village, virtually every family, had sons, daughters, or other relatives on the other side of the Atlantic. They remained absent yet active members of the community — they wrote letters, sent money home, financed the emigration of siblings or other relatives, and followed events in Ireland through the Irish-American press. The anthropologists Arensberg and Kimball observe that often many members of the same family or village emigrated to the same place, even over several generations, a practice that forged lasting international connections with specific foreign localities. These diasporic relations between emigrants and those at home were quite continuous with local affiliations; they were 'part of the general "friendliness" by which the Irish countryman sums up the family obligations' and were expressed in the same terms. There were also various uniquely Irish cultural traditions organized around the departures of emigrants, many of whom viewed themselves as unwilling exiles, such as American wakes, the all-night parties resembling wakes that were often held before a boat sailed.[22] The sheer size of the international Irish diaspora and its intimate incorporation into everyday social and cultural life in Ireland meant that rural communities did not coincide with the local territories they occupied. We might call them communities of mourning or melancholy, or see in them something resembling an Irish Atlantic.[23]

The ambiguous modernity of rural Ireland posed a problem for the cultural nationalism that symbolically appropriated the Irish countryside, and especially the West of Ireland, as the archetypal site of Irishness. In many ways a bourgeois, modernizing movement, cultural nationalism sought less to return to or re-create this version of the West than to unify the Irish people around the idea of its (safely distanced and enclosed, both temporally and geographically) worth. In Joyce's works, the geographical mode of inscribing the problematic of the nation traced here centres on characters

20 Seamus Deane, 'Joyce the Irishman', in Derek Attridge, ed., *The Cambridge Companion to James Joyce* (Cambridge, 1990), 37–54, 40; Fredric Jameson, 'Ulysses in History', in W. J. McCormack and Alistair Stead, eds., *James Joyce and Modern Literature* (London, 1982), 126–41; Duffy, *Subaltern 'Ulysses'*, 53–92; Joep Leerssen, *Remembrance and Imagination: Patterns in the Historical and Literary Representations of Ireland in the Nineteenth Century* (Cork, 1996), 224–31; James Fairhall, *James Joyce and the Question of History* (Cambridge, 1993), 64–79

21 Joseph V. O'Brien, *Dear, Dirty Dublin: A City in Distress, 1899–1916* (Berkeley, CA, 1982)

22 Conrad M. Arensberg and Solon T. Kimball, *Family and Community in Ireland* (Cambridge, MA, 1968 [1940]), 144; Miller, *Emigrants and Exiles*, 558

23 Paul Gilroy's *The Black Atlantic: Modernity and Double Consciousness* (Cambridge, MA, 1993) offers a model that is suggestive for the Irish experience, though of course it is by no means strictly analogous to it.

like Gabriel Conroy and Stephen Dedalus, who reject the conventional forms of national belonging offered to them by cultural nationalism only to find themselves drawn in some manner into alternative narratives of the nation. The narrator of 'Cyclops' is, in a minor way, another such figure. This paradigm is well established in Joyce studies, and represents a dominant view of Joyce himself. Joyce organizes his alternative narratives of the nation around a series of distinctions enabled by the recognition of rural Ireland's perverse partial modernity: material versus metaphorical geographical movement, the complex materialities of spatial scales versus their symbolic appropriation or metaphorization, and movement over space versus movement from one scale to another.

Scale and the West in 'The Dead'

Questions of national ideology and community lie at the heart of 'The Dead' and are organized around two related regions — the West of Ireland and 'that region where dwell the vast hosts of the dead' — and their crucial, ambiguous role in the versions of the national to which various Dubliners subscribe.[24] Much of the story does what the imagination of the cultural nationalism Joyce overtly scorned also did: it merges the two regions into one, a conflation that Joep Leerssen has described as 'one of the dominant modes of nineteenth-century Celticism'.[25] Each region represents something that Gabriel Conroy feels able to reject or master early in the story, but that threatens to overwhelm him at its close. Gabriel's resolution not to 'linger on the past' in his speech gives way to his helpless subordination to the dead, and he resists the critical but flirtatious Miss Ivors's invitation to 'come for an excursion to the Aran Isles', only to 'swoon' before the ominous seductions of another 'journey westward', this one associated with Gretta and Michael Furey.[26] Gabriel's self-conscious cosmopolitanism is, in Bernard Benstock's words, 'mere window-dressing'; in his worship of things foreign, Gabriel is simply the last and most sympathetic in a series of provincial Dubliners.[27] Miss Ivors looks west, Gabriel looks east, and they are linked through their competing versions of Irish provincialism, as well as through their commensurate educations, professions, and superior intellectual status (in Gabriel's mind, at any rate).[28]

Miss Ivors's nationalism and Gabriel's cosmopolitanism represent equally undesirable relations to the national. Much critical debate has revolved around what Emer Nolan calls 'a revivalist sub-text' in the story, which raises the question of what, if any, alternative relation to the national Gabriel establishes or is forced into by his 'journey westward'. Nolan's provocative reading of 'The Dead' incorporates a number of competing interpretations by appealing to formulations of the nation's doubleness suggested by Anderson and Bhabha. She argues, following Anderson, that Gabriel's final epiphany represents both death and immersion in the community because it is the job of nationalism to transform mortality into continuity. Nolan also asserts that readings which claim that Gabriel capitulates to the communal or Irish lures of the West and those that claim he achieves a self-realization that isolates him from any larger community are in fact complementary because 'national belonging is an enabling illusion for individuals who, in spite of it, live in real social isolation'. Gabriel's 'intensely solitary, but

---

24 James Joyce, *Dubliners* (New York, 1992 [1914]), 224

25 Leerssen, *Remembrance and Imagination*, 189

26 *Dubliners*, 189, 205, 225

27 Bernard Benstock, *James Joyce: The Undiscover'd Country* (New York, 1977), 5

28 *Dubliners*, 188, emphasizes the parallels between Gabriel and Miss Ivors: 'He wanted to say that literature was above politics. But they were friends of many years' standing and their careers had been parallel, first at the University, and then as teachers: he could not risk a grandiose phrase with her', marking an obvious contrast to the superiority Gabriel feels in relation to all the other guests.

yet shared experience' is his incorporation into the community-in-anonymity of the nation, symbolized by the reference to the unifying snow in the newspapers, one of the cultural forms that Anderson uses to exemplify the homogeneous, empty, clock-time of the modern nation.[29]

Nolan's reading synthesizes elements in the ending that had often appeared as alternatives to critics: death and continuity, isolation and national belonging, the West as social or literal death and the West as Ireland. She focuses on Gabriel, while other analyses emphasize that the West signifies a diverse and even conflicting constellation of entities and concepts for different characters. Luke Gibbons suggests that 'The Dead' presents a struggle, which Joyce outlined in his 1907 essay on Fenianism, between two competing forms of nationalism: constitutional nationalism and a 'dissident, insurrectionary tradition'.[30] This struggle is 'articulated through the competing strategies of the newspaper, and the popular ballad'; the former is allied with Gabriel's symbolic appropriation of the West, the latter with 'The Lass of Aughrim' and the meanings the song and the West have for Gretta.[31] In a similar vein, Cóilín Owens claims that

> To Gretta [the West] is that which she can never recover; to Gabriel, it is that which he can never know; to the reader it is a radically ambiguous symbol of the differences between Gretta's and Gabriel's temperaments, and of the differences between Gaelic Ireland as a cultural ideal and the impossibility of a reconciliation between it and the 'thought-tormented age' into which modern, urban, bourgeois Ireland is being assimilated.[32]

Nolan, Gibbons, and Owens all read the West as embodying the national, whether as a vehicle of reconciliation or of division. But there is another, related set of ambiguities surrounding the West in 'The Dead', one that is organized through competing geographical scales and the perverse modernity of rural Ireland. This set of ambiguities resists the conflation of the West with the dead. To the aporias about what the West *means*, the text adds a related series of uncertainties about what it *is* as a physical region. Joyce crosses the complexities of the movement over space — the journey westward — with the problem of scale in defining the region that represents the destination. The West is a shifting, semi-modern, marginal set of regions that both enables and defies the fantasies that Gabriel, Miss Ivors, and Gretta construct, and the text carefully renders it ambiguous in geographical and scalar terms.

Miss Ivors combines her invitation to the Aran Isles with an observation about Gretta's origins: 'She's from Connacht, isn't she?' Voicing her enthusiasm for the trip, Gretta says 'I'd love to see Galway again.'[33] Terence Brown's note to Gretta's remark comments, 'Presumably she means Galway city, the principal city of County Galway and of the province of Connacht.'[34] The slippage in these exchanges between the particular places and geographical scales that stand in for the West — a set of islands, a city, a county, a province — gives the West a physical ambiguity that is related but not reducible to its symbolic richness. Other elements of the story give the region a further geographical complexity. Michael Furey's people live in Oughterard, a small village seventeen miles north of Galway city, and he works in the gasworks of Galway city, a typical rural-urban migrant in a semi-developed region. Gretta lived in a district of Galway city called Nuns' Island, which suggests both the inner differentiation of the city-scale and a Catholic alternative to supposedly pagan, primitive Aran. And, as Vincent J. Cheng

29 Nolan, *Joyce and Nationalism* 29, 34, 36
30 *CW*, 188
31 Gibbons, 'Identity without a Centre', 146
32 Cóilín Owens, 'The Mystique of the West in Joyce's "The Dead"', *Irish University Review*, 22, 1 (1992), 84–85
33 *Dubliners*, 189, 191
34 See *Dubliners*, 311 n.46.

has argued, the town of Aughrim in County Galway evokes two catastrophic Irish military defeats in the face of British imperialism: the Battle of the Boyne and the Battle of Aughrim.[35] Various private and public histories — imperial, industrial, romantic, nationalist — are embedded in competing scales and geographies.

Five years later, Joyce again combines a consideration of the West's relation to the past and the dead with an analysis of its ambiguous and uneven modernity. In his 1912 essay on Galway, he begins by invoking the ideas, which he describes as both right and wrong, of 'the lazy Dubliner, who travels little and knows his country only by hearsay', and who thinks of Galway as the exotic 'Spanish city'. Joyce goes on to offer his own blend of fantasy and reality, lamenting the city's decline from a vibrant international trading centre and cultural contact zone to its current isolated, decaying modernity: 'Outside the city walls rise the suburbs — new, gay, and heedless of the past, but you have only to close your eyes to this bothersome modernity for a moment to see in the twilight of history the "Spanish city".' What we might call the true modernity of Galway, with its surprising and energizing contradictions and juxtapositions of the archaic and the modern, regional particularity and international connection, in contrast to its current backward modernity, Joyce finds in a sixteenth-century travel narrative, 'in which the writer says that, although he had travelled throughout the world, he had never seen in a single glance what he saw in Galway — a priest elevating the Host, a pack chasing a deer, a ship entering the harbour under full sail, and a salmon being killed with a spear'.[36]

One might be tempted to read the inclusion of so many actual western locations in 'The Dead' as an instance of the kind of Joycean referential mapping that means, for example, that contemporary readers who visit Dublin can retrace Lenehan's walk in 'Two Gallants' and that the route and landmarks of this walk assemble a fairly coherent set of references to English domination, or that Leopold Bloom and Stephen Dedalus can be read as versions of the *flâneur*.[37] In contrast, the point in 'The Dead,' with its emphasis on different scales, rather than on streets, buildings, and monuments, is to portray the region as rich, problematic deep space, rather than to define it as something readily mappable or easily traversable. The West as Miss Ivors's Aran may be that clichéd embodiment of Irishness worshipped by cultural nationalism. But Gretta's reference to Galway, which introduces a tension between the city and the county, is ambiguous; it signifies cultural nationalism's idea of the primitive rural heartland, the perverse modernity of its material space, an idealized, cosmopolitan past for the 'Spanish city', and the backwardness of Ireland's industrial centres.

Taken together, these references to different material features of the region's uneven modernity, embodied in different geographical scales, both multiply the possible nationalist appropriations of the West and highlight the obstacles that the area in question presents for them. Similarly, the last paragraph of 'The Dead' accomplishes the unifying, symbolic journey westward, but at the same time it suggests a material journey by including the 'dark central plain', 'the treeless hills', and the 'Bog of Allen', all of which belong to the supposedly uninspiring midlands that travellers from Dublin to the West must cross.[38] Joseph Valente has suggested that Gabriel's failure of vision at the end of 'The Dead' springs from 'his inability to identify with the *otherness* of the other' and his penchant for Revivalist myth-making, arguing that the primitive and self-immolating Michael Furey is not an alternative to

35 Cheng, *Joyce, Race, and Empire*, 143–44
36 *CW*, 229, 230
37 Duffy, *Subaltern 'Ulysses'*, 53–92; Clair Wills, 'Joyce, Prostitution, and the Colonial City', *South Atlantic Quarterly*, 95, 1 (1996), 79–96
38 *Dubliners*, 225

such myth-making but a symptom of it.[39] Furthermore, Gabriel is 'humiliated', not simply by Furey's romantic, archaic death, but by the contrast between that death and Furey's mundane, modern working life, as his exchange with Gretta makes clear:

— He is dead, she said at length. He died when he was only seventeen. Isn't it a terrible thing to die so young as that?
— What was he? asked Gabriel, still ironically.
— He was in the gasworks, she said.
Gabriel felt humiliated by the failure of his irony and by the evocation of this figure from the dead, a boy in the gasworks.[40]

The conflict Joyce stages between the symbolically freighted journey westward and the material, geographical ambiguities of its destination indicates that the real otherness of the other is symbolized, not by the fiery depths of Furey's passionate heart, but by the flames of the gasworks where he earned his living.

Scale and Exile in A Portrait of the Artist as a Young Man

In A Portrait of the Artist as a Young Man, Stephen, like Gabriel, rejects conventional Irish nationalism and finds himself engaging with an ambiguous and sometimes threatening alternative mode of narrating the nation. Rather than emphasizing the scalar ambiguities of the West or the local as material regions, Portrait highlights the role different conceptions of scale play in different versions of the nation. And instead of focusing primarily on a largely symbolic journey to the West, Portrait's analysis of the impulses and obstacles to the formation of Stephen's national consciousness foregrounds the importance of his mundane travels between home and school. Stephen is a complex version of Anderson's exile, struggling with competing ways of transforming the local affiliations he has lost into membership in a national community. This process depends upon two major factors: first, Stephen's geographical movement, other displacements, and the homesickness they produce, and, second, fantasized but threatening constructions of rural Ireland.

Early in the novel, Stephen, unable to learn the geography lesson that maps the spatial divisions of the New World in straightforward topographical terms — through 'the names of places in America' — thinks about a different conception of space. In the flyleaf of his geography book he has written:

Stephen Dedalus
Class of Elements
Clongowes Wood College
Sallins
County Kildare
Ireland
Europe
The World
The Universe

39 Joseph Valente, 'Joyce and the Cosmopolitan Sublime', in Mark A. Wollaeger, Victor Luftig and Robert Spoo, eds., Joyce and the Subject of History (Ann Arbor, MI, 1996), 69–73
40 Dubliners, 220–21

Stephen's alternative geography involves an extensive but incomplete list of different scales; he wonders 'What was after the universe?' It also signifies one potential avenue for Stephen's incorporation into a conventional nationalist community. Stephen's list of scales does not include the United Kingdom; instead he places Ireland in Europe. His formulation offers a model of the relations among scales as orderly and commensurate, with each scale neatly enfolding the smaller ones, something it has in common with the explicitly nationalist verse that Fleming has written on the opposite page:

> Stephen Dedalus is my name,
> Ireland is my nation.
> Clongowes is my dwelling place
> And heaven my expectation.

Fleming's verse harmonizes the individual and national scales through a narrative of salvation that links the individual's affiliation with the national — his recognition of Ireland as his nation — with a projected movement from home — his dwelling place — to heaven.[41] Both inscriptions figure the individual climbing the geographical scales from himself to the Irish nation (and beyond) according to the dictates of conventional nationalism.

This process takes place at school, and is catalysed by the kinds of exile school represents. Torn from his home, which is associated with the maternal and the local, Stephen is encouraged to transfer his loyalties to the proto-nationalist community of males who express their resentment of authority through a parody of insurrection: 'Let us get up a rebellion, Fleming said. Will we?'[42] As critics have often noted, this change involves his incorporation into a related set of discourses succinctly described by Vicky Mahaffey as 'the necessity of homosocial bonding, homophobia, and misogyny'.[43] The fact that there is no right answer to the question 'Do you kiss your mother before you go to bed?' indicates that local affiliations are both mandated and forbidden by nationalism; they acquire a problematic doubleness or ambivalence, the experience of which binds the members of the national community together.[44] Stephen is interpellated into the community, not by answering correctly, which is impossible, but by 'try[ing] to laugh with them' at his own newly created discomfort with his maternal origins.[45]

The forms of transportation that brought Stephen to school — trains and hired cars — figure heavily in the first chapter of Portrait, and are associated with his feelings of exile. When Stephen feels that he is 'sick in his heart if you could be sick in that place' he consoles himself by alternately covering and uncovering his ears, comparing the resulting auditory changes to those that occur when a train enters and leaves a tunnel. They are also connected with the vehicle that enables Stephen simultaneously to reject and reconstitute his local, maternal loyalties as part of his membership in a nationalist community: a fantasized construction of rural Ireland. This fantasy revolves around a vision of the women another boy has seen in the village of Clane 'as the cars had come past from Sallins' on the way to Clongowes: 'he had seen a woman standing at the halfdoor of a cottage with a child in her arms'. Stephen finds the rural Ireland they represent both appealing and frightening. While he thinks, 'It would be lovely to sleep for one night in that cottage before the fire of smoking turf', he also feels afraid, and his fear focuses on the road that enables his transportation from home to school, from the local to the national,

41 James Joyce, A Portrait of the Artist as a Young Man (New York, 1976 [1916]), 12–13
42 Portrait, 44
43 Vicki Mahaffey, 'Père-version and Im-mère-sion: Idealized Corruption in A Portrait of the Artist as a Young Man and The Picture of Dorian Gray', in Joseph Valente, ed., Quare Joyce (Ann Arbor, MI, 1998), 124
44 I do not agree with those critics such as Trevor Williams, Reading Joyce Politically (Gainesville, FL, 1997), 106–07, who claim that 'I do not' would have been a correct initial answer; when Stephen does give that answer, it is wrong.
45 Portrait, 11

by way of such rural areas: 'But, O, the road there between the trees was dark!'[46] The roads, signs of rural Ireland's perverse modernity, of Stephen's exile from home, and of his partial return home via national identification, are dark and threatening because they do not resolve the conflicts of scale, between the local/maternal and the national, that they initiate.

Such resolution is only possible at a further remove of fantasy, in the context of imagined rather than actual geographical movement homeward. Anticipating the holidays, Stephen imagines the cars carrying him past the same emblematic women at Clane, and the journey creates an image of community through geographical movement:

> The cars drove past the chapel and all caps were raised. They drove merrily along the country roads. The drivers pointed with their whips to Bodenstown. The fellows cheered. They passed the farmhouse of the Jolly Farmer. Cheer after cheer after cheer. Through Clane they drove, cheering and cheered. The peasant women stood at the halfdoors, the men stood here and there.[47]

Bodenstown is where Wolfe Tone is buried, and in his note to this passage Seamus Deane speculates that the drivers are pointing their whips towards his grave. This vision includes the peasant women of Clane, but their threat has been neutralized, the drive is merry, and the nationalist community is based more on the reciprocal (masculine) cheering and the unifying memory of a nationalist hero than on the attractive but disturbing female figures.[48]

The topographical geography that the exiled Stephen rejects in favour of an ambiguous journey from the local to the national scale is allied with the stridently anti-Parnellite Dante: 'A little boy had been taught geography by an old woman who kept two brushes in her wardrobe. Then he had been sent away from home to a college.' It also displays imperialism's preoccupation with the mapping and territorial conquest of exotic places: 'She had taught him where the Mozambique Channel was and what was the longest river in America and what was the name of the highest mountain in the moon.'[49] Of course, a major lesson of Stephen's actual visit home (and of chapter 1 generally) is that nationalist politics are more about division and ambivalence than they are about the kind of cheery, unproblematic unity figured in Stephen's imagined journey. In addition, Stephen later rejects the nationalism fostered at schools and other institutions while groping his way towards some alternative exilic relation to the Irish nation.

When an older Stephen contemplates his ambivalent relation to the category and ideology of the nation — his rejection of nationalism, his separation from the national community, his desire to learn 'the hidden ways of Irish life' and to 'hit their conscience' to help revive his nation — his imagination returns to the women of Clane, now remembered in the context of his own geographical movement, and associated with the woman who tries to seduce Davin:

> The last words of Davin's story sang in his memory and the figure of the woman in the story stood forth, reflected in other figures of the peasant women whom he had seen standing in the doorways at Clane as the college cars drove by, as a type of her race and his own, a batlike soul waking to the consciousness of itself in darkness and secrecy and loneliness and, through the eyes and voice and gesture of a woman without guile, calling the stranger to her bed.

46 Portrait, 10, 15, 19
47 Portrait, 17
48 Portrait, 282 n.32
49 Portrait, 7, 98

It has become possible for Stephen to see the 'peasant women' of villages like Clane as representatively Irish figures and himself as part (however problematically) of the national community they embody — from the window of a car or train. His conflation of these women and Ireland consistently involves versions of a contrast between a stationary rural woman and a travelling man: 'A woman had waited in the doorway as Davin had passed by at night.'[50] Stephen's actual travel through the space of rural Ireland has helped him produce an imaginary and specifically national geography, in which a national male subject performs the integration of the local into the national by his movement through space and his symbolic appropriation of the peasant women as national types.

But the country roads that link rural and urban areas, carry the displaced into exile, and create the modern, travelling national subject continue to frighten Stephen: 'I fear many things: dogs, horses, firearms, the sea, thunderstorms, machinery, the country roads at night.' The processes they represent are ambiguous and incomplete; Stephen cannot complete a 'project for coming home from exile' by embracing a national scale and narrative.[51] The other regions and scales such a narrative seeks to integrate are not as commensurate as Stephen once believed. As in 'The Dead', the West emerges as both necessary and recalcitrant to a national narrative, a problematic embodied in a different representatively Irish figure: the Irish-speaking old man with red eyes. Critics usually assume that the old man represents the cultural nationalist ideal of primitive Irishness that Joyce rejected. But he also signifies an alternative, and problematic, conception of scale to match Stephen's ambivalent alternative to conventional nationalism: 'Mulrennan spoke to him about universe and stars. Old man sat, listened, smoked, spat. Then said: — Ah, there must be terrible queer creatures at the latter end of the world.' Mulrennan's remarks, so to speak, give the old man a chance to repeat Stephen's earlier trip up-scale from his own individual being, through the nation to the universe. But the old man refuses, and his reply figures space in terms of immense, mythic geographical distance and utter alienation, rather than in terms of linkage and commensurability. What the young Stephen, along with conventional nationalism, imagined as a progression of ever-widening frameworks, each one neatly enclosing the smaller ones, has become the radical incommensurability of scales. Like the country roads, the old man represents something that is both enabling and crippling for a national narrative, and, like them, he is ambiguous and threatening. Stephen's initial claim, 'I fear him', and his conclusion that he means the old man 'no harm', indicate that his famous resolution to narrate the Irish nation, to forge in the smithy of his soul the uncreated conscience of his race, must incorporate or acknowledge these contradictory elements.[52]

Both Gabriel and Stephen fail to arrive at coherent visions of the Irish nation or, more precisely, they arrive at visions of the nation notable for their ambiguity, in part because the real rural landscape both supports and resists the imagined national geography they attempt to project on to it. The material geographies of Ireland's uneven development, and their various possible relationships with imaginative appropriations of space, form a basis for Joyce's critique of cultural nationalism as well as for his alternative narratives of the nation. Both 'The Dead' and Portrait combine a focus on the materiality of space and physical journeys with an investigation of the metaphorical uses of geographical movements, regions, and scales. They figure versions of the 'double-time' of the nation, not by simply metaphorizing the nation as a space, but by teasing out the complex relations between metaphorical and material space, between the Gorts that are in Ireland, and the Gorts that are not.

50 Portrait, 196, 198, 259
51 Portrait, 264; Anderson, Spectres, 65
52 Portrait, 274

How Many People has Gretta Conroy Killed? James Joyce

Two related sets of issues were raised in the preceding essay. The first involves the question of the text's embrace and/or critique of cultural nationalism and the forms of Irish tradition produced and valued by cultural nationalism. Critics who take up this question often focus on Gretta Conroy's Galway origins, Michael Furey's passionate self-sacrifice, and Gabriel Conroy's final 'journey westward'. The second involves the issue of gender and the argument that Gretta, Lily, and other female figures in the story are victims of male public authority, sexual predation, and masculinist aesthetics. These narratives are haunted, disrupted, and countered by an additional, and previously unremarked, narrative in 'The Dead'. This alternative narrative exposes and exploits the gendered cultural meanings of modernity, migration and domestic service, and casts Lily and Gretta neither as emblems of tradition nor as victims. It is also a narrative that Joyce's text and John Huston's 1987 film of 'The Dead' share, though they figure it in different ways.[1]

Considerations of Joyce's engagement with cultural nationalism and gender in 'The Dead' are often closely linked. In many readings, Gretta emerges as a figure for a particular kind of Irish national identity or tradition. Vincent Cheng sees in Gretta an allegory of colonized Ireland, arguing that she is 'a modern-day Lass of Aughrim', and that 'Aughrim, its Lass, Gretta, and Michael Furey in the rain all merge into a composite image of the loss of the Irish soul and autonomy to the imperial masters'.[2] For Luke Gibbons, Gretta is allied with a marginalized, fragmented form of national identity or tradition in which 'the memories of the vanquished … attach themselves to fugitive and endangered cultural forms such as the street ballad'.[3] In contrast to the abstract national identity offered by print culture, this form of the national, found in fragmented, hybrid bits of oral culture, mixes the personal and political, rather than allegorizing the latter through the former. Gibbons extends this argument in two important and provocative ways: first, by connecting Gretta to Lily and to the figure of the servant generally, and, second, by casting the servant's story as a national narrative.[4] There is indeed a coincidence between

---

1   I would like to thank Luke Gibbons and Kevin Kenny for their insightful comments on an earlier draft of this essay.

2   Vincent J. Cheng, *Joyce, Race, and Empire* (Cambridge, 1995), 144

3   Luke Gibbons, 'Identity Without a Centre: Allegory, History and Irish Nationalism', in *Transformations in Irish Culture* (Cork, 1996), 145

4   Luke Gibbons, '"The Cracked Looking Glass" of Cinema: James Joyce, John Huston, and the Memory of "The Dead"', *Yale Journal of Criticism*, 15, 1 (2002), 127–48

Gretta's story and the servant's; but some aspects of the servant's story are antithetical to a national narrative, even (or perhaps especially) one that constructs national identity or tradition as fugitive, marginalized, broken and inarticulate.

There is a feminist critical tradition that focuses less on the potential national significance of Gretta and Lily than on their status as victims of predatory men, patriarchal power, and narrative obfuscation. The title of this essay gestures towards Margot Norris's excellent '"Who Killed Julia Morkan?": The Gender Politics of Art in "The Dead"'. She argues that in Joyce's text the greatest artist is the martyred Julia Morkan, thrown out of the choir by the pope, marginalized by Gabriel and the narrative voice, and dead, as we learn in *Ulysses*, within months of the party. For Norris, 'the narrative itself, the story's "telling"', has a 'performative function': Joyce, she claims, has 'the narrative voice of the story act out the same disavowals of art's oppressiveness that the characters themselves act out'. This narrative voice 'successfully stifles a series of back answers that it cannot prevent from erupting in the text'. As a result, in the text 'the ubiquitous oppression of women is both blatant and discounted, unmistakable and invisible at the same time'. Rather than posit a relation, allegorical or otherwise, between the story's female figures and national tradition, Norris asserts that the narrative voice of 'The Dead' 'maneuvers its emphasis in such a way that Irish nationalist political issues eclipse sexual politics'.[5]

Other critics have assigned different performative functions to the aestheticizing act and/or to the narrative itself in 'The Dead'. Vincent Pecora argues that, rather than dramatizing 'a movement from blind egotism to moral selflessness and sympathetic humility', 'The Dead' reveals Gabriel's repeated embrace of his own heroic 'generosity' as 'the ideologically supported transformation of one set of illusions into another'.[6] Seamus Deane claims that the story's end 'surrenders critique for aesthetics', and Paul Muldoon asserts that text's final passages are 'deliberately overwritten', and that, in them, 'Joyce undercuts the rhetoric of cultural nationalism, revelling in the very thing he repudiates, delighting in what he disdains'.[7] Clearly, there is room for debate over what exactly the narrative is performing; in addition, different elements of 'The Dead' engage in different kinds of performance.

Accordingly, it is useful to appeal to another sense of 'performance,' one that is part of 'orature', as Joseph Roach defines it. Roach borrows the term from Ngugi wa Thiong'o, and uses it as an alternative to traditional conceptions of oral culture. Orature, argues Roach, is best treated as performance. It is an act or site of collective memory that comprises a range of popular forms, such as 'gesture, song, dance, processions, storytelling, proverbs, gossip, customs, rites, and rituals'.[8] It exists in a constantly changing relation to various kinds of literacy and literate culture, and its performances are mediated by them. It is possible to expand Roach's definition of orature to include various kinds of geographical movement, grouped under the heading of 'migration': emigration, tourism, rural–urban migration, and 'going out to service' as a domestic servant. Both Joyce and Huston treat these forms of migration as performances, as part of orature, as forms of bodily movement in which alternative forms of memory, conceptions of tradition, and models of gender difference are embedded.

These two senses of performance — narrative as performance, migration as performance — can be employed in order to give Norris's thesis a further twist. Another argument about gender difference lies buried in 'The Dead', one that is rendered both explicit and marginal by the narrative itself. This element of the story connects Gretta and Lily, neither as sexual victims nor as emblems of tradition,

5   Margot Norris, '"Who Killed Julia Morkan?": The Gender Politics of Art in "The Dead"', in *Joyce's Web: The Social Unraveling of Modernism* (Austin, TX, 1992), 97–101

6   Vincent Pecora, '"The Dead" and the Generosity of the Word', *PMLA*, 101 (1986), 237

7   Seamus Deane, 'Dead Ends: Joyce's Finest Moments', in Derek Attridge and Marjorie Howes, eds., *Semicolonial Joyce* (Cambridge, 2000), 34. Paul Muldoon, *To Ireland, I* (Oxford, 2000), 66. Vincent Pecora's reading of 'The Dead' as a critique of 'the myth of generous self-sacrifice' is also relevant here; see '"The Dead" and the Generosity of the Word', 242.

8   Joseph Roach, *Cities of the Dead: Circum-Atlantic Performance* (New York, 1996), 11

but as modern female migrants. It aligns them with a view of migration that registers the traumas and dangers involved, but that nevertheless finds migration positive and enabling; it acknowledges that Gretta is from Galway, but emphasizes that she left there. While it notes Gretta's submission or subjection to various kinds of authority — male, bourgeois, and urban — it also foregrounds the fatal effects she has on representatives of such authority. This gendered construction of Gretta as a modern female migrant depends more on her body and its movements than on her self-awareness or explicit mental processes. Such performances constitute a form of consciousness, but not necessarily self-consciousness. And, oddly enough, their existence and meanings are pursued by both Joyce's text and Huston's film, each in its own particular way.

Huston and the Gender of Tradition

Norris very rightly laments the fact that Huston's film disregards Joyce's clear, explicit description of Julia's excellent performance of an extremely difficult musical piece:

> Her voice, strong and clear in tone, attacked with great spirit the runs which embellish the air and though she sang very rapidly she did not miss even the smallest of the grace notes. To follow the voice, without looking at the singer's face, was to feel and share the excitement of swift and secure flight.[9]

In the film, her singing is rendered pathetic. Huston's treatment of Gretta and Lily, however, is critical, insightful, and provocative. The film investigates the same issues that interest Gibbons and Norris: the servant's relation to a national narrative and the gendered performative functions of the narrative itself. It examines and revises the relationship between gender and tradition often offered by conventional cultural nationalism, and it casts migration as a performance in Roach's sense.

Huston's film makes three significant additions to Joyce's text that indicate its rigorous, complex engagement with gendered formulations of the relationship between tradition, modernity, and cultural nationalism. The first is Freddy Malins's joke, which has no specified content in Joyce's text, but is supplied (at least partly) by the film, about a rural Sligo woman who treats a baby pig as a substitute for a human infant. The joke adopts a strategy, identified by Rita Felski's *The Gender of Modernity*, of aligning a female figure with 'the dead weight of tradition and conservatism'.[10] It illustrates the bourgeois Dubliner's scorn for the backwardness of country ways, a scorn that in Joyce's text most clearly attaches to Gabriel's mother, with her 'sullen opposition' to Gabriel's marriage and her characterization of Gretta as 'country cute'.[11] In the film, it is also illustrated by Bartell D'Arcy's description of an understudy's poor diction as that of 'an auctioneer at a cattle fair'. That Huston also intends a reference to cultural nationalism of a more or less Yeatsian variety is indicated by the reference to Sligo. In this context, the joke rebukes the tendency of some cultural nationalists to idealize rural dwellers, revealing their 'folkways' as absurd reiterations of hoary slurs on the Irish 'Paddy and his (or, in this case, her) pig'. Of course, most cultural nationalists were also bourgeois Dubliners, and while they venerated the virtues they imagined places like Sligo possessed, they often scorned or suppressed the actual conditions, practices, and populations of such places.

9   James Joyce, *Dubliners* (New York, 1992 [1914]), 193
10 Rita Felski, *The Gender of Modernity* (Cambridge, MA, 1995), 2
11 *Dubliners*, 187

The second example illustrates, but also frustrates, the bourgeois cosmopolitan's eagerness to invest the local, the marginalized, and the past with exotic, non-modern ways of knowing and being. Upstairs in the Morkan house, the pretentious, worldly, and mildly predatory Bartell D'Arcy and Miss O'Callaghan are flirting. As they look out the window at the snow, she tells him, 'My grandmother's old gardener said in November it was going to be a hard winter.' Intrigued, D'Arcy asks, 'How did he know?' and she responds 'the almanac'. The gardener is an overdetermined, exaggerated figure for the past, and for the kind of tradition and folk wisdom that cultural nationalists often imputed to the peasantry. As a gardener, he engages in a form of labour that is linked to the rhythms of nature and to pre-industrial forms of cultivation and community. His status as an avatar of tradition and folk wisdom is reinforced by the fact that he is old, and further reinforced by the antiquity of his employer, Miss O'Callaghan's grandmother, and, of course, by the fact that his prediction was (apparently) correct. The effect of this overdetermination verges on parody. It is not surprising, then, that Miss O'Callaghan's answer to D'Arcy's question punctures the vision of the alternative, non-modern form of knowledge that he expects. These two examples show Huston actively engaging, in a manner both critical and humorous, with several issues that are central to a specific reading of 'The Dead': urban versus rural life, mainstream cultural nationalists' idealization of the West of Ireland, hostile stereotypes of the Irish, and socially marginalized figures (peasants, women) as emblems of, or conduits to, a symbolically central tradition.

Huston's third addition centres on Mr. Grace's recitation of Lady Gregory's translation of the Irish song, 'Dónall Óg'. Yeats, who interested himself early on in the distinction between mass culture and the culture of the masses, included the poem in his 1901 essay 'What is Popular Poetry?' He used it to illustrate the difference between the shallow popular poetry favoured by the middle classes, which did not grow out of and depend upon a tradition, and what he called 'the true poetry of the people', which was grounded in the 'unwritten tradition' of Irish oral and folk culture.[12] 'Dónall Óg' means 'Young Donal', but Huston uses 'Broken Vows', the title that Gregory gave her translation instead. Thus at first glance it might seem that in this instance, in contrast to my first two examples, Huston's film confirms Yeats's Revivalist vision of a truly popular oral tradition whose organizing themes are memory and loss, whose emblem is the wronged and sorrowful woman, and which moves a literate, bourgeois audience because it is startlingly exotic and, at the same time, restores to that audience its own buried and fragmented cultural past. Kevin Barry has read the audience's response to the performance as a 'generalizing of affective response to the Gaelic West' to include, at the least, the other ladies in the room. As a result, Barry argues, 'the East now welcomes the West into the party scene, in a manner that simply does not happen in Joyce's story, except when Gabriel hears Gretta's story in the lonely hotel bedroom'. For Barry, the main purpose of this insertion is to 'connect the party to the story's denouement' narratively, so that in 'the film the affective encounter between East and West happens in both halves of the narrative, and binds them together'.[13]

Barry's astute argument can be extended in several directions to illustrate the critical nature of Huston's engagement with the idea of East welcoming West. First, Barry acknowledges that despite the 'generalizing of affective response to the Gaelic West', Gretta remains 'distinctive' in the film, although it is possible further to define her distinction as a privileged and exceptional audience for the poem.[14] The others utter inarticulate praise, emphasizing the poem's foreign, exotic qualities:

12   W. B. Yeats, 'What is Popular Poetry?', in *Essays and Introductions* (New York, 1961), 8
13   Kevin Barry, *The Dead* (Cork, 2001), 59–62
14   Barry, *The Dead*, 62

AUNT KATE: Very strange ... but beautiful.
MR. BROWNE: I never heard anything like it.
MISS FURLONG: Very mysterious.
MISS HIGGINS: Can you imagine being in love like that?
MISS DALY: I thought it was beautiful.
BARTELL D'ARCY: It would make a lovely song.

These utterances are somewhat at odds with the screenplay's directions for a shot of 'Mary Jane's Young Ladies' as they listen to the poem: 'Clearly the author of the anonymous piece is a girl like themselves except that she is passionately in love.' Huston's effort to cast 'Dónall Óg' as not simply alien, but as also intimate — as a buried, alienated portion of the self — is split, somewhat awkwardly, between the visual, which conveys intimacy, and the verbal, which conveys foreignness. Gretta's response, on the other hand, suffers no such awkwardness or division; she is rapt and silent, 'almost as if she were in a trance'. The screenplay describes her this way: 'Though her gaze is inward, an enigmatic beauty pours from her like that of a fine unsentimental picture of the Annunciation' and comments that Gabriel is 'Slightly baffled' by her expression.[15] While the other audience members ponder the exotic, mysterious nature of the poem, and, by extension, of themselves, Gretta becomes an exotic mystery, not to herself, but to Gabriel and to the filmic audience, as indicated by her 'enigmatic' beauty, Gabriel's bafflement, and the reference to the Annunciation. What sets Gretta apart from the other members of the audience is that she does not merely respond to the poem; in an important respect, she becomes the poem, an enigmatic and beautiful object that both solicits and frustrates the spectator's efforts to understand it.

This emphasis on the baffled gaze of the spectator and of the narrative itself is related to literary critical investigations of the narrative's performative function in Joyce's text, a connection Barry also makes. He observes that Huston's film, like most critical interpretations of Joyce's text, idealizes Gretta. But he also claims that this idealization 'once called into focus by its overdetermination in Huston's film ... becomes questionable', and he invokes Norris's injunction to 'give a more sceptical attention both to the narrator's complicity in idealizing Gretta and to the story's feminist devices that undermine what she [Norris] judges to be the story's suffocating narrator'.[16] To return to the performance of 'Dónall Óg' with this in mind, during the lines 'You have taken the East from me, you have taken the West from me', the camera focuses on Gabriel, looking off-camera, presumably at Gretta, and then on Gretta, looking introspective and sorrowful. This aligns Gabriel and Gretta with East and West — more specifically, with a contrast between a modern, future-oriented East with its desiring, appropriative eyes focused on the West, and a traditional West whose gaze is directed inwards and back into the past. The scene, then, does not simply cast Gretta, or Irish tradition, as insular, and unselfconscious. Rather, it dramatizes the spectator's and the narrative's desire to do so; Lesley Brill has emphasized the independent agency of the camera, remarking, 'with its mobility, energy, and initiative, the camera in effect functions as the central character in the film'.[17]

The camera links Gabriel with the line 'you have taken what is before me', and associates Lily, rather than Gretta, with 'and what is behind me'. Lily remains in the doorway during the remaining few lines of the poem. In the screenplay, Lily interrupts Gabriel's baffled meditation on Gretta's enigmatic, inward beauty: 'Slightly baffled by the look on his wife's face. There is movement behind him. He looks round. It is Lily.'[18] Barry notes the enlarged role that Huston's film gives Lily; for him, the significance of

15 From Tony Huston's screenplay, quoted in Barry, The Dead, 60–61
16 Barry, The Dead, 64–65
17 Lesley Brill, John Huston's Filmmaking (Cambridge, MA, 1997), 222
18 From Tony Huston's screenplay, quoted in Barry, The Dead, 61

this enlarged role lies in the differences between her and Gretta, differences of class and attitude. According to Barry, unlike the young ladies, Lily knows something about love's promises, and so is not moved by Mr. Grace's recitation. And unlike Gretta and the other middle-class party-goers, she does not 'aestheticize loss'. Barry claims that Huston makes Lily into 'a counterpoint to a dreamy female gaze which she undercuts by her matter-of-factness'.[19] Thus the figure of Lily becomes a point where the film counters its own idealization of Gretta, a kind of 'stifled back-answer', as Norris would have it, to the aestheticizing agenda of the narrative itself. Like Freddy's joke and Miss O'Callaghan's reply to Bartell D'Arcy about the almanac, Lily helps Huston foreground and criticize the process by which marginal figures like women and rural dwellers are appropriated as emblems of Irish tradition by a central consciousness or narrative apparatus.

However, the figure of Lily is even more complex and important than Barry indicates; she has an additional function in the film. Underlying the contrast between Lily and Gretta, the film posits a significant identification between the two women. By showing us Lily when, based on the preceding camera work, we might expect Gretta, and by associating Lily with 'what is behind me', the film aligns Lily with Gretta's past. Similarly, when Lily approaches Gretta at the dinner table to tell her something about the meal, her mundane remark does startle Gretta out of a reverie, indicating the kind of contrast Barry notes. But Huston frames the shot of Lily bending over Gretta so that it highlights the similarity in their profiles, an effect he went to considerable trouble to achieve.[20] Huston contrasts Lily and Gretta, only to counter that contrast with suggestions that they are similar, even interchangeable. The film also encodes the coincidence of domestic servant and beloved wife in Huston's cryptic dedication, 'for Maricela'. As Barry observes, 'by this gesture Huston dedicates The Dead to his last and, in his own words, his most beloved companion, an illegal alien in the United States, Maricela Hernandez, a Mexican who had worked as a maid to Huston's fifth wife, Cici'.[21] It is to the interrelatedness of these figures — wife, servant, migrant — in Irish cultural history, and to the kinds of memory or tradition embodied in the movements they share, that I now turn.

Gender, Migration, and Domestic Service

In his introduction to Irish Women and Irish Migration, Patrick O'Sullivan quotes E. G. Ravenstein, who observed in 1885, 'Woman is a greater migrant than man. This may surprise those who associate women with domestic life, but the figures of the census clearly prove it.'[22] It is now known that in the second half of the nineteenth century Ireland experienced massive female migration. Indeed, Irish migration patterns were virtually unique worldwide because the number of women migrating equalled or exceeded the number of men; this was true whether they moved from rural Ireland to metropolitan centres within that country or migrated across national borders. In contrast to earlier periods, the majority of these female migrants were young, single women travelling alone rather than with families. Kerby Miller's Emigrants and Exiles demonstrates that many Irishmen migrated voluntarily and then later came to see migration as forced exile.[23] Irishwomen, on the other hand, according to Miller and several other scholars, left Ireland more willingly and with less emotional trauma than men, and, in Kevin

---

19 Barry, The Dead, 60, 66
20 I owe this point to Luke Gibbons.
21 Barry, The Dead, 7
22 Patrick O'Sullivan, ed., Irish Women and Irish Migration (London, 1995), 2
23 Kerby A. Miller, Emigrants and Exiles: Ireland and the Irish Exodus to North America (Oxford and New York, 1985)

Kenny's words, 'often saw in America a land of opportunity rather than exile or banishment'.[24] Female migrancy, as the term is intended here, denotes a complex set of relationships among several things: the fact of widespread female migration; women's attitudes towards migration, which were different from, and often more positive than, men's attitudes; migration's relation to domestic service and to marriage; and the ways in which Irish-Atlantic culture imagined female migration and domestic service.

As Ravenstein's remark indicates, female migrancy existed in tension with some conventional gender norms and dominant cultural narratives of the period. But if such migrancy was in some respects, or in some discourses, a sexual and cultural scandal, it was also a mundane fact of post-Famine life, and it contributed to, as well as violated, contemporary conceptions of gender. For example, Tom Inglis's analysis of the alliance between Irishwomen and the Catholic Church argues that 'It was from within the home that the practices central to the modernization of Irish agriculture — postponed marriage, permanent celibacy, and emigration — were developed. In this respect mothers became a major power behind the modernization of Irish society, and not mere servants of their menfolk.'[25] Inglis also claims that while Irish mothers often raised at least one son to be overly dependent upon them and poorly able to function in the wider world, 'daughters, on the other hand, were reared to be responsible, competent and independent, which gave them a greater sense of autonomy, prepared them for early emigration from the village, and allowed them to feel less guilty about severing ties with old people'.[26] Irishwomen, according to Inglis, were the arbiters of a repressive sexual morality and the vehicles of an agricultural modernity that required both this morality and the migration of single women. These mothers reared daughters who were better equipped than men to emigrate with success and without regret. By migrancy, then, I do not mean to suggest transgression, or to romanticize the figure of the migrant; migrancy has much to do with negotiating women's relations to the dictates of various institutions and authorities. It is best thought of in terms of survival rather than resistance, and in terms of performance rather than self-awareness or coherent ideology.

A few selective aspects of the history of Irish female migration and domestic service follow, which will offer some tentative generalizations about the cultural meanings of female migrancy. Historically, of course, these generalizations need to be qualified, and to take into account differences among women in age, region, class, religion, skill level, and marital status. They are offered here as part of an effort to understand why and how various forms of Irish-Atlantic culture produced generalized and interrelated ideas about women, domestic servants, and female migration, ideas with which Joyce and Huston engage critically.

Scholars disagree about the causes and significance of Irish female migration and its relation to various economic, social, religious and cultural changes.[27] For example, there is some debate about whether Irishwomen's migration was a mark of abjection, a sign of empowerment, or both. Several historians have argued that female migration increased during the latter part of the nineteenth century because the social status of rural women, which had been fairly favourable in pre-Famine Ireland,

24 Kevin Kenny, *The American Irish: A History* (London and New York, 2000), 139. See also Hasia Diner, *Erin's Daughters in America: Irish Immigrant Women in the Nineteenth Century* (Baltimore, MD, and London, 1983), 19. In a study of a slightly later period, Pauric Travers, 'Irish Female Emigration, 1922–71', in O'Sullivan, *Irish Women and Irish Migration*, 164, concludes, 'it certainly seems probable that emigrant women would be less likely to embrace the "Erin's children in exile" interpretation of emigration'.

25 Tom Inglis, *Moral Monopoly: The Rise and Fall of the Catholic Church in Modern Ireland*, 2nd edn. (Dublin, 1998), 187

26 Inglis, *Moral Monopoly*, 197–98

27 The salient issues in these debates include the declining importance of women's economic contributions to family farms, the emergence of something closer to a Victorian bourgeois ideology of separate spheres, the erosion of extended family ties and the consolidation of the nuclear family in urban life, the increasing hegemony of impartible inheritance and matchmaking and therefore the importance of dowries for women, high rates of permanent celibacy and late marriage age, the rise in the influence of the Catholic Church and the regularization of religious practices.

deteriorated as the century progressed.[28] But Miller has suggested that low female migration may indicate powerlessness rather than contentment, and that higher female migration actually reflected an improvement in the social condition of women, who now had greater access to the things that enabled migration — literacy, proficiency in English, money, and some degree of family support.[29] Similarly, some scholars have argued that the rise of bourgeois ideals, the increased emphasis on housework and the movement of women from waged labour outside the home to unwaged labour within it represented the confinement of women in the home and a decrease in their social status. On the other hand, Joanna Bourke argues that 'for the women who made the decision to leave paid employment, or never to engage in it, housework offered a chance to increase their status and improve the quality of their lives'.[30] She claims, moreover, that 'the move into the home allowed women to expand into other areas of life, outside the strictly economic realm'.[31] While such issues need not be addressed in either/ or terms — empowerment or disempowerment, constraint or freedom — they can help us determine how and why various experiences of migration changed women's lives and the individual and cultural perceptions of those lives.

Central to much scholarly debate about the history, causes and effects of Irish female migration is the question: what did women want? There is a debate in the literature over whether women migrated seeking better marriage prospects, material prosperity, or both. Janet Nolan contends that Irishwomen migrated to increase their chances of marrying and establishing families; Hasia Diner argues that women migrated primarily to secure greater financial security and independence.[32] Miller finds that previous scholarship has drawn the distinction between 'marital and economic motives for emigration' too sharply, arguing that Irishwomen migrated seeking 'both economic opportunity *and* domestic bliss' and that 'they viewed the successful appropriation of the former as the key to the successful acquisition of the latter'.[33] Much research remains to be done on which combinations of marital and economic motives led particular categories of Irishwomen, and particular Irishwomen, to migrate. But it is clear from the historical record that the major personal and cultural meanings of female migration were organized around women's sexuality, women's labour, and upward economic mobility.

This is borne out by an examination of contemporary discourses on female migration, which addressed all of these themes, with sexuality emerging as the paramount concern. As Katherine Mullin has shown, turn-of-the-century anti-emigration propaganda saw migration, both male and female, as a national crisis, and periodicals like the *Irish Homestead* often expressed 'nationalist anxieties over the vulnerability of young female emigrants to sexual dangers abroad'.[34] Such periodicals produced numerous cautionary narratives in which an innocent Irish girl rejects the prospect of a traditional rural marriage in favour of the combination of dangerous sexuality and upward economic mobility represented by emigration: 'balls, parties and big wages and theatres and fine clothes'.[35] Female migration was, in mainstream Irish culture, a 'fatal act of un-Irish sexual impropriety', and, as such, it forced contemporary observers to confront the mystery and intransigence of several kinds of female

---

28 See, for example, David Fitzpatrick, 'The Modernisation of the Irish Female', in Patrick O'Flanagan, Paul Ferguson, and Kevin Whelan, eds., *Rural Ireland, 1600–1900* (Cork, 1987).

29 Kerby A. Miller, with David N. Doyle and Patricia Kelleher, '"For Love and Liberty": Irish Women, Migration and Domesticity in Ireland and America, 1815–1920', in O'Sullivan, *Irish Women and Irish Migration*, 41–65

30 Joanna Bourke, *Husbandry to Housewifery: Women, Economic Change, and Housework in Ireland, 1890–1914* (Oxford, 1993), 270–71

31 Bourke, *Husbandry to Housewifery*, 274–75

32 See Janet Nolan, *Ourselves Alone: Women's Emigration from Ireland, 1885–1920* (Lexington, KY, 1989); Diner, *Erin's Daughters*.

33 Miller, Doyle and Kelleher, '"For Love and Liberty"', 53

34 Katherine Mullin, 'Don't Cry for Me, Argentina: "Eveline" and the Seductions of Emigration Propaganda', in Attridge and Howes, *Semicolonial Joyce*, 172

35 Quoted in Mullin, 'Don't Cry for Me, Argentina', 181

desire.[36] For women themselves, migration involved sexual freedom and possibility as well as sexual danger and scandal. On one hand, the fairly straightforward point can be made that female migration was sexualized in a way that male migration was not. On the other hand, the history of how, culturally, female sexuality itself was conceptualized through material and metaphorical migration has yet to be written.

In Irish-Atlantic culture, female migration was also intimately bound up with domestic service, for several reasons. Mona Hearn notes that the choice facing the daughters of 'small farmers, estate workers, the semi-skilled and the unskilled' was usually domestic service or emigration. But choosing migration most often involved domestic service; the vast majority of female migrants to Dublin or cities abroad went into this sector of employment, at least for a period of time. And choosing service also involved migration on some scale: abroad, to Dublin, to the next parish, or the next house. Indeed, domestic service itself was a kind of migration, as in the phrase 'go out to service'. It removed young women from their homes, and made them ambiguous semi-members of other households. It usually involved bringing young Catholic girls into Protestant homes.[37] In contrast to the kinds of labour available to men, it also brought women into contact with a bourgeois culture that provided a means of organizing their aspirations to upward mobility; servants had to learn new standards and techniques in cooking, house cleaning, laundry, and other domestic chores. When and if they married, their experience in service could become a conduit for introducing middle-class mores into their own homes, though the extent to which this actually occurred is unclear.[38] Domestic servants also engaged in another kind of migration; studies routinely note that employee turnover was very high.[39]

Like migration, and as a version of migration, domestic service for women involved a host of sexual meanings and sexual potential. Service was less an alternative to marriage than a prelude to it; most servants saw it as a temporary occupation before marriage.[40] Diner remarks that by the end of the nineteenth century, 'there was reasonable chance within an Irish marriage that the wife had lived away from home, as a domestic in Dublin or a shopgirl in Cork or even in London'.[41] So the transition from servant to wife was a common one, though the transition from lower-class servant to middle-class wife was far more common in fantasy than in fact. Domestic service was also fraught with more threatening kinds of sexual potential. Young and inexperienced migrants from rural areas confronted an unfamiliar urban sexual culture, and they were vulnerable to sexual exploitation by employers. Hearn argues that seduction and premarital sex were fairly common among servants in Ireland, and notes that 'the mothers of illegitimate children were frequently domestic servants'.[42] Employers and bourgeois culture perceived a different kind of sexual threat in domestic service, often worrying about the morals of servants and their influence on children in particular.

36 Mullin, 'Don't Cry for Me, Argentina', 181

37 Mona Hearn, *Below Stairs: Domestic Service Remembered in Dublin and Beyond 1880–1922* (Dublin, 1993), 2, 13

38 For a discussion of the differences between the ideas of upward mobility available to women and men, and an analysis of the various possible relations, from complete embrace, to partial appropriation, to rejection, that Irishwomen could adopt towards assimilation and bourgeois mores, see Patricia Kelleher, 'Young Irish Workers: Class Implications of Men's and Women's Experiences in Gilded Age Chicago', *Éire-Ireland*, 36, 1–2 (2001), 141–65. For an analysis of how domestic servants both accepted the dictates of bourgeois culture and resisted forced assimilation, see Diane Hotten-Somers, 'Relinquishing and Reclaiming Independence: Irish Domestic Servants, American Middle-Class Mistresses, and Assimilation, 1850–1920', *Éire-Ireland*, 36, 1–2 (2001), 185–201.

39 Hearn, *Below Stairs*, 83–100. This was the case in Ireland and in the United States; see Diner, *Erin's Daughters*, 85, and Sarah Deutsch, *Women and the City: Gender, Space, and Power in Boston, 1870–1940* (Oxford, 2000), 66.

40 Hearn, *Below Stairs*, 83

41 Diner, *Erin's Daughters*, 17

42 Hearn, *Below Stairs*, 97. See also Kenny, *American Irish*, 153–54.

A number of cultural historians have explored the sexual attractions, threats, and ambiguities of domestic servants for turn-of-the-century British bourgeois culture.[43] Three points that are important for the purposes of this essay emerge from this body of scholarship. One is that the servant's sexual meanings depended in part upon her ambiguous relation to another female figure: the mother and lady of the house.[44] Underlying the apparent contrast between them, bourgeois culture discerned, and often disavowed, an unsettling identification between the lower class servant and the bourgeois wife and mother. Histories of psychoanalysis have often observed that, in order to construct the theory of the Oedipal complex as a universal theory of human psycho-sexuality, Freud had to suppress the role of the nurse in middle-class households (including the household he was raised in) of the period.[45] As Bruce Robbins observes, 'it is thanks in large part to the success of this theory that the massive intrusion of desire for servants into the lives of the servant-keeping classes in this period has not attracted more attention'.[46] When such desire was revealed, it created major scandals. In 1910, 'every newspaper' in England reported the story of the clandestine cross-class relationship between Arthur J. Munby, a prominent English barrister, and Hannah Cullwick, a domestic servant.[47] In his will, Munby revealed that Cullwick had been his beloved companion for forty-five years, and his wife for thirty-six of those years. Ann McClintock argues that Cullwick's appeal for Munby, and her lifelong power over him, lay in her ability to combine the contrasting figures of servant and wife: 'Cullwick offered Munby the delicious promise of embodying in one person the contrast of mother and nurse, woman and man, that so excited him.'[48] But if Cullwick's appeal for Munby lay in the contrast rather than the simple conflation of these figures, Cullwick herself also refused the kind of upward mobility that would have transformed her from a servant into a bourgeois wife. As McClintock notes,

> As a barrister's wife, Cullwick could have 'entered society,' but chose instead to live as a maidservant among her own class, spending very little time under the same roof as her beloved husband. In an age when wifely services were void of economic value, she insisted that her husband pay her monthly wages.[49]

McClintock's unwillingness to read Cullwick's choices as pathology or as pathetic submissions to Munby's wishes (indeed, they sometimes involved defying Munby) is instructive.

The second point that emerges from studies of the servant in British culture is that they had much contact with and authority over children, and often initiated children to the physical pleasures of bathing, caressing and, further, sometimes initiated them sexually. As a result, in many turn-of-the-century cultural discourses and private fantasies produced by adults, servants were figures of considerable power, associated with male sexual impotence, as well as arousal.[50] Cullwick was unusual

---

43 See, for example, Bruce Robbins, *The Servant's Hand: English Fiction from Below* (Durham, NC, 1983); Ann McClintock, *Imperial Leather: Race, Gender and Sexuality in the Colonial Context* (New York, 1995); and Stephen Marcus, *The Other Victorians: A Study of Sexuality and Pornography in Mid-Nineteenth-Century England* (New York, 1966).

44 Hotten-Somers examines the ways in which, for their part, Irish-American domestic servants' experiences and attitudes were profoundly shaped by their relationships with their female employers.

45 See McClintock, *Imperial Leather*, 86–95

46 Robbins, *Servant's Hand*, 196

47 Derek Hudson, *Munby, Man of Two Worlds. The Life and Diaries of Arthur J. Munby, 1828–1910* (London, 1972), 437, quoted in Hearn, *Below Stairs*, 20

48 McClintock, *Imperial Leather*, 145

49 McClintock, *Imperial Leather*, 141

50 See Robbins, *Servant's Hand*, 184–203, and McClintock, *Imperial Leather*, 75–180, *passim*. This was, of course, belied by the actual facts of servant life. For some useful cautions about assuming that domestic service was chosen by Irish women in the United States because it was to some extent liberating, see Kenny, *American Irish*, 152–54.

in that she appears to have chosen to exercise this kind of authority (to the extent that it could be translated from the symbolic into the material realm) rather than the kind of authority that she would exercise as a bourgeois wife. Finally, the kinds of appeal, threat, and power that bourgeois culture located in servants were connected to modernity rather than tradition. McClintock argues that, for writers like Baudelaire, Zola and Freud, the servant or nursemaid, who first introduced the child to 'the shocks and sights of urban space', became a figure for the modern city, and for modernity itself.[51] Servants and migrants had opportunities to investigate the spectacle of modernity but, in contrast to the modernist *flâneur*, they did so within the constraints of their employment. Rather than simply consuming the sensations of the modern city, such figures mediated them, performing them in their movements, introducing others to them, and surviving by wrenching temporary and marginal forms of authority from their disadvantaged positions. That Gretta's past in 'The Dead' is aligned with the figure of the servant indicates her upward mobility, her migration from lowly servant to bourgeois wife. It also associates her with a complex set of threats to bourgeois male self-possession: childhood, sexual impotence, and the shocks of modern urban life.

Joyce and Modern Female Migrants

In the famous opening of Joyce's text 'Lily, the caretaker's daughter, was literally run off her feet.' The play on 'literally' — literally put to metaphorical use to suggest the extent of Lily's haste and fatigue — has often been seen by critics as Lily's 'sloppy' language.[52] A preferable reading would acknowledge Joyce's strategic use of a domestic servant to foreground transactions between material and metaphorical spatial movement. The opening sentence raises a question that can be formulated in terms similar to those that Gabriel will use later: what is a housemaid, 'scampering' along a 'bare hallway', a symbol of? She is a symbol of female migrancy, of a way of surviving Irish modernity that will elude, threaten, and possibly destroy Gabriel. Her hurried physical movement suggests (and we should not be too quick to say, parodies) travel, and the tag 'the caretaker's daughter' (applied to her twice) emphasizes that she has left her original home and gone out to service, becoming an ambiguous semi-member of the Morkan family (hence Gabriel's memories of her as a child). And the way she pronounces Gabriel's name indicates that, like Gretta, she has migrated to Dublin from the West of Ireland.[53] Gabriel's questions about school and marriage invoke the combination of material and marital aspirations that drove young women from rural areas to urban centres, and the transition from service to marriage. Lily's bitter retort and Aunt Kate's complaint that she is 'not the girl she was at all' reveal such migration as both sexually liberating and sexually dangerous.[54] Lily is a classic female migrant, undergoing both upward mobility and abuse, with no visible nostalgia for the home she has left and no investment in Gabriel's patronizing, and possibly predatory, version of her various movements.

Having focused our attention on the material and metaphorical significance of Lily's feet and movement, the narrative remains obsessed with feet, footwear and walking. When Gabriel enters, he 'stood on the mat, scraping the snow from his galoshes'; he then 'continued scraping his feet vigorously' but still has snow 'on the toes of his galoshes'. He then 'looked up at the pantry ceiling, which was shaking with the stamping and shuffling of feet on the floor above'.[55] Feet repeatedly

51 McClintock, *Imperial Leather*, 82
52 Clive Hart, quoted in Gibbons, '"Cracked Looking Glass"', 131
53 Donald Torchiana, *Backgrounds for Joyce's Dubliners* (Boston, MA, 1986), 227
54 *Dubliners*, 181
55 *Dubliners*, 176–77

organize Gabriel's separation from other characters in the text. But Gabriel's preoccupation with his own and other people's feet and footwear is not to be confused with the narrative's use of them, which comments critically on Gabriel's interrelated misunderstandings of women and travel on various scales. For example, after his unnerving encounter with Lily, Gabriel 'waited outside the drawing room door until the waltz should finish, listening to the skirts that swept against it and to the shuffling of feet. He was still discomposed by the girl's bitter and sudden retort.'[56] A few lines later, he manages to transform the same sound of feet into an indication of his assumed superiority. As he worries that his after-dinner speech will be above the heads of his listeners: 'the indelicate clacking of the men's heels and the shuffling of their soles reminded him that their grade of culture differed from his'.[57] And galoshes signify the loving control he seeks to exercise over Gretta, his continental pretensions, and her resistance to both — she has refused to wear them tonight.

Gretta's western origins, her migration to Dublin, and the fact that the Conroy's servant, Bessie, will look after the children while they are staying at the Gresham hotel all establish a subtle identification between domestic servant and bourgeois wife. Like Lily, Gretta is an apparently subordinate female figure who thwarts Gabriel's appropriative desires through an alternative model of modernity embodied in her gendered migrancy. While Gabriel spends a good deal of time getting the snow off his shoes, Gretta would 'walk home in the snow if she were let'.[58] In Galway she lived with her grandmother, not altogether unusual, but indicating that her origins are already somewhat migrant, not attached to a nuclear family. Her sexuality, and Gabriel's inability to comprehend or control it, are organized around various kinds of migrancy. She narrates her desire for Michael Furey through the notion of walking: she twice describes their relationship by using a rural idiom for courtship, saying 'we used to go out walking'.[59] And Gabriel initially suspects that her wish to travel to Galway springs from this desire. Her Galway origins and her association with the ballad 'The Lass of Aughrim' invoke cultural nationalism's preoccupation with folk culture and the West of Ireland. But they also invoke the relationship in folk culture between travel and sexuality; Paul Muldoon has argued that an association of the West with sexuality is 'part and parcel of the folk-song and ballad tradition'.[60]

Both Gretta and Michael Furey are rural–urban migrants, and they embody different, gendered, relations to mainstream cultural nationalism, its conception of tradition, and modernity. As Joseph Valente has argued, Furey is quite compatible with Revivalist myth-making.[61] He embodies a nationalist model of tradition as simple and passionate, broken and self-immolating, and profoundly incompatible with modernity. For Furey, modernity and migration — his job in the gasworks, his movement from Oughterard to Galway, his peripatetic romance with Gretta, and his journey from his sickbed to her back garden — are fatal. Joyce's text also associates this fatality with the ideological opposite of migration, a movement towards home and origins. When Furey appeared in her garden on that wet night, Gretta says she 'implored of him to go home'. Her conversation with Gabriel continues:

— And did he go home? asked Gabriel.
— Yes, he went home. And when I was only a week in the convent he died and he was buried in Oughterard where his people came from.[62]

---

56 *Dubliners*, 178
57 *Dubliners*, 179
58 *Dubliners*, 180
59 *Dubliners*, 220, 222
60 Muldoon, *To Ireland*, I, 119
61 Joseph Valente, 'James Joyce and the Cosmopolitan Sublime', in Mark A. Wollaeger, Victor Luftig, and Robert Spoo, eds., *Joyce and the Subject of History* (Ann Arbor, MI, 1996), 69–73
62 *Dubliners*, 223

Joyce's use of repetition inextricably links Furey's death, not just to his migration, but to migration in combination with an attachment to going 'home', and, further, to the idea of stable family or community origins, where one's people come from. Furey, not Gretta, stands for an Irish folk tradition organized around memory and loss, rendered fractured and broken by modernity, and for a model of modern migration as exile from home. It is Furey who stands in the rain, is not admitted but sent away, and is abandoned when Gretta leaves for the convent.

If Furey cannot survive modernity and its attendant migrations, Gretta, on the other hand, thrives on them. She leaves Galway for a Dublin convent, seeking the upward mobility represented by urban schooling or work, a process that the text associates with a change for the worse in Furey's condition: 'And then when it came to the time for me to leave Galway and come up to the convent he was much worse …'[63] A further migration results in her marriage to Gabriel. While her rural origins are a potential liability during this process, the text associates them, not with tradition or powerlessness, but with the death of Gabriel's mother, whose 'sullen opposition' to Gabriel's marriage posed an obstacle to her mobility: 'she had once spoken of Gretta as being country cute and that was not true of Gretta at all. It was Gretta who had nursed her during all her last long illness in their house at Monkstown.'[64] Obviously, this passage suggests that Gretta is a devoted daughter-in-law despite the hostility she encounters. But this unresentful, unselfish devotion, like her passion for Furey, is the opposite of self-immolating; deadly for someone else, it is coupled with, and even a vehicle for, her own survival, migration, and upward mobility. It is well known that Joyce drew on his own life, and on Nora's, when he was composing 'The Dead'.[65] He was struck by 'The Lass of Aughrim' when Nora sang it to him; he was also struck by the idea that romance with Nora was, literally as well as figuratively, fatal to young men. Brenda Maddox argues that Michael Furey is a composite figure, combining two of Nora's young admirers, both of whom died, and comments that, in Joyce's notes for the figure of Bertha in Exiles, he wrote under the heading 'N. (B.).': 'Bodkin died. Kearns died. At the convent they called her the mankiller …'[66] And years later, in Trieste, Joyce created some vignettes based on what Nora told him about her early life and his own free association; the scenes combine snow, 'buttoned boots', emigration, and sexual longing and, while Nora is saddened by 'the pain of separation', Joyce also comments, 'Her sadness is brief.'[67]

In emphasizing the text's characterization of Gretta as a migrant and a 'mankiller', I do not mean to suggest that 'The Dead' invests Gretta with individual agency or locates her embrace of modernity and migration in her explicit mental processes or self-awareness. Her story delivers Gabriel into that final epiphany — a moment of ultimate awareness inseparable from oblivion and death. But by this time she is fast asleep. Gabriel contemplates his sleeping wife before moving into his meditation on the dead, and focuses briefly on the objects that mark her migrancy: 'One boot stood upright, its limp upper fallen down: the fellow of it lay upon its side.'[68] Like the human couple, this pair consists of an ambiguous element that is both upright and fallen, powerful and powerless, and a 'fellow' that is more clearly in a deathlike swoon. Critics often comment that the 'vague terror' that seizes Gabriel when Gretta says, 'I think he died for me', testifies to the seductive, destructive power of the kind of romantic nationalism embodied in Yeats's Cathleen ni Houlihan. But Gretta's fatal qualities have another source, too, in the fact that for Gretta the confrontation between tradition and modernity, home and

63 Dubliners, 222. It is not clear whether she leaves Galway for work or schooling; see Terence Brown's note in Dubliners, 316–17 n.92.
64 Dubliners, 187
65 See Richard Ellmann, 'The Backgrounds of "The Dead"', in James Joyce (Oxford, 1982 [1959]), 243–53.
66 Brenda Maddox, Nora: A Biography of Nora Joyce (New York, 1988), 17–18
67 See Peter Costello, James Joyce: The Years of Growth 1882–1915 (New York, 1992), 241.
68 Dubliners, 223

migration, is far from disabling. Against the regret and nostalgia Gretta feels for Furey and for Galway, Joyce's text sets the physical movements of her body, which encompass both the fact that she loved Furey, and the fact that she left him. Against the impulse to identify Gretta with the Lass of Aughrim, the text sets Furey's greater fitness for the part, and Gretta's inability to 'think of the name' of the song until prompted by Bartell D'Arcy, who admits, 'I couldn't remember it properly.'[69] Against Gretta's subordination to Gabriel, to his mother, and to the performative designs of the narrative, the text sets the fatal performances of her migration.

Huston and Modern Female Migrants

To return to Huston's film, it is also obsessed with feet, footwear and travel. In the opening scenes, carriages pull up in front of the house, and inside, the film emphasizes Lily's hurried movement, contrasting it to the stillness of the sisters, who stand on the stairs and peer over the railing. Lily helps Gabriel off with his galoshes when he arrives, and brings them to him at the end of the evening — both additions Huston made to Joyce's text. Mrs. Malins, whose daughter has migrated to Glasgow while her alcoholic and incompetent son Freddy has stayed in Dublin, bores Gabriel by telling him that her daughter's house is ideally situated because it is at the edge of the city, just where the tram line starts. While Aunt Julia sings 'Arrayed for the Bridal' so badly, the camera leaves the room and surveys various memorabilia in the Morkan household, including a collection of ceramic and glass shoes. Brill calls these 'traces of Cinderella', and Cinderella's transformation from lowly servant to queen is a fairy-tale version of the migration from domestic servant to bourgeois wife.[70] Early in the film, shortly after Gabriel and Gretta arrive at the party, the camera focuses in strikingly on Gretta's feet as she changes her shoes and says that Bessie will look after the children. Gretta's feet, and the movements they imply, are used to assert both her temporary freedom from domestic responsibilities and her connections with a servant, in this case, a servant who is acting as a surrogate mother for her children.

Gretta and the other women in Huston's film are migrants, and the almanac is an apt figure for the kind of modernity, and the kind of tradition, that they share and embody. Both Luke Gibbons and Emer Nolan have suggested that the reference to the newspapers at the end of Joyce's text invokes an Andersonian conception of the community-in-anonymity of the modern nation, and Gibbons has further argued that Joyce's text stages a confrontation between this kind of nationalism and the more resilient, insurrectionary nationalism embodied in that 'remnant of oral culture', the ballad.[71] Miss O'Callaghan's almanac is something else again. The almanac would have been primarily of interest to gardeners and farmers by the early twentieth century. It has evolved, as a source of astronomical and commercial data, since the sixteenth century, to its present day mix of scientific information and traditional lore. Thus, it is a modern, scientific up-to-date resource for people whose livelihoods depend on the traditional rhythms of the working agricultural year, a part of literate culture with especially close ties to non-modern forms of knowledge, and to oral and folk culture.

While we watch Gabriel, and the camera, work to transform Gretta into a symbol of native Irish tradition, the film also subtly positions her, along with Lily, as a modern female migrant, someone whose way of living, loving, and working is equally deadly to Gabriel's cosmopolitan pretensions, Furey's self-immolating passion, D'Arcy's exoticism, and the bourgeois scorn for the country illustrated by Gabriel's mother and Freddy's joke. The performance of the narrative is made visible and, as Norris

69 Dubliners, 213
70 Brill, John Huston's Filmmaking, 225
71 Nolan, Joyce and Nationalism, 34–36; Gibbons, 'Identity Without a Centre', 134

claims in her reading of Joyce's text, is aligned with Gabriel's sympathetic but suspect designs. Barry points out that the embarrassing exposure and disruption of these designs in 'The Dead' continues the preoccupation with 'male failure and its incapacity to express itself' which recurs throughout Huston's films.[72] One of the agents of this exposure and disruption lies in another set of performances, those embodied in the physical details of migration. If we accede to the desires of the camera and the performance of the narrative, the memories of Michael Furey she has 'locked in her heart' may cast Gretta as both a sorrowful female victim and a national type, an exemplary figure of modernity as loss, migration as exile, Irish tradition as broken, inaccessible, yet haunting.[73] But the memories locked in her gendered body tell a different story. They suggest a practical and at least partly enabling means of negotiating between what is behind her and before her, a way embodied neither in the newspaper nor in the ballad, but in the almanac.

---

72 Barry, *The Dead*, 81
73 *Dubliners*, 224

Culture and Enlightenment: W. B. Yeats

Over the last two decades, the conjunction of Irish studies and postcolonial studies has produced several different versions of a 'postcolonial Yeats'.[1] Most of them revolve around assessments of Yeats's nationalism, his Romanticism, and the particularities of Irish history and culture. An alternative postcolonial reading of Yeats is possible, however: one that does not depend upon, or even take up, the question of whether or not Yeats is a postcolonial writer or Ireland a postcolonial country.[2] In this reading, postcolonial studies is useful, not because it applies to or explains Yeats, but because postcolonial studies and Yeats wrestle with some of the same major commitments, issues, and dilemmas.[3] My postcolonial reading of Yeats is thus a reading that is enabled or provoked by some aspects of postcolonial studies, and makes connections between the current state of that field and some problematics in Yeats's works. What Yeats and postcolonial studies share is a troubled political conception of culture in which an enormous faith in culture's transformative and emancipatory power confronts a series of issues that are both foundational and damaging to that faith. These issues involve the public sphere, the political and public role of intellectuals, and the need to negotiate, theoretically and practically, between the universal and the particular, between the abstract and the concrete. They involve, in other words, some political and intellectual legacies of the Enlightenment.

Yeats and postcolonial studies conduct some of their most sustained and important engagements with the Enlightenment through its opposite: a Romantic culturalism. This general claim is not in

1 Seamus Deane characterizes Yeats as a 'colonialist' writer: 'Yeats and the Idea of Revolution', in *Celtic Revivals: Essays in Modern Irish Literature, 1880–1980* (London, 1985), 49. Edward Said, in contrast, casts him as a 'poet of decolonization': 'Yeats and Decolonization', in Seamus Deane et al., *Nationalism, Colonialism and Literature* (Minneapolis, MN, 1990 [1988]), 84. Later, Jahan Ramazani parses some definitions of the 'postcolonial' in order to answer the question 'is Yeats a postcolonial poet?' with 'a qualified yes': 'Is Yeats a Postcolonial Poet?', *Raritan*, 17, 3 (1998), 66. Declan Kiberd places Yeats's work in the context of anti- and postcolonial nation-building in Ireland: *Inventing Ireland* (Cambridge, MA, 1996). My own *Yeats's Nations: Gender, Class and Irishness* (Cambridge, 1996) examines the various formulations of 'Irishness' he constructed or embraced over the course of his career. Gregory Castle, in *Modernism and the Celtic Revival* (Cambridge, 2001), emphasizes Yeats's engagement with a modernist form of anthropology which was derived from imperialism but also critically engaged with it.
2 I take up these questions, and stress the ways in which they are not reliably answerable, in 'Yeats and the Postcolonial', in Marjorie Howes and John Kelly, eds., *The Cambridge Companion to W. B. Yeats* (Cambridge, 2006), 206–25.
3 While I claim that Yeats's works and postcolonial studies have some procedures and problems in common, I am also well aware of the equally important differences between them; my focus on establishing some continuities or genealogies has as much heuristic as historical value.

itself surprising; it is well known that several major elements of postcolonial studies have their origins in critiques of the Enlightenment. Postcolonial studies needs to reinvigorate the 'universal' and the 'abstract' as terms that are necessary and enabling, even though they are also problematic. In addition, Yeats scholars should investigate more fully Yeats's attachment to a variety of abstract principles, both artistic and political, over the course of his career. Finally, Yeats scholarship and postcolonial studies need to supplement their frequent focus on the 'national' with analyses of an important set of related terms: the public, the public sphere, and public intellectuals.

Yeats himself often employed terms like 'Enlightenment' and 'Romantic' to describe his politics and poetics. His professed hatred for the Enlightenment, his invention of an Irish counter-Enlightenment, his denigration of anything in politics or poetry that he labelled abstract, and his claim to be part of the Romantic tradition are widely acknowledged. In casting him as an exemplary figure for my arguments, then, I am challenging some established critical assessments of Yeats, both those sponsored by the poet himself and those that inform the current gallery of figures that make up the postcolonial Yeats. Seamus Deane opens his elegant reading of Yeats this way:

> Yeats began his career by inventing an Ireland amenable to his imagination. He ended by finding an Ireland recalcitrant to it. His readiness to include the actuality of modern Ireland gave substance to his intricate system of symbols. But in the end the actuality overbore the symbolism, and left his poetry hysterical when he let his feeling run free of the demands of form, and diagrammatic when he imposed wilfully formal restraints upon his feeling. 'The Statues' best exemplifies this dilemma.[4]

This is a persuasive reading of the shape of Yeats's career, and versions of it dominate current views of the poet. It sketches a movement from nationalist commitment to disillusioned isolation, and from a healthy desire to engage the concrete actualities of Ireland to being overwhelmed by them and, in consequence, lapsing into abstraction. The dilemma exemplified by 'The Statues', Deane suggests, involves two kinds of abstraction: an alienated individual fails to connect his feelings to the national community that provoked them, and rigid literary forms fail to register the sensuous, concrete qualities of the emotion the poet wishes to convey through those forms. This essay concludes by offering another way of thinking about how that poem figures community, feeling and form, one that focuses on Yeats's engagement with conceptions of the 'public', rather than the 'national', and his considerable, if ambivalent, investment in abstractions, rather than his rejection of them. This alternative focus produces a somewhat different outline of the shape of his career.

Culturalism and Its Enlightened Discontents

The political conception of culture on which I focus is perhaps best defined as 'culturalism'. On one hand, it is a theory of politics and a method of political action. Arjun Appadurai defines culturalism as 'the conscious mobilization of cultural differences in the service of a larger national or transnational politics'.[5] On the other hand, culturalism is also a dominant mode of analysis in historical and literary studies, so dominant that some recent scholarship has begun to ask what might lie 'beyond the cultural

---

4   Deane, 'Yeats and the Idea of Revolution', 38
5   Arjun Appadurai, *Modernity at Large: Cultural Dimensions of Globalization* (Minneapolis, MN, 1996), 15

turn'.[6] Culturalist scholarship defines culture variously, sometimes through references to cultural artefacts or art, and other times more anthropologically, through everyday beliefs and practices. This variety reflects culturalism's most established disciplinary home in literary and cultural studies. More important, however, it also reflects culturalism's democratizing political impulses, impulses that are central to my arguments here. Because culturalism defines culture very broadly, it allows scholars to investigate various forms of subalternity among diverse populations who have little or no access to conventional means of making political demands, such as political institutions, mass movements, guns, or money, and little or no access to the modes of conventional high cultural production, like writing poems or painting pictures. Culturalist analyses tend to treat culture in terms of cultural particularity or difference. Often (though not always) this means national particularity or difference. Culturalist arguments place enormous faith in the subject-constituting or 'soul-making' power of culture, and are preoccupied with the relationship between 'culture' and 'politics' or 'public life'. Culturalism involves the privileging of culture as both an instrument of colonization and a vehicle of resistance to it. Much culturalist work contains a tension between transformation and tradition; it casts culture as a powerful agent of change and simultaneously looks to culture as a source of tradition and continuity.

These elements of culturalist analysis are, for better and for worse, characteristic of much current academic work in postcolonial studies. They are also recognizable features of the Irish Literary Revival in general and Yeats's early cultural nationalism in particular. The Revival was far from a monolithic movement or institution, and Yeats's version of it was complex. Yeats, along with other Revivalist writers, participated in debates over whether or not literature should be explicitly subordinated to politics, whether it should be national or cosmopolitan, and on what basis the Revival should define 'Irishness'. Nevertheless, virtually all the arguments put forward in the context of Revivalist discourse were, in one way or another, culturalist arguments. That English rule had uprooted a vigorous native cultural tradition, and that the regeneration of this tradition would have important political as well as cultural benefits, were founding assumptions of Revivalism in its unionist, constitutional, and physical force varieties.

After his work 'went Irish' in the 1880s, Yeats was preoccupied with the national qualities of Irish literature, and combined this with a deep and abiding interest in folk culture. But a number of scholars have argued that Yeats's early cultural nationalism was less a coherent ideology than a series of strategic engagements with different audiences or potential audiences. During the 1880s and early 1890s, when Yeats was struggling to establish himself as a writer, he contributed to periodicals with vastly differing ideological stances — the Protestant nationalism of the *Dublin University Magazine*, the hardline Catholic nationalism of *United Ireland*, and the anti-Irish unionism of the *Scots Observer*. Writing for such different publics involved some inconsistencies on Yeats's part. Yug Chaudhry has argued at meticulous length that the Yeats of this period displayed what Joyce called his 'treacherous instinct for adaptability' and adroitly altered his political views to suit the tastes of various editors and audiences, while Joep Leerssen draws the more measured conclusion that 'Yeats, with his complex cultural attitude, voiced different emphases and different aspects at different times and for different audiences.'[7] Roy Foster's biography of Yeats emphasizes the poet's tireless pursuit of publicity for himself and his friends, and his skilful orchestration of public controversies and events.[8] However tactical and varied his pronouncements and activities, and however alert his awareness of the vagaries of the Irish public sphere, it was culturalism,

---

6   For several discussions of this question centred on Victoria E. Bonnell and Lynn Hunt, eds., *Beyond the Cultural Turn* (Berkeley, CA, 1999), see *American Historical Review*, 107, 5 (2002).

7   Yug Mohit Chaudhry, *Yeats: The Irish Literary Revival and the Politics of Print* (Cork, 2001); Joep Leerssen, *Remembrance and Imagination: Patterns in the Historical and Literary Representation of Ireland in the Nineteenth Century* (Cork, 1996), 211

8   R. F. Foster, *W. B. Yeats: A Life*, vol. I, *The Apprentice Mage 1865–1914* (Oxford, 1997)

in the sense I have been using it here, that governed and gave coherence to them all.

In current postcolonial studies, culturalism is now fairly widely seen as a significant problem. Stephen Howe's largely hostile survey of postcolonial approaches to Ireland, which is at many points admirably judicious, has little but dismissive scorn for literary and cultural critics, citing their 'overwhelming culturalist bias'.[9] More important, scholars sympathetic to postcolonial work have also launched critiques of culturalism. For example, the inaugural issue of *Interventions* (1998–99), which announced itself as an international journal of postcolonial studies, featured Terry Eagleton critiquing the version of the postcolonial he dislikes for being 'a brand of culturalism, which inflates the significance of cultural factors in human affairs'.[10] In *A Critique of Postcolonial Reason* Gayatri Spivak displays a newly sharpened sense that culturalism is to blame for the shortcomings of postcolonial studies. The chapter entitled 'Literature' begins with a version of Spivak's well-known essay 'Three Women's Texts and a Critique of Imperialism'. Spivak revised the essay slightly, giving a name to the neo-imperialist tendency she deplores in literary studies in the age of decolonization — the name 'culturalist'.[11] The problem is the same: 'the consideration of the old Third World as distant cultures, exploited but with rich intact literary heritages waiting to be recovered, interpreted, and curricularized'; but in the later version Spivak explicitly calls that state of affairs 'culturalism'.[12]

This new emphasis appears elsewhere in Spivak's *Critique*, which opens with her assertion of an affinity between Kant and the contemporary forms of postcolonial reason she criticizes.[13] According to Spivak, in the Kant's third *Critique*, the idea of cultural difference functions to exclude non-European peoples from the category of the human, the 'subject as such'. 'The subject as such in Kant,' Spivak explains, 'is geopolitically differentiated.' As a result, Kant's concept of civil society operates within the axiomatics of imperialism: 'The civil organization of society in *bürgerliche Gesellschaft* is recommended for societies that have already acceded to a general level of culture. Kant's philosophical project, whether sublime or bourgeois, operates in terms of an implicit cultural difference.' Spivak also observes, 'This limited access to being-human is the itinerary of the native informant into the post-colonial.' Accordingly, the chapter entitled 'Culture' takes up current developments in academia, and finds that 'One of the alarming developments of the recent past is the wave of academico-cultural "postcolonialism" that seems to be hitting the elite migrants in Europe.' As a result of this development, she warns, 'Everything is being made "cultural".' The 'distorting culturalism' of postcolonial studies performs much the same function that Kant's references to non-Western peoples did, and postcolonial studies' preoccupation with 'the discourse of cultural specificity and difference' often obscures 'the implicit collaboration of the postcolonial in the service of neocolonialism'.[14]

The fact that Enlightenment universals turn out to be the privilege of a particular culture, race, or gender is nothing new. More significant is the fact that Spivak characterizes the problems of contemporary postcolonial studies as a version of those inequities associated with Enlightenment universals. Spivak's critique of culturalism is (among other things) a critique of an Enlightenment conception of civil society that has a damaging political theory of culture and cultural difference at its heart. Culturalism, for Spivak, means more than the conflation of 'culture' and 'politics' and the inflation of the significance of culture in human affairs, though it does mean those things too.

---

9   Stephen Howe, *Ireland and Empire* (Oxford, 2000), 109

10   Terry Eagleton, 'Postcolonialism and "Postcolonialism"', *Interventions*, 1, 1 (1998–99), 26

11   Gayatri Spivak, *A Critique of Postcolonial Reason* (Cambridge, 1999), 114. For the original version, see 'Three Women's Texts and a Critique of Imperialism', *Critical Inquiry*, 12, 1 (1985), 243–61.

12   Spivak, *Critique*, 114

13   This assertion, and her reading of Kant, is of course open to question. For a discussion of 'misreading' and 'mistakes' as central to Spivak's text, see Mieke Bal, 'Three-Way Misreading', *Diacritics*, 30, 1 (2000), 2–24.

14   Spivak, *Critique*, 26–27, 30, 32, 358, 361, 397, 412

It denotes, more specifically, a political theory of culture based on a conjunction between a political discourse that is liberating and universalist and a cultural discourse preoccupied with particularity and difference. Spivak concludes,

> From my arguments above it would follow that feminists with a transnational consciousness would also be aware that the very civil structure here that they work to shore up for gender justice can continue to participate in providing alibis for the operation of the major and definitive transnational activity, the financialization of the globe, and thus the suppression of the possibility of decolonization — the establishment of a civil society there, the only means for an efficient and continuing calculus of gender justice everywhere.[15]

Protecting civil society in Western nations can prevent the establishment of civil society in other places. As in Kant, the concept of civil society and the category of the human are geopolitically differentiated, and this differentiation is shored up by an implicit concept of cultural difference.

Rather than reject Kant, or the concept of civil society, however, Spivak claims that it is the particular job of intellectuals to cultivate our awareness of the contradictions involved in engaging with them. She continues,

> The painstaking cultivation of such a contradictory, indeed aporetic, practical acknowledgement is the basis of a decolonization of the mind. But the disenfranchised new or old diasporic woman cannot be called upon to inhabit this aporia. Her entire energy must be spent upon successful transplantation or insertion into the new state, often in the name of an old nation in the new.

Spivak's migrant must try to insert herself into existing structures of civil society and public life, structures that are exclusionary and based, like Kant's theory, on implicit notions of cultural difference. But in future generations, Spivak hopes that the migrant's 'daughters or granddaughters' will be able to begin revising those structures, and that 'the interventionist academic can assist them in this possibility rather than participate in their gradual indoctrination into an unexamined culturalism'.[16]

Spivak's reading of Kant and contemporary postcolonial studies is certainly not self-evident, and cultivating our awareness of contradictory structures may not be the most satisfying or effective form of political intervention for academics.[17] But her critique of culturalism has three features that make it particularly relevant for my purposes here. First, rather than oppose culturalism and the Enlightenment, she foregrounds the similarities and exchanges between them. Second, she treats the idea of civil society or the public sphere as problematic but necessary. Finally, she contemplates the function of criticism and the public role of the intellectual. These are features Spivak's critique shares with Gerry Smyth's analysis in *Decolonization and Criticism*, a book that notes the culturalism of postcolonial studies and argues that this culturalism is a particularly severe problem in the Irish context. Smyth observes that in Irish studies, for quite some time, 'an entire academic industry has assured us [that] culture and politics are to all intents and purposes one and the same thing'. As a result, he contends, the recent culturalist emphasis in postcolonial studies has had a conservative rather than a radicalizing effect on critical discourse. In Irish studies culturalism 'represents an essential continuity with older, more established and conservative models', and has 'helped to shore up a fundamentally quietistic model

---

15 Spivak, *Critique*, 399
16 Spivak, *Critique*, 399–402
17 For a thoughtful consideration of her interpretation of Kant, see Chetan Bhatt, 'Kant's "Raw Man" and the Mining of Primitivism', *Radical Philosophy*, 105 (2001), 37–44.

of the relations between the two spheres'. Smyth points out that Irish culturalism has a history, and that it emerged as a result of 'institutional and intellectual struggles over different ways of configuring the relationship between an imagined political community and the cultural forms through which that community could know itself'.[18] He calls the location of these struggles 'criticism'.

Smyth's argument stands much postcolonial and Revivalist work on its head by locating the crucial encounters between colonialism and resistance to it not in primary or creative texts, but in criticism: 'Irish culture cannot express, reflect, embody — or any of the other favoured metaphors — the decolonising nation until it is so constituted by an enabling metadiscourse: criticism.' He claims that the intimate and enabling relationship between criticism and decolonization he is positing arises 'from their problematic engagement with the characteristic discursive modes of the Enlightenment', and he bills his project as a '(re)turn to the question of "the function of criticism"'. Like Spivak, he foregrounds the slippery exchanges between culturalism and the Enlightenment, and scrutinizes the public role of intellectuals. Smyth also points out that the forms of critical discourse that emerged in the eighteenth century were 'crucial for the emergence of a bourgeois public sphere, itself part of the process whereby a modern English identity was constituted' in opposition to peripheral others like the Irish.[19] Smyth shares with Spivak a critique of culturalism that turns to an Enlightenment notion of the public (civil society or the public sphere) in response, and that does so even while demonstrating the ethnocentrism and imperialism that underlie that notion's supposed universality.

Both Spivak and Smyth think that the culturalism of current postcolonial scholarship asks 'culture' to do too much work, to do work that belongs to other domains. They offer genealogies of this problem that trace it to an Enlightenment political project that is both potentially emancipatory and compromised by its relation to imperialism. What they propose strikes me as worth pursuing, partly because I think they have read culturalism's political desires correctly. In the wake of anti-imperial critiques of universalism and abstraction, an insistence on culture, especially on culture as cultural difference, proved attractive to postcolonial critics because it seemed to offer a way of respecting embodiment and irreducible particularity, of furthering political emancipation without replicating Eurocentric versions of universalism. The way to capitalize on culturalism's usefulness while curbing its excesses, according to Spivak and Smyth, is to focus less on culture, the nation, and national culture, and more on civil society, the function of criticism, and the role of intellectuals — to focus, in other words, on various aspects of the public or the public sphere.

Publics, Reasonable and Unreasonable

There are other publics and public spheres in Yeats; for example, the public as theatre audience, as the site of demagoguery and mob politics, or as the falsely benign pose of the 'smiling public man' in 'Among School Children'. Here, however, I focus on versions of the classic, normative model of the public sphere defined as a disinterested and democratic realm of debate and critique, distinct from state sovereignty and from the market economy.[20] It is a bourgeois public sphere that, in Jürgen Habermas's account, was most fully achieved during the nineteenth century and then declined during the twentieth with the rise of consumerism, mass media, and the state's encroachment into the private realm of the

---

18 Gerry Smyth, *Decolonisation and Criticism* (London, 1998), 35–36, 38
19 Smyth, *Decolonisation*, 39, 51–52, 56
20 Bruce Robbins addresses the question of definition helpfully in his editor's Introduction to *The Phantom Public Sphere* (Minneapolis, MN, 1993), xiii.

family.[21] It is an Enlightenment invention, perhaps, according to Geoffrey Harpham, 'even the defining Enlightenment invention'.[22] Kant's famous 'Answer to the Question, "What is Enlightenment?"' insists that 'the freedom to make public use of one's reason in all matters' is the foundation of enlightenment, and for Kant, publicness (rather than reason) is central. What he calls the 'private use of reason' does not have to be free and, indeed, often cannot be free.[23] Its universalism is of course compromised and incomplete, but many theorists have argued that any meaningful model of the public sphere must involve forms of universalism and abstraction. Michael Warner, for example, argues that when we enter the public sphere and become 'the subjects of publicity' we imagine, if imperfectly, that the position we occupy involves indifference to our 'particularities of culture, race, gender or class'. Warner points out that different thinkers will see such abstraction differently: 'There are any number of ways to describe this moment of public subjectivity — as a universalizing transcendence, as ideological repression, as utopian wish, as schizocapitalist vertigo, or simply as a routine difference of register.'[24] But, positive or negative, such abstraction from our ordinary selves is an inescapable element of the public sphere.

Warner outlines a tension, within a general Enlightenment conception of the public sphere, between two models that respond differently to the necessary dis-unity of public and private selves. The 'republican virtue' model denies alienation and insists on unity and continuity: 'The republican was to be the same as citizen and as man. He was to maintain continuity of value, judgment, and reputation from domestic economy to affairs of public nature. The liberal bourgeois model involves a 'dialectic of embodiment and negativity in the public sphere'. It promises a public sphere that offers self-abstraction — 'a utopian universality that would allow people to transcend the given realities of their bodies and their status'. At the same time, it denies its darker side, the fact that such abstraction is a privilege available only to some particularities, some bodies (originally those of propertied white men). This model of the public sphere is one whose universalism is compromised, and it displays ambivalence about whether the public is a space of abstraction or a space of embodiment where one's inner particularity can express itself. The contemporary 'mass public sphere', which struggles with the founding logic of the Enlightenment public sphere, 'promises a reconciliation between embodiment and self-abstraction' that neither it nor, according to Warner, any model of the public, can deliver.[25]

Both the Enlightenment model of the public sphere and Habermas's historical account of it have been criticized for their inability to accommodate counter-publics or different, simultaneously existing, forms of publicity. Warner's essay helpfully outlines two versions within the Enlightenment model and reminds us that, in the contemporary period, 'the discursive genres of mass publicity vary widely'; he insists that some form of self-abstraction is proper to all of them.[26] There are, however, different forms of abstraction, and therefore very different grounds upon which to base notions of the public. This is illustrated by Anthony Cascardi's effort to reformulate the public sphere in *Consequences of Enlightenment*. Like Smyth and Spivak, Cascardi wants to 'challenge the view that the pursuit of constructive social and ethical goals requires an anti-Enlightenment stance'.[27] But while Smyth opts for 'criticism' and Spivak for critical awareness, Cascardi offers a public sphere based on a Kantian aesthetic. Through a

---

21 Jürgen Habermas, *The Structural Transformation of the Public Sphere*, trans. Thomas Burger (Cambridge, 1989 [1962])
22 Harpham says, 'the philosophical establishment of unencumbered public conversation, answerable to the truth but not to prince, church, or nation, could be said to be an Enlightenment invention, perhaps even the defining Enlightenment invention'; see 'So ... What is Enlightenment?: An Inquisition into Modernity', 20, 3 *Critical Inquiry* (1994), 527.
23 Immanuel Kant, 'An Answer to the Question, "What is Enlightenment?"', in James Schmidt, ed., *What is Enlightenment? Eighteenth-Century Answers and Twentieth-Century Questions* (Berkeley, CA, 1996), 59
24 Michael Warner, 'The Mass Public and the Mass Subject', in Robbins, *Phantom Public Sphere*, 234
25 Warner, 'Mass Public', 235, 239, 241, 248, 251
26 Warner, 'Mass Public', 254
27 Anthony J. Cascardi, *Consequences of Enlightenment* (Cambridge, 1999), 5

reading of the third *Critique*, Cascardi proposes feeling, rather than reason or concepts, as that which mediates community and creates a potential public. He is very critical of Habermas's late work, in which Habermas derives from Kant, especially from 'What is Enlightenment?', a model of the public sphere based on communicative action. In Habermas's formulation, it is concepts that are communicated in the public sphere, so his public is ultimately grounded in and reconciled through reason. For Cascardi, in contrast, it is judgements of taste that are communicated, the feelings of pleasure or pain that the beautiful and the sublime produce in us; he thus proposes a community of sense rather than a community of concepts. Cascardi perceives the problem of the *Third Critique*, and of the kind of public that might be enabled or theorized by a Kantian aesthetic, as the problem of negotiating between embracing a necessary, problematic universalism and respecting irreducible particularity, remarking,

> The difficulty inherent in deriving the principle of aesthetic judgment suggests that we are challenged to make binding claims that would preserve and validate the particularity of subjective experience over against the universal categories to which reason in its cognitive operations would otherwise subsume such experience, all the while recognizing that the validity of those claims would have to count on the existence of a community which it is also their purpose to (re)create.[28]

Spivak and Smyth propose models of the public in which the necessary universalizing abstraction is based on reason and criticism; Cascardi offers a model in which such abstraction is grounded in feeling and the aesthetic.

Thus abstraction, and the models of community and the public it enables, comes in different forms. It can be grounded in reason or in feeling. It can be indifferent to concrete bodies, or, alternatively, it can emanate from them. Alan Richardson has argued that the widespread critical view that casts Enlightenment universalism as fundamentally based on abstraction and sees 'Romanticism in terms of a flight from Enlightenment universalism toward an obsession with difference and diversity — individual, national, cultural, and racial' is deeply flawed. It would be more accurate, Richardson claims, to say that

> a number of Romantic writers — poets and scientists alike — rejected the 'timeless' universalism of the Enlightenment, which located human uniformity in reason, language, and logic, with a time-bound and biological universalism that instead grounded 'primary' human features in the body, in the material organization of the mind, and in the emotions.

Richardson calls this 'embodied universalism', and argues that Romanticism involves 'not so much an abandonment as a radical reformulation of human universals'.[29]

In what follows, I trace a few of the ways in which Yeats imagined different kinds of abstraction and engaged with various aspects of the public, both theoretical and practical, over the course of his career. This element in Yeats's work displays a number of features similar to those Spivak and Smyth outline in contemporary postcolonial studies. I suggest that Yeats's culturalism pursues radical reformulations of human universals rather than rejections of them, that these abstractions were grounded, at various times, in both reason and feeling, that they were sometimes indifferent to concrete bodies and sometimes emanated from them, and that Yeats was as much a theorist of the public and the abstract as he was a thinker preoccupied with the nation and the particular.

---

28 Cascardi, *Consequences of Enlightenment*, 19
29 Alan Richardson, 'Embodied Universalism, Romantic Discourse, and the Anthropological Imagination', in *British Romanticism and the Science of the Mind* (Cambridge, 2001), 152

From Justice to Culture: Yeats and O'Leary

John O'Leary is usually thought to have exercised a formative influence on Yeats's engagement with nationalism, but he exercised an equally important influence on Yeats's early conception of the public sphere. Towards the end of his life, when Yeats composed 'A General Introduction for my Work', which was to be the introduction to a complete edition of his poems that was never published, he looked back and claimed, 'It was through the old Fenian leader John O'Leary I found my theme.'[30] O'Leary (1830–1907), who edited the Dublin Fenian journal the *Irish People*, had been arrested in 1865, convicted of treason, and sentenced to twenty years' imprisonment. He was released after nine years, on condition that he went into exile in Paris. He returned to Dublin in 1885, where he met Yeats, and became an influential friend and mentor. O'Leary introduced Yeats to a number of significant books by Irish authors, and helped him get his early work published in nationalist journals like the *Gael*, the *Boston Pilot*, and the *Sunday Providence Journal*.[31] Most critics have followed the later Yeats in casting O'Leary's nationalism as paramount and in characterizing that nationalism as one that opposed the rigid abstractions of much nationalist ideology and respected the irreducible particularity of the individual. Elizabeth Butler Cullingford, for example, comments that 'the old nationalism of O'Leary was essentially individualist and libertarian'.[32] More specifically, as fewer critics have noted, for the early Yeats, O'Leary's nationalism was about the limits of nationalism. O'Leary subscribed to two principles to which nationalist goals and ideas were ultimately subordinated. One was the integrity of art. The other was an Enlightenment embrace of universal principles and strict standards for regulating public behaviour. One of the most notable features of this philosophy was precisely its embrace of the abstract, an embrace Yeats found necessary, positive, and problematic all at once.

When Yeats reviewed O'Leary's memoirs, *Recollections of Fenians and Fenianism* (1896) for the *Bookman* in 1897, he faced a quandary; he had hated the book. He negotiated this dilemma by reviewing the man instead, and his portrait of O'Leary emphasized his mentor's role as one of Ireland's 'public men', his embrace of the universal principles that ultimately took precedence over his nationalist aspirations, and his commitment to various abstractions. Yeats introduced a saying that would become his favourite example of the qualities that drew him to O'Leary: the dictum that 'there are things which a man should not do, perhaps even to save a nation'.[33] He would return to this saying again in his autobiography, remarking that O'Leary 'would speak a sentence like that in ignorance of its passionate value, and would forget it the moment after.'[34] This republican virtue model of public behaviour demanded complete continuity between public and private life. In Yeats's review, such continuity was guaranteed by a series of abstractions: O'Leary's 'passion for abstract right', his sense of 'abstract ideas, of abstract law', and his capacity for 'abstract emotion'. O'Leary's devotion to abstract principles gave him a 'detachment from his own enthusiasms' and his book a 'strange impartiality'. Yeats also offered the somewhat Arnoldian idea that these universals were a peculiarly Celtic form of idealism: they embodied 'the Celtic passion for ideas', a quality that Celtic peoples had preserved 'longer than more successful and practical races'.[35] Yeats's review grounds the abstract equally in reason and feeling: he emphasizes passion, emotion, and enthusiasm in combination with impartiality, law, and principle.

---

30 W. B. Yeats, *Essays and Introductions* (New York, 1961), 510; hereafter cited as EI
31 See Foster, *Apprentice Mage*, 42–44.
32 Elizabeth Butler Cullingford, *Yeats, Ireland and Fascism* (New York, 1981), 1
33 W. B. Yeats, *Uncollected Prose*, vol. 2, ed. John P. Frayne and Colton Johnson (New York, 1976), 36
34 W. B. Yeats, *The Autobiography of William Butler Yeats* (New York, 1968), 64
35 *Uncollected Prose*, vol. 2, 36–37

Yug Chaudhry has argued that Yeats's relationship with O'Leary became strained earlier than most commentators have realized. He cites Yeats's participation in an 1892 controversy in the nationalist *United Ireland* over Trinity College, Dublin, in which O'Leary defended the college, and Yeats, who had attacked Trinity in print before, did so again, even though the paper had been hostile to O'Leary since his return to Ireland, and even though in the context of the debate such an attack would be seen as a personal attack on O'Leary as well.[36] This makes it less surprising, then, that the poor quality of O'Leary's writing was not the only source of Yeats's ambivalence in the 1897 review. The model of public behaviour O'Leary exemplifies, and its various abstractions, also provoke ambivalence. While O'Leary's attachment to abstract principles makes him superior to other contemporary nationalists, it also has negative consequences for Irish public life: 'The very inhumanity of Irish journalism and of Irish politics comes from a tendency to judge men not by one another, not by experience of the degree of excellence one may hope to meet in life and in politics, but by some abstract standard.'[37]

Given Yeats's later hatred for abstraction, this early review may simply seem anomalous. It is not anomalous, however, if we focus on the model of the public sphere that Yeats attached to O'Leary. One way to think of Yeats's culturalism as an ambivalent continuation of an Enlightenment project would be to say that it asked culture to do the work that abstract, civic political ideals like Liberty, Justice, and Equality did for Enlightenment republican nationalism: to unite the members of the nation in a common endeavour and provide some of the organizing principles of that endeavour. For the Yeats of 1897, O'Leary represented a Romantic cultural nationalism that had not completely made this substitution, and whose patriotism was still explicitly regulated by a transnational idealism based on reasoned Enlightenment principles of public conduct. Later in Yeats's career, 'abstract' would come to have entirely negative connotations, and would become a kind of Yeatsian swear word. In the first portion of his autobiography, written in 1916, Yeats again stresses the 'passionate' value of O'Leary's sayings, but only invokes the abstract to characterize the book's literary shortcomings: 'When it was finished, it was unreadable, being dry, abstract, and confused; no picture had ever passed before his mind's eye.'[38]

Yeats did continue to emphasize O'Leary's commitment to both an impassioned nationalism and to the 'cold intellect' of abstract universals.[39] However, he began to shift some of the terms he employed to do so. In 'Poetry and Tradition', written after O'Leary's death in 1907, Yeats said that O'Leary belonged 'to the romantic conception of Irish nationality' that Yeats himself worked for.[40] This characterization of O'Leary as 'romantic' does not indicate that Yeats had abandoned the notion of O'Leary's fidelity to Enlightenment doctrines. Rather, it reveals how loosely and widely Yeats applied that term, and how, in Yeats's thought about O'Leary, there was no clear distinction between Enlightenment universals and the Romantic. Yeats repeated the saying that there are things one must not do to save a nation and added another, whose purpose was 'that we might not forget justice in the passion of controversy'. The new dictum was 'there was never cause so bad that it has not been defended by good men for what seemed to them good reasons'.[41] This, too, became part of his permanent characterization of O'Leary, and found its way into his autobiography.[42] By this time Yeats has rephrased the part of this characterization that formulated O'Leary's devotion to abstract principles; he has replaced his earlier emphasis on the

36 Chaudhry, *Yeats*, 6–8
37 *Uncollected Prose*, vol. 2, 37
38 *Autobiography*, 142
39 *Uncollected Prose*, vol. 2, 37
40 EI, 246
41 EI, 247
42 *Autobiography*, 63

abstract as such with various forms of the assertion that 'life is greater than the cause'.[43] 'Life' was one of Yeats's favourite abstractions because it masqueraded as a concrete opposite of abstraction.

O'Leary was a nationalist who also embraced a transnational conception of public good and public behaviour. His idealism contained a conception of the public sphere that involved both the republican virtue model, in which the individual's public behaviour remained faithful to the dictates of private conscience, no matter what the practical costs — there are things one should never do, even to save a nation — and the self-abstraction aspect of the liberal bourgeois model which (theoretically) guarantees that all positions and participants must be accommodated in reasoned debate, all views assumed to be those of good men (and it is clearly a male ideal) with potentially good reasons. O'Leary was a committed nationalist, but he was also a theorist of a disinterested public sphere whose principles regulated and ultimately took precedence over nationalist aims. He represented passionate attachment to the national cause and, simultaneously, an impartial detachment from it.

As this suggests, Yeats drew on Enlightenment thought less to separate reason from passion than to distinguish between desirable and undesirable alternatives to reason. His devotion to passion actually consists of a series of highly regulated distinctions between the right and the wrong kinds of passion. O'Leary is a figure for this series, which included distinctions between the abstract and the ideal — conflated in the early essay but later separated — between the material and the concrete, between the 'delirium of the brave', which was activated by the ideal, and the hysteria of mere political opinion, which was provoked by the abstract. These distinctions appear in Yeats's poetry in a number of ways. The 'excess of love' that may have bewildered the martyred rebels of 'Easter, 1916' is at least a potentially positive kind of political delirium, this possibility being one source of the poem's ambivalence. But in his prose writings, Yeats repeatedly linked 'nationalist abstractions' with sexual abstinence and hysteria. In 'On Those that Hated the Playboy of the Western World, 1907', the 'eunuchs' who run through hell and 'rail and sweat' as they 'stare' at 'great Juan' are both sexually frustrated and (therefore) insufficiently passionate although overly excited — hence their frenzied jealousy of the great lover's 'sinewy thigh'. They are hysterical rather than delirious.[44]

Over time, the initial agent that enforced those distinctions and theoretically enabled a public sphere that organized them — O'Leary's abstract universalism — was replaced in Yeats's writings by another agent — culture. In 1907, in 'Poetry and Tradition', he had proposed to regulate the passions aroused by public debate or controversy (and a controversy is distinguished from a disagreement precisely by its publicness) through an appeal to 'justice'. By 1910, however, we find Yeats stating in a newspaper interview that 'passion in public life without culture was ignoble',[45] and he held to versions of this formulation for the rest of his career. Now Yeats's culturalism offers a public sphere grounded in and regulated, not by the abstract, but by a common devotion to culture. It is a critical commonplace that Protestant writers like Yeats looked to culture in their search for a non-sectarian model of Irish community that could include them, or by which they could include others. Revivalists understood culture as cultural difference, but they also believed in culture as a universalizing medium of unification and transcendence. Culture offered a utopian abstraction from one's individual particularities, and such abstraction could, Yeats hoped, wrest a united Irish public from the divisive controversies of contemporary Irish politics.

In tracing Yeats's changing treatment of O'Leary thus far, I have argued that, for Yeats, the old Fenian's conception of 'the public' was the most important aspect of his commitment to 'the nation', and that, in Yeats's thinking, a culturalist theory of the public gradually emerged out of an initial embrace of a

43   EI, 260
44   I take up this topic at greater length in ch. 3 of Yeats's Nations.
45   Quoted in Donald Torchiana, W. B. Yeats and Georgian Ireland (Evanston, IL, 1966), 30

more traditional Enlightenment model of the public. As Spivak and Smyth show, such a transformation is neither surprising nor unusual; rather, these slippery transactions between justice and culture are central to contemporary postcolonial studies, which often tries to pursue universal values like human rights through respect for irreducible specificity and cultural difference. In addition, as this transformation proceeded, Yeats, like the Kant of Spivak's argument, began to imagine a public sphere in which culture was less a guarantor of universal access than a marker of difference between those who could sustain a public sphere and those who could not. The vision of public good represented by O'Leary increasingly operated in terms of an implicit cultural difference. To illustrate this point I take up Yeats's most famous representation of O'Leary, 'September 1913'.

O'Leary in the Grave

The central question 'September 1913' raises is: what, exactly, is buried with O'Leary? What constitutes 'Romantic Ireland' and what do it and O'Leary share? A number of traditional readings have identified Romantic Ireland with a self-sacrificing republican or Fenian nationalism, in part because it features O'Leary so prominently, and in part because after 1916 Yeats appended a note to the poem that encouraged such readings. In the note, Yeats suggests that the qualities represented by Romantic Ireland were revived by the Easter Rising:

> 'Romantic Ireland's dead and gone' sounds old-fashioned now. It seemed true in 1913, but I did not foresee 1916. The late Dublin Rebellion, whatever one can say of its wisdom, will long be remembered for its heroism. 'They weighed so lightly what they gave', and gave too in some cases without hope of success. [July 1916].[46]

Yeats was able to transform 'September 1913' into a poem about nationalism and martyrdom effectively because his reading of the Rising focused on qualities that are indeed present in the text: reckless, generous self-sacrifice, idealism, the right kind of passion. But when the poem was first published, it invoked these qualities in the service of a different cause: imagining an Irish public sphere in which passion was regulated by culture.

The poem was first published in The Irish Times on 8 September 1913, under the title 'Romance in Ireland'. Its subtitle read: 'On reading much of the correspondence against the Art Gallery'.[47] When Yeats wrote to Lady Gregory of his plans to publish it, he commented, 'I had not thought I could feel so bitterly over any public event.'[48] The public event to which Yeats refers here is the controversy over Hugh Lane's offer to donate his collection of modern art to Dublin if the city would build a suitable gallery to house it. The Dublin Corporation ultimately refused.[49] Recently, Yug Chaudhry has offered a provocative reading of the poem in its original contexts. He reminds us that Yeats was careful to place 'September 1913' and 'The Gift' in The Irish Times, that The Irish Times was a conservative, unionist paper with a largely Protestant readership, that the paper had supported the art gallery, and that the editor would be very unlikely to publish a poem advocating armed rebellion. He also points out that, during

---

46 *The Variorum Edition of the Poems of W. B. Yeats*, ed. Peter Allt and Russell K. Alspach (New York, 1957), 820; hereafter cited as *VP*
47 *VP*, 289
48 Quoted in Chaudhry, *Yeats*, 20
49 The other public event that scholars have found relevant is the Dublin strike and lockout of 1913, though there is little evidence of this connection in the poem itself or in Yeats's letters, and he had begun thinking about the poem seven months before the strike was called, and had finished it on 9 August, seventeen days before the strike began; see Chaudhry, *Yeats*, 29–30.

the period when Yeats was thinking about and composing the poem, his letters are full of references to Catholic intolerance and Protestant marginalization. Chaudhry argues that 'September 1913' is a Protestant, sectarian poem that castigates the Catholic middle classes, celebrates Protestant superiority and laments Protestant marginalization. What is important about the poem's heroes, according to Chaudhry, is not their political opinions, nationalist or otherwise, but their 'Protestant panache'.[50]

Chaudhry supports his argument by offering a revised portrait of O'Leary as a public figure during the 1880s and 1890s. Rather than the respected elder statesman and radical Fenian Yeats claimed him to be, O'Leary was a conservative, anti-democratic élitist who favoured a constitutional monarchy. Chaudhry calls him an 'honorary Protestant'; he was also a landlord with a reputation, one that he shared with the rest of his family, for requiring that his tenants adhere strictly to the letter of their agreements. After his return to Ireland, he expressed his opposition to the most widespread and successful forms of protest against British rule: the Land League, the Irish Parliamentary Party, and agrarian agitation. In return, he was 'relentlessly attacked and ridiculed in the nationalist press'.[51] As Marcus Bourke observes, around 1890, 'by older folk in the town, dead within the past decade, John O'Leary was remembered principally, not as an Irish patriot, but as a "hard landlord".'[52] By 1913, O'Leary's conservatism and élitism had become more congenial to Yeats than they had been in the 1890s. Like Yeats, O'Leary castigated the middle classes for their materialism and timidity. In *Recollections of Fenians and Fenianism* O'Leary called the middle class 'distinctly the lowest class morally' and said that its 'prudential virtues', while good in themselves, were not 'the stuff out of which patriots are made'.[53] In addition, O'Leary had always shared Yeats's respect for the integrity and public effectiveness of culture. Thus the 'romance' O'Leary embodied for the Yeats of this period had little to do with his Fenianism; rather it arose out of his literary taste and his conviction that 'a certain leaven of ... aristocratic feeling' came naturally to the Irish.[54]

Chaudhry's insistence on the Protestant sectarianism of the poem does not paint an attractive portrait of what Yeats meant by Romantic Ireland in 1913, but it is compellingly argued, and he deals more thoroughly and effectively with the various public contexts of 'September 1913' than any other scholar to date.[55] One weakness of Chaudhry's argument is that his characterization of O'Leary as an armchair Fenian and an isolated crank is overly harsh; Bourke insists that O'Leary was active and respected in the Irish Republican Brotherhood after his return to Ireland.[56] Another is that Chaudhry launches a scathing critique of O'Leary's 'political philosophy — "there are things that a man must not do to save a nation"'. Chaudhry asserts that this philosophy was 'derived from the romantic idealism of Young Ireland', and, quoting F. S. L. Lyons, that this movement was 'at its weakest in action'. 'His aristocratic, high-principled conception of patriotism,' concludes Chaudhry, 'was hopelessly out of touch with *realpolitik*.'[57] This is disturbing, as it suggests that regulating the pursuit of nationalist goals through adherence to universalist principles is not only hopelessly impractical, but also somehow in collusion with aristocratic privilege. The 1848 Rising was certainly not an effective movement in action. But Chaudhry's argument links its failure to the abstraction of 'romantic idealism' and 'high-principled' philosophy from the concrete realities of *realpolitik* — a word that itself entered the common vocabulary after the failure of the 'impractical' and idealist revolution of 1848 in Germany. Under what conceptual

---

50 Chaudhry, *Yeats*, 22
51 Chaudhry, *Yeats*, 12
52 Marcus Bourke, *John O'Leary: A Study in Irish Separatism* (Tralee, 1967), 198
53 John O'Leary, *Recollections of Fenians and Fenianism* (New York, 1969 [1896]), vol. 1, 31
54 O'Leary, *Recollections*, 245
55 The other serious analysis of these contexts, which comes to very different conclusions, is George Bornstein's 'Yeats and Textual Reincarnation', *Material Modernism* (Cambridge, 2001), 46–64.
56 Bourke, *John O'Leary*, 200–35
57 Chaudhry, *Yeats*, 12

scheme does the obviously Enlightenment notion that certain universal human values trump nationalist aims appear as a species of Romantic idealism? Clearly, only a conceptual scheme that, like that of Yeats himself for most of his career and of much contemporary postcolonial scholarship, automatically denigrates anything it believes to merit the label 'abstract'.

'September 1913' is, as Chaudhry suggests, a Protestant *cri de cœur* rather than a nationalist call to arms or a non-sectarian critique of modern cowardice and materialism. But it is also a poem about the Irish public sphere that continues Yeats's engagement with how that public sphere should be regulated. In a 1914 note to the group of poems in *Responsibilities* that addressed the Hugh Lane controversy ('To a Wealthy Man who promised a Second Subscription to the Dublin Municipal Gallery if it were proved the People wanted Pictures', 'September 1913', 'To Friend whose Work has come to Nothing', 'Paudeen', and 'To a Shade'), Yeats commented: 'In the thirty years or so during which I have been reading Irish newspapers, three public controversies have stirred my imagination.'[58] These were the controversies over Parnell, Synge's *Playboy*, and Hugh Lane; what brought them together for Yeats was that they all illustrated 'how base at moments of excitement are minds without culture'.[59] In 'September 1913', O'Leary stands for a public sphere in which culture — embodied in the art gallery and in the example of cultured individuals like him — should function as justice did earlier; it should provide the civilizing influences the masses need and provoke the right kinds of public-spirited passion. But 'culture' has come to mean something different from either private integrity or self-abstraction; the 'public' now connotes more a passive audience to be shaped than a democratic sphere of reasoned debate, and the poem emphasizes the incompatibility of Yeats's ideal with Irish public life.

The poem's major figures for positive action in the public sphere are expenditure, self-sacrifice, waste, the gift. Romantic Ireland is embodied in the wind, the flight of the Wild Geese, the shedding of blood, and the excesses of madness and passion. It is dominated by varieties of centrifugal motion, by gestures that annihilate the individual subject. In the grave with O'Leary is the time when such gestures had a positive, public effect, when 'the names' of the heroes 'stilled' the 'childish play' of Catholic Ireland. Catholic Ireland, on the other hand, is defined through its preoccupation with forms of retention — reasoning, saving, praying:

What need you, being come to sense,
But fumble in a greasy till
And add the halfpence to the pence
And prayer to shivering prayer, until
You have dried the marrow from the bone?[60]

All of these suggest centripetal motion and privacy, as the individual subject seeks to enclose, to contract, to gather things to its centre. This centre, however, is empty, like the bone without marrow. Catholic Ireland, in effect, does not have a public sphere, only a series of private aspirations to acquire and retain things — reason, money, God's blessing, self-control. The 'high-principled philosophy' that Yeats had earlier ascribed to O'Leary, his concern for the dictates of private conscience, his insistence that each individual point of view must be accommodated in reasoned debate, do not appear here. Indeed, they would be antithetical to the self-negating generosities of Romantic Ireland, and more in keeping with the private selfishness of Catholic Ireland. The varieties of self-restraint that Yeats said gave O'Leary a 'detachment from his own enthusiasms' and his book a 'strange impartiality' in 1897 have become the

58 *VP*, 818
59 *VP*, 819
60 *VP*, 289

'wasteful virtues' of Protestant panache. The abstractions of Enlightenment thought have given way to a different kind of abstraction, one that is indeed a kind of transcendent, Romantic idealism, but that bears little relation to the philosophy Yeats ascribed to O'Leary elsewhere.

The point I want to make here is not that Yeats was inconsistent or changed his mind about O'Leary. Instead, I want to emphasize the ease with which detachment became self-sacrifice, reasoned impartiality became unreasoning devotion, and how one kind of abstraction modulated into another. The model of the public that Yeats organized around O'Leary was founded on radical ambiguities between Enlightenment and Romance, justice and culture, individual integrity and individual disintegration. Yeats's faith in the transformative public and political effects of culture was originally rooted in political doctrines that were legacies of the Enlightenment, combined with democratizing impulses indicated by his interested in Irish folk culture. In 'September 1913' this culturalism confronted the actual public sphere in Ireland and found it recalcitrant; neither cultural artefacts, like Lane's paintings, nor public intellectuals like Yeats, had the ability to regulate public controversies and passions. In response, Yeats imagines a form of 'publicness' that belongs exclusively to Romantic Ireland, and he excludes Catholic Ireland from the public as such. Romantic Ireland is not nationalist Ireland, nor is it simply idealistic Ireland. It is an Ireland in which culturalism works, both as a political method and a mode of analysis.

O'Leary Turns to Stone

We also find Yeats's interest in the public, mediated by an ambiguous process of abstraction that seemed to work either through universals like justice or through a Romantic conception of culture, in his very late works. In fact, his last two volumes — New Poems (1938) and Last Poems (1939) — display a renewed interest in the idea and fact of the 'public': that word does not appear anywhere in the preceding two volumes. In his later years, Yeats launched bitter critiques of Irish government and public life. Indeed, in poems like 'Roger Casement', and 'A Model for the Laureate', 'public' has become another Yeatsian swear word. But along with his disgust for the public sphere as an arena of betrayal and dishonesty, Yeats also continues to meditate on the public and communal functions of art or culture. Here I focus on 'The Statues', a difficult poem, whose version of the public is confusing. Some critics have read it as an admirable statement about the public role of art, while others have found it repellent.[61] For Seamus Deane, Yeats turns to abstract form in 'The Statues' to impose order on the chaotic feelings a recalcitrant Ireland provoked in him. I argue, on the other hand, that the poem invokes abstract form because it carries on the negotiations between universal and particular, reason and feeling, Enlightenment and culture, that Yeats organized around O'Leary earlier.

'The Statues' is a kind of ultimate culturalist argument, which imagines the power of art to bring about the rise and fall of civilizations. It is also a hymn to a particularly corporeal version of Enlightenment rationality — to intellect, calculation, number, and measurement, as they are embodied in cultural artefacts. The abstract qualities of Greek art, based on the mathematical theories of Pythagoras and embodied in the statues of Phidias, 'put down all Asiatic vague immensities'.[62] They, rather than military victory at Salamis, produced the movement of the gyres in which one civilization gave way to its antithesis. The poem charts a Yeatsian theory of history, as the triumph of Greek abstraction

---

61   Examples of the former judgement can be found in Edward Engelberg, The Vast Design: Patterns in W. B. Yeats's Aesthetic (Washington, DC, 1988), Thomas R. Whitaker, Swan and Shadow: Yeats's Dialogue with History (Chapel Hill, NC, 1964), and F. A. C. Wilson, Yeats's Iconography (London, 1960). Harold Bloom's Yeats (New York, 1970) takes the latter position.
62   VP, 610

becomes by extension 'Buddha's emptiness' and so declines towards formlessness again. The last stanza describes 'we Irish' as 'wrecked' by another such 'formless' age and proposes a return to the number and discipline of Greek statues.

'The Statues' is also a poem about the public sphere, and this is how Michael North has read it. He argues that 'sculpture has an ambiguous significance in Yeats's work, especially in its monumental aspect, because of the peculiar quasi-public nature of the art'. North also observes that, for Yeats, the 'publicness' of statues depends upon their 'abstract proportions'. In 'truly public' statues, 'the standardization of their forms overcomes the idiosyncratic and the temporary'. His reading of 'The Statues' argues that the poem offers 'an image of a society founded on the repudiation of collective life' through a representation of 'public art founded on the ideals of privacy'. North points out that Yeats draws on two conflicting ways of thinking about sculpture. On the one hand, the 'repose' (a word Yeats got from Pater) of the statue represents health, serenity and the fusion of body and thought for Pater and for Winckelmann; on the other hand, it suggests disease and death in Gustav Moreau. The statue is a public art that represents collective tradition, an ideal balance between individual and society; at the same time, it embodies an ultimate privacy, an indifference to the social. North concludes that 'Yeats's mature poetry ... uses the ambiguous nature of sculpture itself ... to place the "statue of solitude" at the center of collective life'.[63]

I would like to recast North's claims to suggest that the ambiguity of sculpture in the poem is a further mutation of the public sphere represented by O'Leary, one which contains elements of both Yeats's earliest characterization of O'Leary and his revision of it in 'September 1913'. The statue by Phidias is ambiguous because it lacks 'character' or particularity — its form is accomplished but potentially dead or empty. It provokes the 'stares' of the people as Don Juan in hell did. Here, as in 'On Those that Hated the Playboy of the Western World, 1907', the people are defined through their sexual frustration, and both poems present public scenes that paradoxically take place at 'midnight'. But these boys and girls channel their passion into solitary erotic encounters with the statue rather than into mass riot: they 'pressed at midnight in some public place / Live lips upon a plummet-measured face'. This moment in the poem seems to offer something like Cascardi's public sphere. It is based on the feelings generated by art — produced by the process in which the irreducible particularity of individual subjective experience — the 'live lips' — has an encounter with the aesthetic — the 'plummet-measured face'. As a result, a new civilization triumphs over 'all Asiatic vague immensities'. On the other hand, the poem's emphasis on form, measurement and calculation also seems to gesture towards reason and criticism. O'Leary's abstract principles have, in a sense, been replaced by the statues — cultural forms whose important features are their abstractness and their capacity to arouse passion and yet contain it.

The other statue in this poem is the statue of Cuchulain erected in the Post Office to commemorate the Rising. Earlier, Yeats had associated the Romantic conception of Irish nationality, and the idealistic rebellion it fostered, with the delirium of the brave and with Protestant panache. In the last stanza of 'The Statues', however, the Rising is assimilated to intellect, calculation, number and measurement. It is associated with the abstract principles, embodied earlier in O'Leary and here in Greek sculpture, that distinguish that passion from the wrong kinds of passion, from the 'formless, spawning fury' of the degenerate modern world. The public, the 'we Irish' of this stanza, comes into being by following the principles, tracing the lineaments, of the statues. This achievement is both arduous and merely asserted, fulfilled in the present and perpetually deferred. It begins in the climb (rather than a descent) to 'our proper dark' — not in Enlightenment, but not in formless chaos either. 'Our proper dark' encapsulates the contradictions of a conception of the public sphere that attempts to rewrite Enlightenment notions of the deployment of reason in public life into the terms of cultural nationalism — passion, culture, and embodiment. It represents the generative powers of the right kind of irrationality, a force that is both unconscious and highly structured. In a related passage from 'A General Introduction for My Work' Yeats records his hatred of 'modern heterogeneity', a hatred that 'comes up out of my own dark'.[64]

Yeats's engagement with the public sphere was structured, both over time and in this particular poem, through the interchangeability of Enlightenment and romance, justice and culture, delirium and calculation. This interchangeability is one reason the poem cannot answer the question: 'What stalked through the Post Office?' It also appears in what North identifies as the ambiguity of sculpture itself: as a figure for that which generates and regulates public passions, do the statues suggest deadly rationalism or healthy critical principles? That question, which is the question of the relationship between culture, Enlightenment thought, and decolonization, is the question that animates Spivak and Smyth, both postcolonial scholars who are interested in reinvigorating abstract and universalist conceptions of civil society and the public sphere. In A Critique of Postcolonial Reason, Spivak reads literature as a way of revealing how culturalism produces a 'soul-making' project that is also an 'imperialist project cathected as civil-society-through-social-mission'.[65] Postcolonial studies shares with Yeats a culturalism which is the extension of an Enlightenment project that has been rendered both tainted and newly urgent. It is appropriate, then, that Spivak's first book was a study of Yeats in which she noted that he 'conceived of poetry as the business of soul-making, not merely as a rhetorical exercise'.[66]

'What stalked through the Post Office?' How should we reconfigure our ideas about what makes significant historical events happen, about the respective roles of reason and culture, Enlightenment and Romance, the universal and the particular, in national and public discourses? If Spivak's famous question, 'Can the subaltern speak?' pointed to the important and inaccessible particularities of subaltern subjectivity, 'What stalked through the Post Office?' indicates the many unanswered questions that surround conceptions of the collective, the public, and the universal in the age of decolonization. An alternative postcolonial reading of Yeats suggests that these questions should and will animate Yeats scholarship and postcolonial studies for some time to come.

64 EI, 526
65 Spivak, Critique, 116
66 Gayatri Spivak, Myself I Must Remake: The Life and Poetry of W. B. Yeats (New York, 1974), 180

Index